Definition in Theory and Practice

Also by Roy Harris

Rethinking Writing

The Necessity of Artspeak

The Semantics of Science

Definition in Theory and Practice

Language, Lexicography and the Law

Roy Harris and Christopher Hutton

BLOOMSBURY
NEW DELHI • LONDON • OXFORD • NEW YORK • SYDNEY

BLOOMSBURY INDIA
Bloomsbury Publishing India Pvt. Ltd
Second Floor, Building No. 4
DDA Complex LSC, Pocket C – 6 & 7
Vasant Kunj, New Delhi 110070
www.bloomsbury.com

BLOOMSBURY, Bloomsbury Academic India and the Diana
logo are trademarks of Bloomsbury Publishing Plc

First published in India 2019
First published in 2007 by Continuum International Publishing Group Ltd
Paperback edition first published by Bloomsbury Academic 2014

This edition published with permission from Bloomsbury Publishing Plc,
50 Bedford Square, London, WC1B3DP, UK

British Library Cataloguing-in-Publication Data
A catalogue record for this book is available from the British Library.

Library of Congress Cataloging-in-Publication Data
Harris, Roy, 1931-
Definition in theory and practice : language, lexicography and the law
/Roy Harris and Christopher Hutton.
p. cm
Includes bibliographical references and index.
ISBN 978-0-8264-9705-5 (hardback), 978-1-4411-7100-9 (paperback),
978-1-4411-7615-8 (epdf), 978-1-4411-3562-9 (epub)
1.Lexicography. 2.Law-Language. 3.Semantics.
I.Hutton, Christopher. II. Title P327.H367 2007
340'.14-dc22
2006038806

ISBN: 978-93-88002-11-0

2 4 6 8 10 9 7 5 3 1

For sale in the Indian subcontinent only

Digitally printed and bound in India by Replika Press Pvt. Ltd.

Contents

Preface

This book is concerned with words insofar as they are related to definitions, and concerned with definitions insofar as they are related to words. There are, it need hardly be said, many other aspects of both words and definitions; but they do not need extensive consideration here. It is sufficient that one recognize a relationship of some kind between words and definitions, and be prepared to attempt an elucidation of it.

Etymologists, who are the archaeologists of the verbal world, tell us that the term *definition* comes from the Latin *definitio*, itself connected to the verb *definire*, said to mean 'delimit, determine, circumscribe, set bounds to'. So some idea of pinning down or making explicit what would otherwise be elusive or vague seems to be the basic motivation for the existence of such a word. This accords with the long history of *definitio* as a technical term in Western logic, where it features as a prerequisite for the operations set out in the Aristotelian syllogism. Traditionally, there were supposed to be 'rules' of definition, and we shall comment on them in due course.

The relationship between words and definitions succeeded in capturing the attention of some of the outstanding thinkers in the Western tradition. This alone should ensure that the topic is well worth the scrutiny of their intellectual heirs and successors. However, the last general book to be published in English on the theory of definition was Richard Robinson's *Definition* (1954). Although we shall have occasion to refer to Robinson's book in several places, we do not think it can still be regarded as a satisfactory introduction to the subject today, for various reasons. Robinson's approach to the subject was that of a philosopher writing in the heyday of 'ordinary language philosophy', and concerned mainly with definitional issues that would or might affect the philosophical treatment of traditional philosophical questions. His coverage of other areas was somewhat perfunctory. Two such areas in particular would nowadays be regarded as weak. These are (1) lexicography, with its associated problems of semantic theory, and (2) the law, with its associated procedures for determining the application of terms for legal purposes.

In our view, both of these areas are important. The actual practice of lexicographers cannot be ignored in any modern literate society, while the law is one of the major supercategories (along with science, history, religion and the arts) that provide the intellectual framework for all modern thinking. Both, therefore, in view of their practical importance in current educational and social affairs, merit special treatment. We have accordingly adopted a tri-partite structure for the present book. In Part 1 we shall deal with general questions relating to the theory and typology of definition; in Part 2 with dictionary definitions; and in Part 3 with definitions in jurisprudence.

A few preliminary comments about our approach are in order here. Unlike Robinson, we assume that any satisfactory account of definition will have to be based on some specific theory of language. Robinson seemed to suppose that all definitions have a bi-partite structure, comprising a correlation between just two independently given items. (On one hand the form: on the other hand the meaning. Or, here the *definiendum*: there the *definiens*. As if the definitional universe consisted of an infinity of possible pairs, each singleton looking for its partner.) From this assumption was derived the plan of Robinson's book. It led directly to his exhaustive classification of definitions into (1) word-thing definitions, (2) word-word definitions, and (3) thing-thing definitions. But it was never very clear what linguistic or epistemological theory underlay and justified this classification.

The theory we adopt here is an integrationist theory (Toolan 1996; Harris 1998; Harris and Wolf 1998; Harris 2006a, 2006b). Exactly how integrationism impacts on our endeavour will emerge in detail in the following chapters. In general terms, the relevant feature of integrationism is the basic assumption that all signs (not only linguistic signs) are semantically indeterminate. In this perspective, semantics is the study and practice of human attempts to impose some degree of communicational determinacy on signs. The successes, failures and limitations of such efforts are, in our view, central to the enterprise of definition.

An integrationist approach to our subject seems particularly appropriate for the following two reasons. First, although all the familiar supercategories of the modern world are, at least to some extent, linguistic constructs (as argued in Harris 2003, Harris 2004, Harris 2005), the law is unique among them in the extent to which it relies overtly upon the possibility of determining verbal meanings. Appeal to the dictionary has become one of the features of contemporary jurisprudence. This presupposes the possibility of integrating lexicographical practice with legal practice. Second, the law is in any case a practical, institutionalized attempt to implement one particular type of integrational procedure; namely, integrating (1) the past verbal activities of legislators and testators with (2) the present and future activities (verbal or non-verbal) of all those affected or potentially affected by (1). The form such integration will take, or should take, it is the function of judges and courts to decide. Without that integrational function, the law would have no *raison d'être*.

Attempts to supply a theory of definition have a long history. But so too has scepticism about definition. This ranges from claims that certain words have meanings that cannot be defined to postmodernist rejections of determinacy for all words and all types of definition. Indeterminacy, however, is a more complex issue than may at first sight appear. The 'radical indeterminacy' recognized by integrationists differs in fundamental respects from the indeterminacy acknowledged by many philosophers, critics and legal theorists. We shall consider these differences in detail later.

Whereas for Robinson the kind of definition that he and others call 'stipulative' is one which features as no more than a sub-class of 'word-thing' definitions, as far as integrationists are concerned – on the contrary – it stands in the forefront of the whole topic. For if sense cannot be made of introducing a meaning by 'stipulation', one might as well give up on any other kind of definitional endeavour. Failure to recognize the centrality of this question accounts, in our opinion, for most of the difficulties that theorists of definition have encountered. We endorse the view of the commentator who observed:

> The problems of definition are constantly recurring [. . .] although there is a widespread tendency to assume that they have been solved. Practically every book on logic has a section on definition in which rules are set down and exercises prescribed for applying the rules, as if the problems were all settled. And yet, paradoxically, no problems of knowledge are less settled than those of definition, and no subject is more in need of a fresh approach.

These words were written some forty years ago (Abelson 1967), but they are no less apt today. The 'fresh approach' that the writer wished for is one we hope this book will provide. At least, we shall ask some questions about definition that have never been asked before. Whether our answers are plausible must be left for our readers to decide.

Except where otherwise indicated, the translations we provide for texts in languages other than English are our own.

R. H.
C. M. H.

I. Definition and Theory

Chapter 1

On Stipulative Definition

What people mean by what they say or write is an unending source of contention. After losing a recent libel suit, a well-known publicist is reported in the London press (*Daily Telegraph* 3 February 2005) as saying: 'I have lost this on what I could have meant rather than what I did mean.' In other words, he denies that he meant what he was interpreted as meaning, while conceding in effect that what he said could have meant what the court construed him as meaning.

In an ideal world, presumably, there would never be any doubt about what we mean by what we say. So court cases of this kind could never arise. The problem of definition, unfortunately, takes its place in a world that is far from ideal.

How far from ideal is evident not only from the fact that the loser in this case had to pay out a sum said to be in the region of a quarter of a million pounds for one misconstrued meaning but also from the fact that the press was noticeably reluctant to report the exact words in contention. Presumably this was because the newspapers feared the charge of repeating the libel. Here we pass all the way from a level of discourse where occasional misunderstandings occur, but often pass unnoticed, to a level of discourse that is booby-trapped throughout by legalities of definition.

How, then, is it possible to distinguish betweeen (1) what people mean by what they say or write, and (2) what they might have meant? That question is at the heart of any theory of definition.

* * *

Is it possible to preclude possible misinterpretation by stating the correct or intended definition in advance? Many speakers and writers seem to have believed this, and the result is what is commonly known nowadays as 'stipulative definition'. Perhaps the earliest authority to make extensive and systematic use of it for expository purposes is Euclid. In his *Elements*, a numbered list of relevant definitions (*horoi*) regularly precedes every topic discussed. A famous example is his Definition 15 in Book I: 'A circle is a plane figure contained by one line such that all the straight lines falling on it from one point among those lying within the figure are equal one to another.' For Euclid, definitions are to be distinguished from postulates (*aitemata*) and from common notions (*koinai ennoiai*). An example of the former is 'All right angles are equal to one another' and of the latter 'If equals are subtracted from equals, the remainders are equal'. In drawing these distinctions Euclid appears to be following Aristotle (*Posterior Analytics*). Definitions, postulates and common notions jointly make up what Euclid regards as having to be taken for granted in geometry.

Euclid's thinking marks a stage at which geometry was being transformed from a collection of empirical observations about measurement into an axiomatic system. Ideally, such a system would consist of the minimum number of basic assumptions, plus the minimum number of steps or procedures required to derive deductively therefrom all the truths of geometry. The role of definitions would be to supply precise meanings for all terms entering into propositions otherwise unprovable. Euclid's progress towards setting up such a system, although an impressive intellectual achievement, leaves a great deal to be desired and was criticized even in antiquity. His definitions have aroused much controversy. From their form it is not obvious what exactly their epistemological status is. Some critics have maintained that Euclid's so-called definitions tacitly rely on a prior intuitive grasp of the notions being presented: 'they reduce to simple empirical descriptions' (Blanché 1970: 21). It is certainly open to doubt whether anyone totally unfamiliar with what a circle is would be able to work it out just from Euclid's definition. It is also arguable that this definition comprises or conflates two quite different notions: (1) that it is actually possible for there to be a figure having the properties mentioned, and (2) the proposal that such a figure should be called (for purposes of exposition) a *circle.* (1) is clearly an assertion that is either true or false, whereas (2) is merely a linguistic proposal contributing nothing at all to the content of geometry. In other words, the objection would be that Euclid confuses definition of a geometrical term with 'real definition' (see Chapter 3).

Aristotle had already made the point that if a geometer's best attempts to draw a certain geometrical figure always contain minor imperfections or inaccuracies, that does not invalidate the definition of the figure in question. In *Posterior Analytics* (I.10.76b. 35ff.) he denies that definitions are hypotheses, 'for they do not assert either existence or non-existence'. Definitions (*horoi*) 'need only to be understood'. This is the source of the claim constantly reiterated later throughout the Western tradition that a definition has no truth value. Whatever view Euclid himself may have taken of the matter, it seems clear that many writers would never have proposed stipulative definitions had they not supposed that these were more than convenient pieces of nomenclature, bearing no relation to the facts of the matter under discussion. On the contrary, their motivation is in many cases quite patently to assist in revealing truths that would otherwise risk being obscured for want of terminological clarity.

A straightforward example of such a case, far removed from the ambitious enterprise of Euclid, is Sir James Frazer's definition of *myth, legend* and *folk-tale.* In the Introduction to his edition and translation of Apollodorus, Frazer wrote:

> As the distinction between myth, legend, and folk-tale is not always clearly apprehended or uniformly observed, it may be well to define the sense in which I employ those terms.

> By myths I understand mistaken understanding of phenomena, whether of human life or of external nature. . . .
>
> By legends I understand traditions, whether oral or written, which relate the fortunes of real people in the past, or which describe events, not necessarily human, that are said to have occurred at real places. . . .
>
> By folk-tales I understand narratives invented by persons unknown and handed down at first by word of mouth from generation to generation, narratives which, though they profess to describe actual occurrences, are in fact purely imaginary, having no other aim than the entertainment of the hearer and making no real claim on his credulity. (Frazer 1921: xxvii–xxix)

It would be absurd to suppose that Frazer introduces these stipulative definitions just for his own terminological convenience, without any implication that they correspond to any actual distinctions detectable among the innumerable accounts which go to make up humanity's vast repertoire of stories.

Stipulative definition is the practice advocated by Bacon in *The Advancement of Learning* when he enjoins his readers in all controversial matters to define their terms at the outset, in order to avoid misinterpretations: for

> . . . words, as a Tartar's bow, do shoot back upon the understanding of the wisest, and mightily entangle and pervert the judgment. So as it is almost necessary in all controversies and disputations to imitate the wisdom of the mathematicians, in setting down in the very beginning the definitions of our words and terms that others may know how we accept and understand them, and whether they concur with us or no. (Bacon 1605: 2. xiv.11)

A long line of eminent writers seem to have followed Bacon's advice. Hobbes in *Leviathan* declares:

> By Manners, I mean not here, Decency of behaviour; as how one man should salute another, or how a man should wash his mouth, or pick his teeth before company, and other such points of the *Small Moralls*; But those qualities of man-kind, that concern their living together in Peace, and Unity.
>
> (Hobbes 1651: I.xi)

Adam Smith in *The Wealth of Nations* forewarns his reader:

> By the money-price of goods, it is to be observed, I understand always the quantity of pure gold or silver for which they are sold, without any regard to the denomination of the coin. (Smith 1776: I.v)

Kant in his *Critique of Pure Reason* announces:

> By the term 'knowledge *a priori*,' therefore, we shall in the sequel understand, not such as is independent of this or that kind of experience, but such as is absolutely so of *all* experience. (Kant 1781: Introduction, I)

Unfortunately, it is not always so clear that the stipulative definition succeeds in elucidating the meaning intended. It may even happen that the definition itself begs more questions than it answers. For example, in *Aesthetics and History*, Bernard Berenson writes:

> By 'spiritual significance', on the other hand, I mean to designate whatever affords us the prospects of easing the dead weight of matter, whatever gives us the hope that our lives will amount to something more than the unwinding of the coil of energy which we brought with us at birth; but promises that our activities will be progressively directed toward the building of a social structure where it will be safe and praiseworthy to live free from care, and greed and cunning; where being will count more than doing, the intransitive more than the transitive; where man may dwell once more in an earthly paradise, but this time feeding as sinlessly from the tree of knowledge as from the tree of life, and blessed by the gods revealed by his own consciousness and conscience. (Berenson 1950: 109)

It seems to us to be dubious whether this definition makes Berenson's use of the expression *spiritual significance* any the less obscure, particularly in its application to works of art.

Our list of examples might easily be continued down to the present day. If stipulative definition were no more than a literary practice confined to the works of scholars it might not be of great practical importance; but such definitions are commonplace in many mundane circumstances. They occur, for example, in insurance policies and legal documents of all kinds – their purpose being to avoid potential misapprehensions concerning the commitments of the parties involved. Arguably, the very notion of a binding contract, whether commercial or political, implies the acceptance of such definitions, even if they are not always made as explicit as they might be. In other words, without the possibility of stipulative definitions it seems that not merely the arts and sciences but the social order itself would lack a sound foundation.

* * *

There is a wide gamut of purposes to which stipulative definition may be put. The most trivial of these is simply as a rhetorical device to delimit a certain field of discussion. For example, in his Gifford Lecture of 1972 on 'The frontiers of psychology', Christopher Longuet-Higgins began by announcing:

> This year our subject is *The Development of Mind*. In case, by some oversight, we should fail to define 'development', let me say at once how I shall be using the word. I want to use it in its biological sense – or, rather, in its two biological senses. The first sense occurs in the name developmental psychology, which is the study of mental development in the individual from conception to senility. . . .

> The other biological sense of the word 'development' is the evolutionary sense. Two billion years ago, we believe, there was a primaeval soup in which the first living things assembled themselves. Whatever one's views about the nature of mind, one can hardly deny that there is a good deal more mental activity going on now than there was then. (Longuet-Higgins 1973: 1)

It is quite clear that what Longuet-Higgins is doing is something which has little in common with what Frazer attempts in the passage cited earlier. There is no concern to distinguish an idiosyncratic or potentially contentious meaning of a term from some more widely accepted or less contentious meaning. Moreover, it is difficult to see that what Longuet-Higgins calls two different 'senses' of the word development are actually different at all. In short, the speaker could have said all he wanted to say simply by announcing that he was going to talk about the development of mind in the individual human being as well as in living creatures in general. The resort to stipulative definition is just window dressing.

Likewise, we find the historian D. C. Somervell stating:

> The title of this book is *A History of Western Europe*, a term that can be variously defined. We take it here to include France, Italy, and Germany; it obviously does not exclude Holland and Belgium, Spain and Portugal, but these are not Great Powers. Our principal study will be the development of France, Italy, and Germany, their relations with each other, and with their other neighbours. (Somervell 1928: 7)

Here the author is not seriously attempting to redefine the term *Western Europe*, but simply announcing the limits of his own discussion.

William Whewell proposes a stipulative definition of *experience* in his *Philosophy of the Inductive Sciences*:

> I here employ the term Experience in a more definite and limited sense than that which it possesses in common usage; for I restrict it to matters belonging to the domain of science. In such cases, the knowledge which we acquire, by means of experience, is of a clear and precise nature; and the passions and feelings and interests, which make the lessons of experience in practical matters so difficult to read aright, no longer disturb and confuse us. We may, therefore, hope, by attending to such cases, to learn what efficacy experience really has, in the discovery of truth. (Whewell 1847: I.62)

Similarly, in *The Laws of Nature*, the distinguished physicist Sir Rudolf Peierls warns his readers:

> When we speak here of matter we mean by this only inanimate matter. The laws of nature which will be discussed throughout this book do not include a description of life or of living beings. (Peierls 1955: 15)

J. B. Priestley's book *The English Novel* begins:

> What is a novel? Sometimes people use the term to describe only certain kinds of fiction. Thus, if a story is filled with tea parties, they will call it 'a novel'; but if it is filled with sea fights, they will call it 'a romance.' When I talk of novels in these chapters, however, I mean any and every kind of fiction. The only definition of the novel I can offer is that it is a narrative in prose treating chiefly of imaginary characters and events. Some novels, such as Scott's *Kenilworth* or Thackeray's *Esmond*, do show us actual historical personages, but nevertheless they all contain far more fiction than fact.
>
> (Priestley 1927: 5)

All the above cases may be described as *ad hoc* definitions, set up arbitrarily to suit the purpose to hand, but claiming or implying nothing further.

* * *

A more serious purpose may be discerned in G. E. Moore's stipulative definition of the word *voluntary* in the opening chapter of his book *Ethics*. Moore sets out a particular theory of ethics as follows:

> This theory starts from the familiar fact that we all very often seem to have a choice between several different actions, any one of which we might do, if we chose. Whether, in such cases, we really do have a choice, in the sense that we ever really *could* choose any other action than the one which in the end we do choose, is a question upon which it does not pronounce and which will have to be considered later on. All that the theory assumes is that, in many cases, there certainly are a considerable number of different actions, any one of which we could do, *if* we chose, and between which, therefore, in *this* sense, we have a choice; while there are others which we could not do, even if we did choose to do them. It assumes, that is to say, that in many cases, *if* we had chosen differently, we should have acted differently; and this seems to be an unquestionable fact, which must be admitted, even if we hold that it is never the case that we *could* have chosen differently. Our theory assumes, then, that many of our actions are under the control of our wills, in the sense that *if*, just before we began to do them, we had chosen not to do them, we *should* not have done them; and I propose to call all actions of this kind *voluntary* actions. (Moore 1912: 10–11)

The reader may initially be puzzled to understand exactly what is at stake here. The example does not have the triviality of Longuet-Higgins' definition of *development*, nor the obvious contentiousness of Frazer's definition of *myth*. The stipulative definition of *voluntary* that Moore proposes seems at first sight entirely uncontroversial, but on closer inspection it turns out not to be so, as Moore goes on to point out.

> It should be noticed that, if we define voluntary actions in this way, it is by no means certain that all or nearly all voluntary actions are actually themselves chosen or willed. It seems highly probable that an immense number of the actions which we do, and which we *could* have avoided, *if* we had chosen to avoid them, were not themselves willed at all. It is only true of them that they are 'voluntary' in the sense that a particular act of will, just before their occurrence, would have been sufficient to *prevent* them; not in the sense that they themselves were brought about by being willed. And perhaps there is some departure from common usage in calling all such acts 'voluntary'. I do not think, however, that it is in accordance with common usage to restrict the name 'voluntary' to actions which are quite certainly actually willed. And the class of actions to which I propose to give the name – all those, namely, which we could have prevented, *if*, immediately beforehand, we had willed to do so – do, I think, certainly require to be distinguished by some special name. (Moore 1912: 11)

In short, the purpose of the stipulative definition is to draw attention to a distinction that is blurred in the common usage of the word *voluntary*. This distinction, as one might expect, will turn out to play a significant role in Moore's account of ethics.

* * *

Different again is Darwin's stipulative definition of *natural selection*. For here is a case in which one can scarcely speak of 'common usage' at all until Darwin's theory focused attention upon that expression.

> This preservation of favourable individual differences and variations, and the destruction of those which are injurious, I have called Natural Selection, or the Survival of the Fittest. Variations neither useful nor injurious would not be affected by natural selection, and would be left either a fluctuating element, as perhaps we see in certain polymorphic species, or would ultimately become fixed, owing to the nature of the organism and the nature of the conditions. (Darwin 1859: 81)

Darwin proceeds to deal with various objections to, and misunderstandings of, the term *natural selection*. In particular he is at pains to make it clear that *selection* here does not imply conscious choice. He goes on to disavow any intention on his part to attribute to Nature a purpose, and supplies to this end two more stipulative definitions:

> it is difficult to avoid personifying the word Nature; but I mean by Nature, only the aggregate action and product of many natural laws, and by laws the sequence of events as ascertained by us. (Darwin 1859: 81)

The way Darwin chooses to formulate his definition of *natural selection*, by coupling it with *survival of the fittest*, raises further questions. Does *natural selection*, as defined, mean the same as *survival of the fittest*? If not, what is the connection between them? Are these two separate definitions, or alternative versions of a single definition?

To the related expression *struggle for existence* Darwin devotes a separate section of Chapter 3, which begins:

> I should premise that I use this term in a large and metaphorical sense including dependence of one being on another, and including (which is more important) not only the life of the individual, but success in leaving progeny. (Darwin 1859: 68)

Whatever one makes of this, it is clear that a series of stipulative definitions is being put in place to support the main argument of *The Origin of Species*. The chain leads back in assured steps to the point of departure for any nineteenth-century naturalist: namely, the understanding of Nature herself.

The effect of adopting stipulative definitions can often be to turn what look at first sight like empirical claims into tautologies. Thus in the example cited above, the proposition that 'variations neither useful nor injurious are not affected by natural selection' is not, as it might seem, the summary of many careful investigations carried out by the naturalist: the proposition is already self-evidently true once Darwin's definition of *natural selection* is accepted.

In this perspective, stipulative definition emerges as a tactic deployed to support a certain line of argument when appeal to observation runs out. (For it would be a gross mistake to suppose that natural selection is observable, however many observers are available, and however many opportunities of observation.) More importantly, in the case of *natural selection* one sees stipulative definition serving to introduce at one stroke a new concept immediately applicable throughout several separate domains of scientific inquiry. And that immediately puts *natural selection* in a different class from any of the other examples considered so far.

* * *

It is interesting to ask how Darwin's use of stipulative definition relates to the modern proliferation of scientific terminology. New discoveries in botany, biology, physics, chemistry and many other fields have called for names, where previously no name existed. Every proposal of such a neologism constitutes, in practice, a stipulative definition. Some individual or group of individuals must at some point make a proposal to the effect that the newly recognized phenomenon (variety, species, force, particle, process, etc.) shall be called by a certain term. The term in question thus acquires by stipulation its definition. Whether such a neologism gains general acceptance is another question, and how it does so is another question again. But its introduction is a matter of stipulation. Names do not drop out of thin air.

In some cases, what is named is an already existing type of observable physical object hitherto unnamed (as in the discovery of a previously unknown kind of plant or insect). This is the model of nomenclature encapsulated in the biblical story of Adam naming the animals. The animals already existed, regardless of what Adam stipulated their names to be.

In other cases, what is named is a 'theoretical object', previously unnamed because the need to identify and discuss it had not yet arisen. In this second type of case, it is the function of a stipulative definition to formalize this recognition. Typical theoretical objects are units of measurement and hypothetical causes. In Genesis, God never asked Adam to name theoretical objects. But since antiquity it has often been assumed that theoretical nomenclature is some kind of extension of Adamic nomenclature. Whether that is the case raises a whole raft of questions that are very pertinent to definition.

It has sometimes been argued that stipulating new names for new theoretical objects is not merely a convenience but an essential part of the advancement of science. Kelvin in his famous paper on electrical units of measurement lamented the lack of a name for the reciprocal of resistance, and proposed one:

> How much we owe for the possession of names, is best illustrated by how much we lose – how great a disadvantage we are put to – in cases in which we have not names. We want a name for the reciprocal of resistance. We have the name 'conductivity,' but we want a name for the unit of conductivity. I made a box of resistance coils thirty years ago, and another fifteen years ago, for the measurement of conductivity, and they both languished for the want of a name. My own pupils will go on using the resistance box in ohms, rather than the conductivity box, because in using the latter it is so puzzling to say 'The resistance is the reciprocal of the sum of the reciprocals of these resistances.'
>
> (Kelvin 1883: 133–4)

Kelvin's suggestion was to write the word *ohm* backwards, thus yielding *mho* as the name of the unit that was missing. He added modestly:

> I do not say that *mho* is the word to be used, but I wish it could be accepted, so that we might have it at once in general use. We shall have a word for it when we have the thing, or rather, I should say, *we shall have the thing when we have the word.* (Kelvin 1883: 135–6. Our italics.)

The neologism *mho* had some success in scientific circles, but was eventually replaced by *siemens* (named after Ernst Werner von Siemens) as the unit of electrical conductance.

* * *

Sometimes what is stipulated is the meaning not of a single word or phrase, but of an entire statement. There is the seventeenth-century example of Robert Boyle's defence, in Part 2 of *The Sceptical Chymist*, of the claim that fire does not necessarily dissolve a substance into its ultimate constituents. This was a live issue in the experimental chemistry of the day.

Boyle writes:

> That I may not make this paradox a greater than I needs must, I will first briefly explain what the proposition means, before I proceed to argue for it.
> (Boyle 1661: 63)

Boyle focuses upon two possible misinterpretations. The first is the following:

> . . . I do not mean that anything is separable from a body by fire, that was not materially pre-existent in it; for it far exceeds the power of meerly naturall agents, and consequently of fire, to produce anew, so much as one atome of matter, which they can but modifie and alter, not create; . . .
> (Boyle 1661: 63)

The second misapprehension is described thus:

> Nor does the proposition peremptorily deny, but that some things obtained by the fire from a mixt body, may have been more than barely materially pre-existent in it, since there are concretes, which before they be exposed to the fire afford us several documents of their abounding, some with salt, and others with sulphur. (Boyle 1661: 63)

Boyle then sums up his stipulation:

> That then which I mean by the proposition I am explaining, is, that it may without absurdity be doubted whether or no the differing substances obtainable from a concrete dissipated by the fire were so existent in it in that forme (at least as to their minute parts) wherein we find them when the analysis is over, that the fire did only disjoyne and extricate the corpuscles of one principle from those of the other wherewith before they were blended.
> (Boyle 1661: 64)

So here a stipulative definition is deployed even when there is no apparent doubt about the *bona fides* of the relevant individual terms (*fire, body, natural agent*, etc.).

* * *

Two hundred years after Boyle, Ruskin took Mill to task for failing, in his *Political Economy*, to give an adequate definition of *wealth*. In the 1871 edition of *Munera Pulveris*, Ruskin complains:

> 'Every one has a notion, sufficiently correct for common purposes, of what is meant by wealth,' wrote Mr. Mill, in the outset of his treatise; and contentedly proceeded, as if a chemist should proceed to investigate the laws of chemistry without endeavouring to ascertain the nature of fire and water, because every one had a notion of them, 'sufficiently correct for common purposes.'
>
> But even that apparently indisputable statement was untrue. There is not one person in ten thousand who has a notion sufficiently correct, even for the commonest purposes, of 'what is meant' by wealth; still less of what wealth everlastingly *is*, whether we mean it or not; which it is the business of every student of economy to ascertain. (Ruskin 1871: §§1–2)

Having taken this intellectual high ground, Ruskin could hardly shirk the task of providing his own stipulative definitions of *wealth, money, riches* and various other terms, which he proceeds to do in the opening chapter ('Definitions') of *Munera Pulveris.* It is on the basis of these definitions that he attacks the economic theorists of his day for being 'without exception, incapable of apprehending the nature of intrinsic value at all.'

* * *

At the opposite end of the spectrum from plugging perceived gaps or remedying uncertainties in scientific or technical vocabulary comes the deployment of stipulative definition for a much more ambitious and dramatic purpose: introducing a new scientific framework altogether. This has much more in common with Euclid's original attempt to systematize the whole of geometry. The classic modern case is Einstein's stipulative definition of *simultaneity.* This was not a question of opting for one of a number of definitions already in circulation; nor of modifying one of them for the author's special purposes. It involved claiming that all previous definitions were inadequate, i.e. based on fundamental misapprehensions about the nature of time.

Nothing as revolutionary as this applies to the majority of stipulative definitions. In Chapter VIII of *Relativity*, Einstein introduces the problem by considering what it means to say that two flashes of lightning occurred simultaneously. He dismisses with something like contempt the suggestion that the meaning is clear from the words in which the statement is expressed. This will not pass muster in physics: the physicist needs a practical test procedure which will show whether the two flashes of lightning were simultaneous or not. And this in turn reflects back upon the definition of *simultaneity.*

> We thus require a definition of simultaneity such that this definition supplies us with the method by means of which, in the present case, he [sc. the physicist] can decide by experiment whether or not both the lightning strokes occurred simultaneously. (Einstein 1961: 22)

At this point in the argument, Einstein goes out of his way to emphasize that this is not a matter of devising some special terminology of interest only to physicists; for he adds:

> As long as this requirement is not satisfied, I allow myself to be deceived as a physicist (and of course the same applies if I am not a physicist), when I imagine that I am able to attach a meaning to the statement of simultaneity.
> (Einstein 1961: 22)

It is worth pausing to note the implications of this. What Einstein is saying is that we do not discover the definition of simultaneity by looking up *simultaneity* or related words in a dictionary. For there we might find, for instance, that *simultaneous* means 'occurring at the same time'. But that brings us back to square one. We are no further forward in knowing how to determine whether two flashes of lightning occur 'at the same time'.

Einstein goes on to consider a practical proposal for determining whether one flash of lightning at point *A* is simultaneous with another flash of lightning at point *B*. The observer is placed exactly at the mid-point *M* of the distance between *A* and *B*. An arrangement of mirrors allows both *A* and *B* to be kept under continuous observation. Then, if the observer at *M* sees a flash of lightning at *A* occurring concurrently with a flash of lightning at *B*, the two flashes are counted as being simultaneous.

But this will not quite satisfy Einstein either. For the experiment depends on assuming that light travels the distance *AM* at the same velocity as it travels the distance *BM*. Unfortunately, no such assurance can be given without a means of measuring time. But then we are back to the problem of simultaneity, where we began.

The only way out of this circle, according to Einstein, is to recognize that requiring the time taken for light to travel from *A* to *M* to be the same as the time taken for the light to travel from *B* to *M*

> is in reality neither a *supposition nor a hypothesis* about the physical nature of light, but a *stipulation* which I can make of my own freewill in order to arrive at a definition of simultaneity. (Einstein 1961: 23. Italics in the original.)

Under the terms of this stipulation, the problem is solved, given what the physicist demands of a definition.

> There is only *one* demand to be made of the definition of simultaneity, namely, that in every real case it must supply us with an empirical decision as to whether or not the conception that has to be defined is fulfilled.
> (Einstein 1961: 23)

This demand is the cornerstone of Einstein's theory of relativity.

* * *

We have now offered a fairly wide range of illustrative examples of what we consider to be, or are willing to call, stipulative definitions. Does that mean we have, in effect, given our own stipulative definition of the expression *stipulative definition*? And if so, is that a legitimate first move in what purports to be a general analytic survey of definition? Is it not question-beggingly regressive (i.e. producing yet another stipulative definition in order to solve the problem of defining *stipulative definition*)?

The procedure we have chosen to adopt, i.e. citing examples, is sometimes called 'extensive definition' or 'denotative definition' (see Chapter 7). But there are authorities, beginning with Plato (see Chapter 3), who deny that this counts as definition at all. What lies behind this disagreement?

Stebbing (*A Modern Introduction to Logic*) approaches it by considering various possible ways in which *A* might explain to *B* what is meant by the word *sonnet.* One of *A*'s answers is:

> 'You know Wordsworth's *Earth has not anything to show more fair,* and Shakespeare's *Shall I compare thee to a summer's day?* and Keats's *Much have I travelled in the realms of gold?* Well, these are sonnets.' (Stebbing 1930: 421)

According to Stebbing, this does not constitute giving a definition of the word *sonnet,* or even of what *A* meant by the use of the word on the occasion that prompted *B*'s question.

> It may . . . be doubted whether the giving of typical examples can rightly be regarded as a process of defining. B must be acquainted with the examples given if he is to understand 'sonnet' by means of them. He would then know more or less how to apply the word 'sonnet' but it seems doubtful whether he would know what 'sonnet' expresses. (Stebbing 1930: 422)

Stebbing's implied distinction between 'understanding' the word and 'knowing what it expresses' is not further elaborated, but the reasoning seems to be as follows: this is not a definition because although *B* now knows more or less what kind of poem counts as a sonnet, *A*'s answer does not explain precisely *what* makes a sonnet a sonnet. If *B* wants to know that, he will have to work it out for himself (if he can). Stebbing adds the finger-wagging admonition:

> We must be careful not to use 'definition' so widely that it comes to stand for any process enabling us to learn the application of words. These processes are so different that to call them by the same name leads to confusion.
> (Stebbing 1930: 422)

It seems to us, however, that no less confusion is likely to be caused by arbitrarily restricting the term *definition* to suit the professional interests of logicians. We are not particularly concerned with whether the procedure we have followed above is itself called *definition* or not. It stands or falls not as the exposition of a type of definition, but as an appropriate introduction to the topic. We do not deny that it can be seen as an attempt to make clear how we will be using the expression *stipulative definition* for purposes of the present discussion. But as far as we can see, there is no culpable evasion or circularity involved in that.

Our examples were chosen in part to bring home the point that questions of definition are not just verbal quibbles, even if lawyers and legislators, not to mention lexicographers and philosophers, spend endless time quibbling over them. Neither Darwin nor Einstein can be dismissed as quibblers. The issues they address go far beyond any pedantic concern for verbal niceties. For them, stipulative definition holds the key to a whole way of thinking.

The examples were also chosen with a view to illustrating our contention (mentioned in the Preface) that explicating definition involves linguistic theory. For in order to make sense of the examples we have cited (whether or not you then accept these particular examples as proper examples of stipulative definition), it is necessary to make certain assumptions about language and linguistic communities. Let us try to spell out the most important of them.

Perhaps the most obvious of these assumptions is that not everyone understands words in the same way. Stipulative definition is a practice which would be quite unnecessary if all words had determinate meanings. The reason for stipulative definition would vanish if one could be quite sure that a word would be understood in the same sense by all its users and interpreters. That the practice of stipulative definition exists at all is the clearest evidence that languages are not regarded by their speakers and writers as fixed codes or repositories of determinate signs. The existence of a familar language affords no assurance whatsoever, even among its highly educated members, of a reliable consensus concerning the meanings of any given set of linguistic forms.

Frazer's case alone provides a clear example of this indeterminacy. It was precisely because Frazer realized he could not rely on any such consensus that he believed it necessary to set out his own definitions of the terms *myth*, *legend* and *folk-tale*. By his own account, he felt it likely that different readers of his English text might well attribute different meanings to these terms, or even fail to distinguish between them.

Frazer's assumption is characteristic of naturally heterogeneous communities. In such communities, participatory membership does not preclude having conflicting individual views about many things, including the meanings of words. It is only against the background of this linguistic assumption that the practice of stipulative definition makes sense.

This conclusion is of some theoretical importance in view of the fact that a great deal of academic linguistics over the past century has been based on a model which explicitly rejects the notion of intralingual heterogeneity. One much-quoted formulation of this model of a 'completely homogeneous speech-community' runs as follows:

> Linguistic theory is concerned primarily with an ideal speaker-listener, in a completely homogeneous speech-community, who knows its language

> perfectly and is unaffected by such grammatically irrelevant conditions as memory limitations, distractions, shifts of attention and interest, and errors (random or characteristic) in applying his knowledge of the language in actual performance. (Chomsky 1965: 3)

Here is an approach which stands the notion of a naturally heterogeneous linguistic community on its head, i.e. eliminating by theoretical fiat all those individual differences that a scrupulous observer might have set out to investigate. The homogeneous model espoused by Chomsky and like-minded linguists represents a totalitarian conception of the role of the individual in society. Nor can this unwelcome conclusion be evaded by insisting that the homogeneous model is merely an 'idealization'. On the contrary, its role as an ideal betrays an underlying obsession with dismissing individual differences as aberrations in a well-conducted collectivity of human beings. It stands at the opposite end of the theoretical spectrum from the integrationist model of communication, on which the present study is based. From an integrationist perspective, the totalitarian idealization is both inappropriate and objectionable on various counts.

Whatever one may think about the wisdom of adapting totalitarian models in the study of language, the relevance to stipulative definition is clear. If Sir James Frazer and his readers had been members of a 'completely homogeneous' community, his professed anxiety about definitions would have been pointless. For either the word *myth* would have been part of their vocabulary, or it would not. Assuming the former, that word would already be known to Frazer's readers in exactly the sense assigned to it. Nor need he have worried that perhaps they had temporarily forgotten its meaning, or confused it with some other word. For the homogeneous model (or Chomsky's version of it) explicitly rules out 'memory limitations, distractions, shifts of attention', etc. The same applies, *mutatis mutandis*, not only to *myth*, *legend* and *folk-tale*, but to every word in their language.

The homogeneous model thus ensures mutual comprehension and rules out any possibility of misunderstanding. It allows no room for divergent assignments of form and meaning by different members of the linguistic community. It not only assumes but demands that a language operate as a fixed code. Furthermore, this assured consensus is envisaged as applying not only to the community's knowledge of internal relationships between one word and another (e.g. between *myth* and *legend*), but also to 'applying . . . knowledge of the language in actual performance' (Chomsky 1965: 3). In other words, given specific cases, it involves identifying some stories as 'myths', 'legends', etc., or refusing to accept those identifications. Otherwise, it would have been vacuous for Frazer to insist on his preferred definitions, i.e. if the definitions in question implied no particular classification of already well-known stories. (Story *A* is a myth, but story *B* is not.)

A related point is made by Wittgenstein:

> If language is to be a means of communication there must be agreement not only in definitions (*Definitionen*) but also (queer as this may sound) in judgments (*Urteilen*). (Wittgenstein 2001: §242)

Here Chomsky and Wittgenstein both fall into the same trap. Certainly it would be fatuous for Peter and Priscilla to agree that 'two eggs plus two more eggs amount to four eggs in all' if they could not agree as to what counts as one egg in the first place. The judgement that *this* object (a particular example) counts as one egg is crucial, and so it must be for each and every egg counted. But it does not follow from this that Peter and Priscilla have somehow reached agreement by sharing a common definition of *egg*. That would be a plain *non sequitur*.

The next point that needs to be made about proposed homogeneous models of the linguistic community is that they are themselves, in effect, stipulative definitions. That is to say, the proposal amounts to announcing: 'By a *language* I mean that common system of verbal communication which all members of a community share (irrespective of loss of memory, lapses of attention, etc.)'. This being so, any attempt to invalidate the practice of stipulative definition by appeal to homogeneous (fixed-code) models of what a language is must be rejected. Such an attempt would be to embark on a semantic regress, given that such models are themselves stipulative. The point has important consequences for the rationale of any inquiry into the kind of definitional practice which Frazer, Darwin, Einstein and so many other writers appear frequently to rely on.

A further theoretical point to which we wish to draw attention is the following. In order to make sense of stipulative definition, it has to be assumed that the linguistic sign is arbitrary (in the sense of Saussure 1922). That is to say, there is no *natural* connection between its form and its meaning. A word does not mean what it does because there is some hidden principle determining what meaning that particular sequence of sounds or letters *must* have. In principle, any form might have any meaning, and any meaning be expressed by any form. If it were otherwise, there would be natural constraints on the freedom of Frazer, Darwin, Einstein, *et al.* to select a linguistic form and assign or re-assign a meaning to it. But there appear to be no such constraints.

Finally, it has to be assumed that at least some efforts at stipulative definition are communicationally effective: that is to say, that the authors of such definitions do sometimes succeed in their professed objective. For if they never succeeded to their own satisfaction (and that of others), it would be difficult to account for the persistence of the practice among intelligent and well educated people who clearly take the task of communication very seriously. If, for example, they had found by experience that attempts at stipulative definition were either ignored or uniformly greeted by incomprehension on the part of audiences or readers, they would presumably have abandoned the strategy long ago.

In short, in order to construct any plausible account of definition, a necessary condition is a theory of language which allows the possibility of definition by stipulation. Not all theories of language meet this requirement. We shall return to this point later. An integrationist approach recognizes definitions as being stipulative not necessarily on the basis of their author's expressed intentions (which are by no means always reliable), but on the basis of the function they fulfil in integrating communication between users. Typically, a stipulative definition serves to provide hearers or readers with an interpretation of an expression that might otherwise be in doubt or unavailable to them. Such definitions do not automatically command assent; nor do they invariably deserve respect. But they provide practical guidelines for the conduct of communicational activities.

Before pursuing these matters further, we shall consider two other types of definition that have been widely discussed ever since the topic first appeared in the curriculum of the Western educational tradition.

Chapter 2

On Definition and Common Usage

The meanings specified in stipulative definitions are often contrasted with those accepted in 'common usage' (as in the passages cited from Whewell and Moore in the preceding chapter). John Stuart Mill in his *System of Logic* distinguished these two kinds of definition as follows:

> The simplest and most correct notion of a Definition is, a proposition declaratory of the meaning of a word; namely, either the meaning which it bears in common acceptation, or that which the speaker or writer, for the particular purposes of his discourse, intends to annex to it. (Mill 1884: I.viii.1)

Sometimes we are told that a non-stipulative definition is 'a form of history'. It is an attempt to state 'what certain persons meant by a certain word at a certain less or more specified time and place' (Robinson 1954: 35). A closely related view is that non-stipulative definitions are 'empirical (and therefore corrigible) reports of linguistic behavior' (Abelson 1967: 314).

The terminology adopted by various writers in drawing the distinction is confusing. Robinson calls non-stipulative definitions 'lexical'. This is the term also adopted by Hurley: 'A lexical definition is used to report the meaning that a word already has in a language' (Hurley 1988: 82). Abelson, however, calls such definitions 'linguistic'. Neither *lexical* nor *linguistic* is a happy choice, since both adjectives could apply to stipulative definitions as well. The same must be said about *verbal*, which is the term chosen by some writers to designate stipulative definitions. In what follows we shall try to avoid these terminological sources of potential misunderstanding as far as possible. We shall reserve the term *lexical* not to distinguish non-stipulative from stipulative definitions, but to distinguish the definition of words from the definition of things (or 'real definition').

The kind of distinction that Mill was trying to draw is by no means a product of modern or even post-Renaissance thinking about language. Perhaps the earliest example on record comes from Book I of Plato's *Republic* when Socrates is arguing with Thrasymachus about justice (*Republic* 336ff.). Thrasymachus is trying to maintain what Cornford calls an extreme version of 'the doctrine that might is right' (Cornford 1941: 14). What is 'just' is simply what is in the interests of the ruler or the ruling party. It does not matter whether power is wielded by a despot, or a democracy, or an oligarchy. 'That is what I mean;' says Thrasymachus, 'in all states alike "right" has the same meaning, namely what is for the interest of the party established in power, and that is the strongest' (Cornford 1941: 18).

Socrates objects to this that rulers can make mistakes about what is in their own interests; so what Thrasymachus is saying is that right is what rulers *think* is in their own interests, whether it really is or not. To counter this objection, Thrasymachus claims that whenever rulers make mistakes about it they are not acting as rulers. They do not, in such cases, deserve to be called 'rulers', any more than a mathematician who gets his sums wrong deserves to be called a 'mathematician'. 'The ruler, in so far as he is acting as a ruler, makes no mistakes and consequently enjoins what is best for himself' (Cornford 1941: 20).

But Socrates is not to be tricked into accepting this novel account of what it is to be a ruler. He protests:

> to prevent any more misunderstanding, when you speak of that ruler or stronger party whose interest the weaker ought to serve, please make it clear whether you are using words in the ordinary way or in that strict sense you have just defined. (*Republic* 341b; Cornford: 21)

In effect, he is telling Thrasymachus: 'Of course, if you wish, you can redefine the term *ruler* in order to win the argument, and no one can prevent you. But that is not what it means in common usage.' Thus Thrasymachus has to choose between opting for common usage – and therefore abandoning his argument – or else sticking to his own definition. He chooses the latter, which is just the corner into which Socrates wishes to drive him.

More than two millennia separate the *Republic* from Mill's *System of Logic*, but there are two parallels worth noting. The first is that when a distinction is introduced between stipulative definition and common usage, it is common usage that wears the trousers. Stipulative definition is cast from the beginning as a *departure* from common usage: it is something not sanctioned in advance. Anyone opting for stipulative definition against common usage is thus automatically put on the defensive, inasmuch as a special *justification* for departing from common usage is implicitly required. Common usage, on the other hand, is tacitly assumed to require no justification. Its meanings are in order just as they are. Or, as Gilbert Ryle put it more explicitly and much later, 'naive users' of ordinary language are not 'in any doubt or confusion about what their expressions mean': nor do they need the results of philosophical analysis in order to 'continue to use intelligently their ordinary modes of expression or to use them so that they are intelligible to others' (Ryle 1931: 13). The well-foundedness of common usage became something of a philosophical mantra in the twentieth century, but it has ancient antecedents in the Western tradition.

The second parallel is that the distinction is invoked only at the point when it is needed to support or defend a position that would otherwise appear vulnerable. In both cases there is a whole philosophical agenda at stake: in one instance Socrates' analysis of justice (on which the entire programme for Plato's ideal state depends) and Mill's theory of logic in the other.

Are these parallels over such a wide interval of time purely fortuitous? We do not think so. What links Socrates/Plato to Mill across the centuries is a common feature in their philosophy of language. They are both committed to a particular version of what integrationists call 'the language myth'. What we understand the language myth to consist in we shall now explain.

* * *

It is difficult to get very far in discussing definition without encountering two widespread beliefs about language that surface time and again in the Western tradition.

(1) One is the belief that *words convey thoughts*. They have a 'telementational' function; that is, they provide the means by which what *A* is thinking may be transferred from *A*'s mind to *B*'s. If *A* is to speak clearly, so as to convey a desired message to *B*, *A* must choose the right words, and if *B* is to understand, *B* must grasp the thoughts conveyed by those words. Languages, on this view, are systems of signs (words and their combinations) which have this telementational or thought-transference function.

(2) The other is the belief that if *A* and *B* both speak the same language, they will both already know the same set of forms and meanings. The assumption is that a language is a *single* set of forms and meanings, known to those whose language it is. In other words, for *A* and *B* their shared language functions as a stable fixed code. They do not each have their own idiosyncratic or variable version of it. If either attaches different meanings to the same forms, or if one uses forms unfamiliar to the other, they do not speak the same language.

These two beliefs are logically independent (assent to either does not entail assent to the other), but when conjoined they can be made to support each other in a remarkable way: that is, the transference process hypothesized in (1) is taken to provide the reason for the fixed code hypothesized in (2), while the latter is taken simultaneously to provide the explanation of how the former is possible. It is the conjunction of (1) and (2) that integrationists call 'the language myth' – a myth because there is no serious independent evidence for either conjunct.

We should make it clear that integrationists have no quarrel with millions of ordinary folk who habitually talk about 'conveying thoughts' to one another or assume as a matter of course that they speak the very same language as their neighbours. What the integrationist objects to is the erection of these lay beliefs and ways of talking about words into theoretical *explanations* or *models* of human communication.

This language myth, according to integrationists, was first elaborated by Greek philosophers. It sponsored Plato's metaphysics of Forms, underwrote Aristotle's formalization of logic, passed into the curriculum of the medieval universities, and was adopted and adapted by a long line of post-Renaissance thinkers right down to the present day. It thus found its way from the very beginning into modern linguistics, when this branch of academic inquiry became established in the nineteenth century.

Integrationists distinguish between different versions – or families of versions – of the language myth. There are 'reocentric' versions, in which the further assumption is made that language provides connections between words and an independently existing reality. There are 'psychocentric' versions, which place more emphasis on the connections that words make between different ideas in the mind. Thus reocentric theorists tend to assume that the meaning of the word *water* depends on and presupposes the existence of the liquid water; whereas psychocentric theorists tend to assume that the meaning of *water* depends on the ideas that people (whether rightly or wrongly) have about water.

What links Socrates/Plato across the centuries to Mill is that they are committed to a reocentric view of meaning, and this has consequences for their approach to definition.

* * *

An initial difficulty that confronts anyone trying to make sense of what Mill says about definition is that it is not necessarily obvious from the form of a definition whether it is stipulative or not. Furthermore, there seems to be no reason in these cases why a definition should not be treated both as a report of common usage and at the same time as a recommendation to use the word in accordance with the definition given. This appears to be how dictionary definitions are often regarded by dictionary-users, regardless of the intentions of dictionary-makers. That is to say, the definitions are treated, simultaneously, as authoritative summaries of current practice and as guidelines for the approved use of the word in question. Dictionaries are as often consulted to find out the right way to use a word as to discover how it is or has been used by others. We shall deal with this ambiguity in more detail in considering lexicographical definition.

The result of adopting Mill's formulation of the distinction between two kinds of definition – and doubtless Mill's primary reason for formulating it thus – is that the whole issue is made to hinge on the reasons for giving the definition. These may or may not be explicit. But one consequence, allegedly, is that a definition has no truth value if construed as merely prescriptive. This is important for reocentric theorists, because it means that one cannot object to a definition on the ground that what it says is false, i.e. does not correspond to what is 'really' the case. (Thus if, for example, someone wants to define *water* stipulatively in such a way as to exclude ice, it is no objection to say that as a matter of fact ice really *is* water.)

The point had already been made before Mill by Whately, who evidently thinks it applies to dictionary definitions in general. Discussing definitions in mathematics, Whately observes:

> A Mathematical Definition . . . cannot properly be called *true*, since it is not properly a *proposition*, (any more than an article in a Dictionary,) but merely an explanation of the meaning of a Term. Perhaps in Definitions of this class, it might be better to substitute (as Aristotle usually does) the *imperative* mood

> for the indicative: thus bringing them into the form of *postulates*: for the Definitions and the Postulates in Mathematics differ in little or nothing but the form of expression: *e.g.* 'let a four-sided figure, of equal sides and right angles, be called a square,' would clearly imply that such a figure is *conceivable*, and that the writer *intended to employ* that term to signify such a figure: which is precisely all that is meant to be asserted. If, indeed, a Mathematical writer mean to assert that the *ordinary* sense of the term is that which he has given, *that*, certainly, *is* a proposition, which must be either true or false; but in defining a *new* term, though the term indeed may be ill-chosen and improper, or the Definition may be self-contradictory, and consequently unintelligible, the words 'true,' and 'false,' do not apply.
>
> (Whately 1840: 296–7. Italics in the original.)

Neither Mill nor Whately challenged a way of looking at the matter that had been current at least since the seventeenth century. In the *Logique* of Port-Royal, we are told that when definitions purport to give the meaning of a word as established in common usage, they may be judged true or false:

> when there is no intention simply to make known in what sense one takes a word, but a claim to explain how it is commonly taken, the definitions given are not arbitrary at all; but are bound and obliged to represent not the truth of things, but the truth of usage (*la vérité de l'usage*), and should be considered false if they do not truly express that usage; that is to say, if they do not join to the sounds the same ideas (*les mêmes idées*) that are joined to them in the ordinary usage of those who use them. And this also explains why these definitions are by no means exempt from contestation, for the meaning that usage assigns to terms is being disputed every day. (Arnauld and Nicole 1683: I.xv)

But if these are matters of constant dispute by the users themselves, as the authors of the Port-Royal treatise freely admit, a major problem that arises is that of establishing criteria for determining what counts as 'common usage' and identifying the meanings current therein. Arnauld and Nicole do not, any more than Whately or Mill, make specific proposals for tackling that problem. The standard move here is for philosophers and logicians to plead that such matters do not fall within the scope of their professional expertise, and pass the buck to grammarians and lexicographers. It is interesting to note that although the scholars of Port-Royal were in the forefront of educational thinking in their day, and produced grammar books (including the famous *Grammaire générale et raisonnée* of 1660), none of them attempted a dictionary. Nevertheless, Arnauld and Nicole seem to be in no doubt that the meanings of words in common usage can, in principle, be ascertained and set down, even though they do not explain how. They even give examples of words of which the meaning, they claim, is known to everyone: *être*, *pensée*, *étendue*, *égalité*, *durée* and *temps*. These are words relating to matters of which 'all men have naturally the same idea' (*tous les hommes ont naturellement la même idée*). But how that can be known without empirical investigation they do not say. We hear echoes at this point of Aristotle's metaphysical assumption that the world is the same for all observers (*De Interpretatione* 16a).

* * *

On tracing its history, it becomes evident that there are even more philosophical underpinnings to Mill's distinction between two kinds of definition. This emerges clearly, for example, in what Locke has to say on the subject. Locke's semantics is manifestly bound up with his epistemology. In his *Essay Concerning Human Understanding*, he maintains that 'the defining of words . . . is nothing but declaring their signification', and more specifically, 'nothing but making another understand by words what idea the term defined stands for' (Locke 1706: III.iii.10). Locke insists on this account of definition several times in Book III of his *Essay*. For Locke, *idea* is a theory-laden term. Locke boldly affirms his commitment to the telementational component of what we are calling 'the language myth' (although for him there is nothing mythical about it):

> The chief end of language in communication being to be understood, words serve not well for that end, neither in civil nor philosophical discourse, when any word does not excite in the hearer the same idea which it stands for in the mind of the speaker. (Locke 1706: III.ix.4)

According to Locke, there are two kinds of ideas. What he calls 'simple' ideas are basic, unanalysable, delivered by the senses and our reflection on sense experience. (Examples Locke offers include the coldness of ice, the taste of sugar and the smell of a rose.) By contrast, 'complex' ideas are constructed by the mind from combinations of simple ideas. (Examples are beauty, gratitude, a man, an army, and the universe.) Locke holds that individuals are free to construct whatever complex ideas they wish, and to associate them with whatever words they choose. Every man, says Locke, has an 'inviolable' liberty 'to make words stand for what ideas he pleases' (Locke 1706: III.ii.8). This liberty is the source of many failures of communication: that is to say, it results in the hearer misunderstanding the ideas which the speaker intended to convey. (The misunderstanding may not be realized by the parties involved, but it occurs nevertheless.)

Further confusion, according to Locke, comes from two sources. Although words 'can properly and immediately signify nothing but the ideas that are in the mind of the speaker', nevertheless men 'suppose their words to be marks of the ideas in the minds also of other men, with whom they communicate' (Locke 1706: III.ii.4). In this way they believe that they have conveyed the ideas they intended to convey, when often they have not. They 'think it enough that they use the word, as they imagine, in the common acceptation of that language; in which they suppose that the idea they make it a sign of is precisely the same to which the understanding men of that country apply that name.' What Locke seems to be suggesting here is, first, that recognizing the form of a word is no guarantee of understanding what the speaker means by it; and, second, that we are apt to delude ourselves in identifying our own usage of terms with that of the linguistic community to which we think we belong. In short, Locke is questioning the 'fixed code' component of the language myth.

The second source of confusion that Locke identifies is that men often suppose that their words 'stand also for the reality of things' (Locke 1706: III.ii.5). This is directed against reocentric assumptions concerning language: people fail to realize that the world is not necessarily as their language represents it. Here Locke echoes the misgivings that Bacon expressed in *The Advancement of Learning* concerning 'the false appearances that are imposed upon us by words' (Bacon 1605: 2.xiv.11). But these are compounded by Locke's contention that complex ideas are inventions of the mind: they may correspond to nothing at all in actuality. The matter is further complicated by Locke's distinction between 'real essences' and 'nominal essences'. The real essence is 'the very being of anything, whereby it is what it is', whereas the nominal essence is 'nothing but that abstract idea which the general . . . name stands for' (Locke 1706: III.iii.15). It follows that it would be a mistake to take the nominal essence for the real essence: human knowledge is limited and cannot claim to have fathomed the mysteries of God's creation.

One need go no further in order to grasp how important definition is for any philosopher who takes a Lockean view of language, communication, reality, God and the human mind. Without the possibility of stipulative definition – however unsatisfactory, provisional, or wanting in exactitude – there would be no guarantee that all exchange of views was not, as Locke puts it, 'nothing but so much insignificant noise'. And this would leave philosophy itself bankrupt.

Locke pours scorn on Aristotle's definition of motion, which he translates as 'the act of a being in power, as far forth as in power'. 'What more exquisite jargon could the wit of man invent?' asks Locke derisively. It would 'puzzle any rational man, to whom it was not already known by its famous absurdity, to guess what word it could ever be supposed to be the explication of' (Locke 1706: III.iv.8). It is important to note here the precise point of Locke's complaint. It is not that Aristotle is mistaken about motion; nor that Aristotle is not clear in his own mind about what motion is; nor even that that is not what most people understand motion to be; but that *the terms of Aristotle's definition are obscure.* The definition does not express Aristotle's idea in a way that is immediately and unambiguously comprehensible.

A defender of Aristotle would doubtless retort that it is hardly to be expected that a person totally unacquainted with Aristotle's philosophy will understand what Aristotle is attempting to do here (*Metaphysics*: 1065b). Locke in short – an integrationist would say – is guilty of deliberately decontextualizing a definition in order to hold it up to ridicule.

This may seem a rather trivial detail on which to take issue with as powerful a philosopher as Locke. But our point is not that this facile jest at Aristotle's expense is unworthy of the rest of Locke's exposition. From an integrationist perspective, it reflects a fundamental weakness that pervades the whole of

Locke's semantics: namely, Locke's failure to recognize that all meanings are context-bound.

Nor does Locke have much to say in favour of the traditional definition *per genus et differentiam* (e.g. 'Man is the rational animal'). Again, the reason is the same. Although it is convenient to define terms in this way, it is not always the best or the only way to express the meaning:

> if it should be said, that man was a solid extended substance, having life, sense, spontaneous motion, and the faculty of reasoning, I doubt not but the meaning of the term man would be as well understood, and the idea it stands for be at least as clearly made known, as when it is defined to be a rational animal. . . . (Locke 1706: III.iii.10)

The reason, Locke suggests, why traditional definitions appeal to the *genus* (in this case 'animal') is 'not out of necessity, but only to save the labour of enumerating the several simple ideas which the next general word or *genus* stands for'. And he adds sarcastically: 'or, perhaps, sometimes the shame of not being able to do it.' Here we come to the core of Locke's doctrine of definition: 'a definition is best made by enumerating those simple ideas that are combined in the signification of the term defined' (Locke 1706: III.iii.10). Definition, in brief, calls for analytic ability: specifically, the ability to analyse complex ideas into their simple constituents.

Various corollaries follow from this, or are alleged to follow. For instance, a definition is not simply the production of an equivalent expression, even when the equivalence is semantically unobjectionable. To say that *reckless* means 'rash' may well be correct and even helpful, but it is not a (Lockean) definition. By the same token, to say that *chien* means 'dog' may be true, but it is not a definition of the word *chien.* A translation is not a definition (Locke 1706: III.iv.9).

A more interesting corollary is that not all words are definable. Locke argues this point as follows. Supposing that all words are definable leads to an infinite regress. 'For, if the terms of one definition were still to be defined by another, where at last should we stop?' Locke here follows the lead of the Port-Royal logicians (Arnauld and Nicole 1683: I.xiii), who claim that definition must ultimately rest on 'primitive terms' (*termes primitifs*) that are themselves undefinable. Locke's primitive terms are the names of simple ideas, and a simple idea is 'an idea which has no composition at all'.

> and therefore a definition, which is properly nothing but the showing the meaning of one word by several others not signifying each the same thing, can in the names of simple ideas have no place. (Locke 1706: III.iv.7)

It would be difficult to trump this in the annals of Western philosophy as an example of circular reasoning. Simple ideas are defined as unanalysable, and then definition is defined in terms of analysis into simple ideas; from which it is concluded that definition is not applicable to simple ideas. All by definition.

As to whether, in principle, it is possible to define the 'common acceptations' of words across a whole linguistic community, Locke does not commit himself. On this issue he may be read as a 'communicational sceptic' (Taylor 1992: 30). All he will venture are the following carefully hedged pronouncements:

> (1) . . . men talk to one another, and dispute in words, whose meaning is not agreed between them, out of a mistake that the significations of common words are certainly established, and the precise ideas they stand for perfectly known; and that it is a shame to be ignorant of them. Both which suppositions are false; no names of complex ideas having so settled determined significations, that they are constantly used for the same precise ideas.
>
> (Locke 1706: III.xi.25)

> (2) . . . the necessity of communication by language brings men to an agreement in the signification of common words, within some tolerable latitude, that may serve for ordinary conversation: and so a man cannot be supposed wholly ignorant of the ideas which are annexed to words by common use, in a language familiar to him. But common use being but a very uncertain rule, which reduces itself at last to the ideas of particular men, proves often but a very variable standard. (Locke 1706: III.xi.25)

The first of these two statements is as far as Locke goes towards the integrationist position on indeterminacy of meaning. He is careful to qualify it as applying only to 'names of complex ideas'. It does not hold for names of simple ideas, the point being that simple ideas are not free constructions of our own but ideas directly derived from sense experience and reflection thereon. Here we reach a level of commonality grounded in the biological constitution of *Homo sapiens.* Thus Locke avoids the implausible conclusion that an individual's ideas, although private, are totally idiosyncratic and bear no relation at all to the ideas of other individuals.

He concedes that no definition can bring a blind man to understand the meanings of words like *red* and *yellow.* Those of us who understand these meanings in common do so in virtue of sharing sensory experience that is denied to the blind. He also argues that it would be pointless for us to form and name our ideas of sheep, trees, clouds, etc. unless such things were perceived by us to exist in the natural world. In this respect, he thinks we accept what Nature offers as a 'standard'. So this goes some way towards explaining why our individual ideas, and hence the meanings of certain words, might tend to coincide.

But does it go far enough? Are these caveats enough to save Locke from the dire consequences of his own assumptions? If common usage reduces in the final analysis to 'the ideas of particular men', and if *all* that a word can signify is an idea (currently) in the mind of the speaker, it is difficult to see how, even in what Locke calls 'ordinary conversation', there can be any well-founded 'agreement in the signification of common words'. That would be like imagining that a currency system could operate on the basis of tokens each of which had a value known only to its current owner. The notion that an individual might make publicly – as distinct from privately – explicit the (private) ideas that words stand for, and could do this by means of defining them in other words, falls foul immediately of the 'infinite regress' argument that Locke himself has deployed against the thesis that all words are definable. For each word in philosopher *A*'s proposed definition of a term would be subject to exactly the same requirements. Thus the very notion of 'agreement' between two or more individuals would be called into question. It would not be sufficient for *B* to say 'I agree with *A*'s definition', since *ex hypothesi* all that could mean is that *B* attaches his own ideas to the words *A* utters and finds *that* (private) interpretation of the definition satisfactory. What would still be lacking is any objective demonstration that *A* and *B* share the same ideas in question, i.e. that *B* understands *A*'s definition.

Did Locke believe that calling for such a demonstration was asking for the impossible? If he did, the whole argument of his *Essay* is flawed by a *petitio principii*. If he did not, it is vitiated by his failure to explain how this demonstration can be given.

* * *

Locke's semantic theory was memorably satirized in the late nineteenth century by Lewis Carroll.

> 'When *I* use a word,' Humpty Dumpty said, in rather a scornful tone, 'it means what I choose it to mean – neither more nor less.'
>
> 'The question is,' said Alice, 'whether you *can* make words mean so many different things.' (Carroll 1871: Ch.6)

Here Humpty Dumpty espouses Locke's thesis that any individual is at liberty to make any word 'stand for' whatever idea he pleases. The particular word they were discussing was *glory*, and whether it could mean, as Humpty Dumpty held. 'a nice knock-down argument'.

When linguists invoke this literary anecdote they usually seem to take it for granted that Humpty Dumpty's position on the question is self-evidently absurd. On closer inspection it emerges that there are two separate questions here which should not be confused. One is the question of what the word *glory* means in English, or meant in the late nineteenth century when Lewis Carroll's story was published. The other is the more general question of whether what a word means is determined by the intentions of those who use it. The first of these might nowadays be regarded as a question of descriptive semantics, and the second as a question of theoretical semantics. However, neither Lewis Carroll nor any of his contemporaries would have described them thus, because at the time the word *semantics* did not exist.

When we reflect on that, the second of the two theses distinguished above begins to seem somewhat less of an absurdity than one might originally have thought. For we have to suppose that somehow, between 1871 and the present, the word *semantics* was brought into existence, together with its meaning, and the *prima facie* difficulty is to see how this could have come about except as the result of deliberate, voluntary activity on the part of speakers and writers. In brief, the very genesis of the term *semantics* already poses a semantic problem that is crucially relevant to the problem of definition. How are lexical meanings brought into existence?

If Humpty Dumpty had just invented the word *glory* and decided it should mean 'a nice knock-down argument' his case would have been stronger. Alice's objections, when viewed in this light, seem to depend rather crucially on two contingent facts: (1) that Humpty Dumpty did not coin the word *glory* and (2) that the word already has a well-established usage in English which has nothing to do with arguments of any kind.

Even so, that does not entirely dispose of the disagreement between Alice and Humpty Dumpty, for at least two reasons. First, Humpty Dumpty might still argue that none of this abrogates his right to coin a new word *glory* which just happens to be homophonous with the old word *glory*. In which case, the worst he can be accused of is perversity or lexical mischief. Second, and more importantly, nothing that Alice has said invalidates the more general contention that what a word means depends on its being used intentionally with that meaning.

Thus Humpty Dumpty, for all his perversity, poses – in the wake of Locke – a genuine theoretical problem. For if what a word means does ultimately depend on its users, and if its users can be quite whimsical in their use of it, then it is difficult to see how there can be any comprehensive science of lexicography. And if that is so, the answer to the question of whether one can give a semantic account of the words in common usage has to be 'No'. Humpty Dumpty's claim, in brief, is one which a soundly based semantics is needed in order to rebut. For if it cannot be rebutted *somehow*, then Humpty Dumpty has pulled the rug from in under most of modern linguistics, as well as much traditional lexicography and grammar, and undermined the foundations of classical logic into the bargain.

Humpty Dumpty's Lockean thesis has a long history in the Western tradition. The form in which it is first stated is that championed by Hermogenes in Plato's dialogue *Cratylus*. According to Hermogenes, we are all free to give whatever names we please to whatever we wish, and indeed *to change them as often as it suits us*. In this perspective, what Humpty Dumpty says can be seen as representing a view that needs to be taken seriously, as indeed it is by Socrates. And in the same perspective, modern semantics can be seen as the culmination of a series of attempts in Western thinking to resolve precisely the problem that Hermogenes, Locke and Humpty Dumpty raise.

It is generally agreed that one cannot have a science of meaning if meaning is at the mercy of arbitrary decisions by individuals, any more than one could have a science of geology if the properties of rocks and minerals were liable to random alteration without prior notice. A science of meaning requires that there should be objectively ascertainable facts about meaning, which individuals do not have the power to override or set aside. Otherwise semantics, one must conclude, does lie outside the domain of science. Its supposed subject-matter defies any possibility of constructing scientific theories about it. The notion that definitions can be given of words in current usage presupposes that it is possible to ascertain what meanings words in current usage have. This is the foundational assumption of modern descriptive semantics. But is it well founded?

In an article entitled 'Is semantics possible?', Hilary Putnam makes a general point which goes to the heart of the matter. In any theory of definition, we have no right to expect that a science of meaning *must* somehow be possible, simply because as a matter of fact there is an already existing discourse about it. Putnam writes:

> Certainly we cannot assume that *there is* a scientific subject to be constructed here just because ordinary people have occasion to use the word 'meaning' from time to time; that would be like concluding that there must be a scientific subject to be constructed which will deal with 'causation' just because ordinary people have occasion to use the word 'cause' from time to time. In one sense, *all* of science is a theory of causation; but not in the sense that it uses the word 'cause'. Similarly, any successful and developed theory of language-use will in one sense be a theory of meaning; but not necessarily in the sense that it will employ any such notion as the 'meaning' of a word or of an utterance. Elementary as this point is, it seems to be constantly overlooked in the social sciences, and people seem constantly to expect that psychology, for example, must talk of 'dislike', 'attraction', 'belief', etc., simply because ordinary men use these words in psychological description.
>
> (Putnam 1975: 146–7)

Although Putnam makes no reference to Humpty Dumpty, one way of reading this is as follows: don't expect that a science of meaning will necessarily turn out to be one which provides a direct refutation of Humpty Dumpty. In other words, a science of meaning may not amount to anything which will allow us to go back to Humpty Dumpty and say: 'You are wrong about the meaning of the word *glory*, because the meaning of the word *glory* is in fact not what you say it is, and semantics can prove it.'

Semantics, as far as Putnam is concerned, does not have to be committed in advance to notions like 'the meaning of the word *glory*'. Now why does Putnam say this? One might suppose that what Putnam fears is that there might not turn out to be any such thing as 'the meaning of the word *glory*'. But that is not in fact his position. The reason why he says this is that he is deeply suspicious of dictionaries; and in particular of the model of meaning that dictionaries and their definitions implicitly offer.

Putnam answers his own question 'Is semantics possible?' in a curiously ambivalent way. He does not say outright that semantics has failed. But he does speak of what he calls 'lack of progress'. And this lack of progress is mainly due, according to Putnam, to the fact that those engaged in semantics have been misled in their enterprise by a misguided trust in the traditional lexicographical model of meaning. He writes:

> you may dress up traditional mistakes in modern dress by talking of 'recursive rules' and 'linguistic universals', but they remain the traditional mistakes. The problem in semantic theory is to get away from the picture of the meaning of a word as something like a *list of concepts*. . . . (Putnam 1975: 146)

The reason why Putnam thinks this model of lexical meaning must be discarded is revealing. He holds that it works only for a very small number of words. These include words like *bachelor* and *hunter*, which Putnam believes can be uncontroversially defined as 'man who has never married' and 'one who hunts'. In short, these are words for which we can state necessary and conditions of application, and such statements formulate analytic truths about the words in question. But this will not work, according to Putnam, for words designating what he calls 'natural kinds'. An example would be the word *lemon*, designating a kind of fruit which exists in Nature. Putnam argues:

> In the traditional view, the meaning of, say 'lemon', is given by specifying a conjunction of *properties*. For each of these properties, the statement 'lemons have the property P' is an analytic truth; and if P_1, P_2, . . ., P_n are all the properties in the conjunction, then 'anything with all of the properties P_1, . . ., P_n is a lemon' is likewise an analytic truth.
>
> In one sense, this is trivially correct. If we are allowed to invent unanalysable properties *ad hoc*, then we can find a single property – not even a conjunction – the possession of which is a necessary and sufficient condition for being a lemon, or being gold, or whatever. Namely, we just postulate *the property of being a lemon*, or *the property of being gold*, or whatever may be needed. If we require that the properties P_1, P_2, . . ., P_n *not* be of this *ad hoc* character, however, then the situation is very different. Indeed, with any natural understanding of the term 'property', it is just *false* that to say that something belongs to a natural kind is just to ascribe to it a conjunction of properties.
>
> To see why it is false, let us look at the term 'lemon'. The supposed 'defining characteristics' of lemons are: yellow color, tart taste, a certain kind of peel, etc. Why is the term 'lemon' *not* definable by simply conjoining these 'defining characteristics'? (Putnam 1975: 140)

The most obvious difficulty, according to Putnam, is that a natural kind may have 'abnormal' members or instances. A green lemon is still a lemon – even if, owing to some abnormality, it never turns yellow. A three-legged tiger is still a tiger. Gold in its gaseous state is still gold. It is only normal lemons that are yellow, tart, etc.; only normal tigers that are four-legged; only gold under normal conditions that is hard, white or yellow, etc.

What bothers Putnam here is that once we admit that definitions like that of the word *lemon* can only hold by reference to 'normal' lemons, we have simply postponed the problem. The problem is now to define normality for lemons, and it is totally unclear how to do this.

No such problem, according to Putnam, arises for words like *bachelor* and *hunter.* For it is nonsense to say, *qua* lexicographer, that bachelors are 'normally' unmarried, or that hunters 'normally' go hunting. If a man is married then he is not a bachelor, by definition, and there's an end to it. Similarly, one who never hunts is not a hunter, by definition. Whereas a lemon can lack any of the properties of colour, taste, etc. that are typical of most lemons, and still be a lemon nevertheless.

What Putnam is arguing, in short, is that there are some words, like *lemon,* which resist definition – at least if a definition is viewed as a conjunction of properties from which the lexicographer can construct a set of necessary and sufficient conditions. And this allows Humpty Dumpty all the freedom he needs to play havoc with the enterprise of descriptive semantics.

At this point in our discussion it is worth asking why, in Putnam's view, there are some words that can be defined but others which cannot be. Putnam does not set out his answer as clearly as Locke; but it seems reasonable to reconstruct the following rationale.

The difference between the meaning of words like *lemon* and the meaning of words like *bachelor* and *hunter* is this. As far as Putnam is concerned, we do actually know what *bachelor* and *hunter* mean, because these are words that human beings have brought into existence for their own purposes. The definition hinges on some particular trait of behaviour that human beings have decided to recognize as significant. Neither bachelors nor hunters are natural kinds: they have been deliberately set up as classes, and the conditions for membership laid down by human fiat. But lemons are quite different: they exist independently of human interests. It is not up to human beings to *decide* what lemons are: only God or Nature can do that. Lemons would be lemons even if no human communities existed.

Regardless of what one thinks of Putnam's argument, what it shows is just how much is – or may be – involved in questions of definition. They may open up a whole ontology, a whole epistemology, a whole understanding of the world and the position of human beings in relation to it. And if that is so, then definitions are too important to be left to the academic concerns either of linguists or of philosophers.

The search for a theory of definition becomes a quest for reassurance about whether human beings really comprehend the world in which they live. And at the same time it becomes *ipso facto* a quest for reassurance that we can really understand one another. The trouble with Putnam's approach – we shall argue – is that, unlike either Locke or Humpty Dumpty, Putnam confuses the definition of words with the definition of things. Now making sense of the definition of things – or 'real definition' as some authorities call it – is a problem in itself, and to this we turn in the following chapter.

Before proceeding that far, however, we would like to go back to an issue that Locke raises and which casts doubt on whether defining the meanings of words in common usage is, in general, an empirically achievable project. Locke has this to say about the meaning of *gold*.

> I think all agree to make it stand for a body of a certain yellow shining colour; which being the idea to which children have annexed that name, the shining yellow part of a peacock's tail is properly to them gold. Others finding fusibility joined with that yellow colour in certain parcels of matter, make of that combination a complex idea to which they give the name gold, to denote a sort of substances; and so exclude from being gold all such yellow shining bodies as by fire will be reduced to ashes; and admit to be of that species, or to be comprehended under that name gold, only such substances as, having that shining yellow colour, will by fire be reduced to fusion, and not to ashes. Another, by the same reason, adds the weight, which, being a quality as straightly joined with that colour as its fusibility, he thinks has the same reason to be joined in its idea, and to be signified by its name; and therefore the other made up of body, of such a colour and fusibility, to be imperfect; and so on of all the rest: wherein no one can show a reason why some of the inseparable qualities, that are always united in nature, should be put into the nominal essence, and others left out: or why the word gold, signifying that sort of body the ring on his finger is made of, should determine that sort rather by its colour, weight, and fusibility, than by its colour, weight, and solubility in *aqua regia*: since the dissolving it by that liquor is as inseparable from it as the fusion by fire; and they are both of them nothing but the relation which that substance has to two other bodies, which have a power to operate differently upon it. For by what right is it that fusibility comes to be a part of the essence signified by the word gold, and solubility but a property of it? Or why is its colour part of the essence, and its malleableness but a property?
>
> (Locke 1706: III.ix.17)

If Locke is right about this, and if *gold* is a fairly typical case, it would appear that one problem with the enterprise of defining the meaning that a word has in common usage is, simply, that there may be no common usage. Individuals 'annex' different meanings to a word as seems, for their own purposes, expedient or reasonable to them. They may all agree on at least one thing – e.g. that gold is of a shining yellow colour; but this agreement is hardly sufficient to yield a definition of *gold* that would distinguish it from words with other meanings. As Locke puts it, 'the signification of that name must unavoidably be very uncertain'; and names of uncertain signification are patently recalcitrant to definition.

This conclusion can be avoided, in our view, only if there is some way of construing 'common usage' as something *other than the sum total of conflicting individual usages*. One theoretical escape route might be to treat meanings as belonging to and determined by the overall organization of 'the language' itself, rather than the vagaries of actual users, i.e. as a matter of *langue* and not of *parole*. This would mean abandoning the psychocentric voluntarism of Locke's approach to language in favour of some version of Saussurean structuralism, or one of its successors. Whether some such move as this can provide the basis for a viable theory of definition we shall consider in due course.

Chapter 3

On Real Definition

Scepticism about definition may take a bewildering variety of forms. The integrationist thesis that meanings are indeterminate is itself sometimes regarded as implying scepticism about the possibility of definition. So it seems advisable early on for us to point out some forms of scepticism that we do *not* subscribe to.

According to J. A. Fodor, 'the view now favoured in both philosophy and cognitive science' has it that 'most words' are not definable. In fact, 'there is now something like a consensus in cognitive science that the notion of a definition has no very significant role to play in theories of meaning' (Fodor 1998: 44). So too, it appears, are 'many psychologists' to be numbered among the sceptics (Fodor 1998: 47). If there is indeed such a consensus as Fodor maintains, we will take this opportunity of distancing ourselves from it, for the uncomplicated reason that the thesis that most words are not definable is *prima facie* false. It ignores some important and conspicuous evidence bearing on the question; in particular the existence of dictionaries. Not that Fodor denies the existence of dictionaries – he even refers to one at one point – so he would appear to be committed to believing that lexicography does not, or cannot, produce definitions (at least, not for 'most words'). This claim is equally silly, and it is accompanied by other anti-lexicographical claims, such as the assertion that there is 'no such thing as polysemy' (Fodor 1998: 53). We imagine that what makes Fodor oblivious to the obtuse perversity of all this is his fixation with certain philosophical requirements that dictionaries do not fulfil. In short, rejecting definability is in fact his way of introducing his own stipulative definition of *definition*. And that in turn renders his denial of definability self-defeating.

Worthy of more serious attention are varieties of scepticism which do not rule out definition *ab initio*. Some philosophers in antiquity had doubts about what it was possible to define. Socrates in *Theaetetus* 201e–202c seems to approve the contention that primary elements can be given names only, but not definitions. If this is so, it would follow that while it is possible to give a substance a name (e.g. *gold*), if this is a primary element it is not possible to add any further account which would yield a definition of what that name means. Aristotle (*Metaphysics* 1043b) says that Antisthenes held that it is impossible to say what things *are*, only what they are *like*. Aristotle himself claims that not everything that is demonstrable is definable: 'there is not definition of everything of which there is demonstration' (*Posterior Analytics* 90b). But in all these cases it is pertinent to ask *of what* a definition is being sought.

Asking what gold is has to be distinguished from asking what the word *gold* means. The reason for drawing this distinction is usually said to be that the former question could be asked (and answered) without ever mentioning (or even knowing) the word *gold*. One is a request for information about a certain metallic substance, while the other is a lexicographical inquiry. In support of this, it is pointed out that gold existed, and was the subject of human curiosity, long before the word *gold*; that the word appears in dictionaries, whereas the substance does not; that the substance has an atomic weight, whereas the word has none, and so on. Nevertheless, it is difficult to convince many people that there is no connection between finding out what gold is and finding out what *gold* means. And understandably so, since the purpose of having a word *gold* is thought of, at least by reocentric theorists, as being to designate the substance in question. From this it would follow that if you have no idea what gold is, you do not know the meaning of the word *gold*.

Nothing in the above reasoning depends on the fact that *gold* happens to be the name of a substance, and a valuable one. The same would apply to such words as *democracy* or *honesty*, which are not names of substances. Here too asking what democracy and honesty are is to be distinguished from asking what these words mean. The question then naturally arises: 'Is it not possible to bypass words (such as *gold*, *democracy* and *honesty*) and give instead 'real definitions' (i.e. directly of gold, democracy and honesty)?'

From very early on in the Western tradition, it was assumed that this was not only possible but preferable. According to Robinson,

> The inventors of the notion of definition, Socrates and Plato, were obviously thinking only of the definition of things and not at all of the definition of words. The search for the definition of piety in Plato's *Euthyphro* is certainly an inquiry about the thing piety, not about the word 'piety'. Socrates does not ask Euthyphro what piety is because the word 'piety' is new to him, or because he cannot think of an effective method of teaching the use of this word to those who do not know it. He is not asking a question about the word 'piety', but using the word 'piety' to ask a question about the thing piety. He assumes that both he and Euthyphro already know the use of the word. The subject-matter of the dialogue falls within the field of ethics, not that of linguistics or lexicography. The same is certainly true of every other place in Plato's writings where there is discussion of a question having the form 'What is *x*?', that is to say, a request for a definition. (Robinson 1954: 149)

Various philosophers in antiquity are credited with works on or collections of definitions, including Aristotle, Speusippus, Theophrastus and Chrysippus. Their predilection for arguing about definitions was a topic for satirical comment. Diogenes the Cynic is reputed to have plucked a chicken and said 'Here is Plato's man' – an allusion to the definition of man as a featherless biped. The short work attributed to Plato under the title *Definitions* is a collection of nearly two hundred definitions, including definition itself (*horos*), which is said to be 'something said, comprised of genus and differentia'. It is almost certainly not due to Plato, but may be assigned to 'school of Plato' (Hutchinson 1997: 1678).

In the Platonic dialogues, Socrates is certainly dealing with real definitions. In *Euthyphro,* he dismisses the notion that a definition can be given by listing examples. He is inquiring after 'the form itself that make all pious actions pious', and eventually extracts from Euthyphro the answer that what is dear to the gods is pious, and what is not is impious. This Socrates accepts as a proper definition, although he does not agree with it. His disagreement with Euthyphro is not over the correct use of the word *piety,* but over whether approval by the gods really *is* what makes pious actions pious. Similarly, in *Meno* Socrates will not rest content with identifying what various kinds of virtue there are. For this, he says, would be like saying that there are many sorts of bees: it does not tell us what a bee is. However greatly one bee many differ from another, there is one thing in which they do not differ: namely, in respect of being bees. Again, the question is not about what creatures are correctly called 'bees', but about what makes a bee a bee.

In Chapter X of *Laws,* the Athenian claims that there are three things to be known with respect to any given thing. One, 'what the object actually *is,* the second is the definition of this, and the third is the name.' 'Sometimes we put forward the mere name and want to know the definition, and sometimes we put forward the definition and ask for the name' (*Laws* 895d). So although name and definition are correlated, they are only so in virtue of the relation of both to the thing.

The reason why a 'real definition' was deemed preferable to a word definition thus becomes clear. We have already touched on it implicitly above: namely, if the word is no more than a name of the thing, concentrating on the name does not go far enough: stopping there can only obscure matters and stand in the way of acquaintance with the thing itself. As Theaetetus is told in *Sophist* 218c, it is no use clinging to the name, because two people may use the same name for a different thing: 'we always need to be in agreement about the thing itself by means of a verbal explanation, rather than doing without any such explanation and merely agreeing about the name.' The name alone tells one nothing about the thing. From the name *Socrates* one learns little about the man, and from the name *daffodil* little about the flower. Better to set aside all verbal labels and focus on the realities if you are genuinely interested in acquiring knowledge.

The first point we should like to draw attention to is that here, once again, an influential view of definition has its roots in linguistic theory. The particular line of theorizing in question is that sketched in Plato's dialogue *Cratylus,* which in effect provides the foundation for all the 'What is *x*?' questions throughout Plato's work. In *Cratylus* Socrates makes mock of the traditional Greek concern with questions of etymology and demolishes the contention that words provide reliable clues to the nature of the things which they designate. Word forms are shown to be labile, subject to change, and names only fortuitously connected to what they are names of. Names may even be grossly inappropriate, as in the case of the name of Cratylus' partner – *Hermogenes* – who is no 'son of Hermes' (*Cratylus* 383b). Inquiry is only valuable – Plato's reader is invited to conclude – when it penetrates beyond words to the realities underlying them. And these realities are independent of language altogether.

> SOCRATES: How realities are to be learned or discovered is perhaps too great a question for you or me to determine; but it is worth while to have reached even this conclusion, that they are to be learned and sought for, not from names but much better through themselves than through names.
>
> (*Cratylus* 439b)

This is the credo underlying all reocentric approaches to language and all forms of real definition. The question then becomes, for those who seek real definitions, how to identify those characteristics of the thing in question that 'really' define it. And that leads straight to the Classical doctrine of 'essences'. An essence is traditionally supposed to be some fundamental property or set of core properties without which the thing in question would be – if it existed at all – something other than what it is. 'Something other' not in the trivial sense that it would not be exactly the same (in appearance, behaviour, etc.), but in the more basic sense that it would lose its original identity and become something else altogether. Thus, for example, a comb might lose one or two teeth without ceasing to be a comb; but if it lost all its teeth it could hardly function as a comb at all. It thus seems to be of the 'essence' of a comb that it has teeth, even though exactly how many it can lose before ceasing to be a comb is doubtless debatable. Similarly, if the colour blue were gradually to alter until it became indistinguishable from green, it would cease to be blue; although at what precise point it was no longer recognizable as blue might never be settled to everyone's satisfaction. People might still cling to the old linguistic habit of referring to the colour of the summer sky as 'blue' even when the sky was as green as grass; but that linguistic archaism would be irrelevant to any real definition of the colour itself.

The acknowledged authority on the Classical doctrine of essence is Aristotle. According to Aristotle 'the essence of each thing is what it is said to be in virtue of itself' (*Metaphysics* 1029b). The problem as Aristotle conceives it concerns the semantics of 'being' and the semantics of 'substance' (*ousía*). If there were no substance, nothing could 'be': there could 'be' nothing to see or touch or hear, no such universe as the one we inhabit. In this universe, a thing is said to 'be' itself ('Socrates is Socrates', 'A man is a man'). But it can also be said to 'be' something else ('Socrates is a philosopher', 'A man is an animal'). How exactly are these two kinds of 'being' related? And what of the non-substantial 'being' that we admit when we identify non-existent things, as when we say 'There is a not-white'? (*Metaphysics* 1069a). It seems obvious to Aristotle that not every attribute of a substantial thing belongs to its essence. But this leads him into all kinds of difficulties. If you are musical, he claims, 'you are not musical in virtue of yourself'. Which seems to mean no more than that you would still be yourself even if you were not musical. But that seems to be, at the very least, debatable; and perhaps, if you happen to be a professional musician, nonsensical. We are left without any clear idea of what Aristotle thinks you are *just in virtue of yourself.* Another question he raises is what it is to be a cloak. Does a cloak have an essence at all? 'Probably not' is Aristotle's view. Aristotle's problem with cloaks seems to be that it is not clear that there is any one feature that makes a garment a cloak: so the suspicion is that cloaks are already a class in which different essences are confused or combined. But again we are left in doubt about the reason.

Those who have attacked the Classical doctrine of essence focus on the obscurities of Aristotle's account. According to Robinson, the 'activity of searching for essence is bad because there is no such thing as essence in the sense intended.'

> We can convince ourselves of this by studying the most serious attempt there has ever been to make sense of the notion of essence, namely, Aristotle's *Metaphysics* Z 4–6. In these bewildering chapters we find Aristotle reaching the mysterious conclusions that some things have an essence and others do not, and that of the things that do have an essence some are the same as their essence and others are not. These doctrines, and the very great obscurity of the chapters, suggest strongly that there is a muddle somewhere. If a man asks Aristotle what he means by the word 'essence' . . . the nearest Aristotle comes to a reply is to say that an essence is what is stated in a definition. This would help if we knew what a definition was, but according to Aristotle a definition is a statement of essence. A definition states essence, and essence is what you find in a definition. This useless circle is the best than can be extracted from Aristotle when we ask what he meant by 'essence', and it is strong evidence that there is no such thing as essence in his sense of the word.
>
> (Robinson 1954: 154)

We do not propose to embark here on an exegesis of the *Metaphysics,* since there are more accessible accounts of 'essence' that pinpoint the same nucleus of problems with respect to real definition. (One of these has already been mentioned in the preceding chapter: Locke's discussion of 'real essence' in Book III of the *Essay Concerning Human Understanding.*) Robinson argues that all these accounts founder on the same reef, which is 'the confusion of real definition with nominal definition': that is, 'wrongly taking a case of word-thing definition to be a case of real definition' (Robinson 1954: 154–5).

This certainly seems to be the error that some philosophers have made and continue to make. An example would be Putnam on the definition of *lemon,* already mentioned in the previous chapter. What appears to worry Putnam is the existence in Nature of abnormal lemons. But if this is a problem, it is a problem for the taxonomist trying to frame a satisfactory real definition of a certain kind of fruit. And that is a quite different enterprise from trying to state how the word *lemon* in practice is already used. If the occasional presence of certain abnormalities does not appear to inhibit people from applying the term *lemon*, that itself is sufficient reason for casting the definition of the word *lemon* in terms wide enough to include the abnormal specimens in question. What lemons 'really' are is not a problem that the lexicographer is obliged to confront; nor one that the lexicographer *qua* lexicographer is equipped to tackle.

Robinson illustrates the confusion of real definition with nominal definition by means of a geometrical example:

> That being bounded by three sides is the essence and not a property of the triangle is merely a confused way of saying that we define the word 'triangle' to mean a figure bounded by three sides. That having the sum of its interior angles equal to half a turn is a property and not the essence of the triangle is merely a confused way of saying that this characteristic is not assigned to be the meaning of the word 'triangle' [. . .]. If we choose, there is nothing in the world to prevent us from defining the word 'triangle' to mean a figure whose interior angles sum to half a turn; and then this would be the essence of a triangle, while its having three sides would be a property. (Robinson 1954: 155)

He concludes that: 'Essence, then, is just the human choice of what to mean by a name, misinterpreted as being a metaphysical reality.' But this is going too far too fast. The whole point of distinguishing real definition from the definition of words, for those who, such as Locke, draw that distinction explicitly, is precisely *not* to conflate how things stand in reality with how they might appear to be from the names human beings happen to give them. Thus, for example, at a time when a geocentric model of the universe was generally accepted, any accurate definition of the word *earth* would presumably have reflected that belief. Now that a heliocentric model has replaced the geocentric model, the definitions of the words *earth, sun* and so on have altered accordingly. The word *sun* is no longer said to designate a heavenly body that rotates about the earth. But no one supposes that the earth itself and its relation to the sun have somehow changed in reality over the past millennium: the fact is simply that a real definition of the earth cannot accommodate both the geocentric and the heliocentric models. Similarly, when it was generally believed that insanity could be caused by changes in the moon, it would doubtless have been accurate to define the word *lunatic* as meaning 'person whose mental health is disturbed by lunar changes'. But modern medicine denies that the lunar cycle is or ever has been a cause of insanity; so any appeal to the effect of the moon is now inadmissible in a real definition of lunacy, irrespective of what ignorant people in the past may have, or perhaps in some cases still do, believe about it, or of how in consequence they use or did use the word *lunatic*.

Thus, *pace* Robinson, belief in real definition – we contend – arises not from confusion of the meaning of a word with the constitution of the thing it designates (although doubtless some such confusions occur in some people's minds) but from a conviction that, when all erroneous beliefs are set aside, there is a definable reality that can be known and stated, even though we may at present be ignorant of it. This is what Locke understands by 'real essence', but with the following proviso. In the case of what he calls 'corporeal substances', the essence is that 'from which flow those sensible qualities which serve us to distinguish one from another, according as we have occasion to rank them into sorts, under common denominations' (Locke 1706: III.iii.17). This proviso, unfortunately, once more takes the lid off Pandora's metaphysical box and blurs the distinction Locke has carefully drawn between the two kinds of essence. For there can be – in our view – no ultimate assurance that human knowledge has reached a point where 'real essences' are finally revealed and understood; consequently, no guarantee either that 'those sensible qualities which serve us to distinguish' one kind of thing from another and give names to them do actually 'flow from' any real essence. Both these assumptions are no more than acts of faith about the way the world of Nature is constituted and related to human language.

Once the mystical notion of essences is abandoned, the notion of real definition, divested of its metaphysical trappings, emerges as much more credible. It has become the bedrock of the natural sciences in the modern world. A real definition in this sense is a summary of what is currently believed to be uniquely distinctive about a certain type of thing found in Nature. Thus a real definition of gold currently tells us that gold is a soft yellow malleable transition element with the atomic number 79, relative atomic mass 196.967, melting point 1064.43 degrees Celsius, and so on. This is not a definition of what those who use the word *gold* mean by it, except perhaps for a small sub-population of scientists. But the community of users extends far beyond this group, and most of the members of that wider community would be hard put to it to guess what the atomic number of gold is or its melting point; so what the word *gold* means for them can hardly be said to include all the information about gold that a real definition of gold would encompass.

A real definition of the kind just indicated is in principle subject to continuous revision, as and when more is discovered about gold. A definition of the word *gold* is likewise in principle subject to continuous revision, but as and when the usage of that term changes. It is not impossible that at some point in the future the two definitions might coincide, but that seems unlikely. It is difficult to envisage a civilization which had achieved such a high level of education that everything discovered about gold was known and understood by all members of the community. Moreover, for purposes of everyday communication, much of that knowledge would be redundant in any case. As is already evident, one needs to know relatively little about gold in order to use the word *gold* effectively for such purposes as buying gold jewellery, or acquiring shares in a gold mine, or ascertaining the current market value of gold, or discussing the pros and cons of a return to the gold standard. (We shall take up this point later in connection with 'communicational' definition.)

A real definition of gold is not an attempt to set out necessary and sufficient conditions for using the word *gold*. Nor is a definition of the word *gold* an attempt to specify what human beings have managed to find out about the substance gold. If this is clearly borne in mind, there is no problem about the two kinds of definition or the relationship between them.

Matters are less straightforward, however, when for gold and the word *gold* one substitutes democracy and the word *democracy*, or honesty and the word *honesty*. Our view is that much confusion arises from supposing that real definitions can be given of democracy and honesty. To believe that they can be is to succumb to the fallacy of reification. There is no empirical investigation of democracy or honesty that parallels the investigation of natural substances like gold. It would be a gross error to imagine that one could conduct an investigation of the nature of democracy by sending out a research team to study a representative number of established democracies, or to reveal the nature of honesty by examining in detail a sufficiently large number of honest acts or honest persons. These would be research activities worthy of the professors in Swift's grand academy of Lagado. The difficulty in such chimerical projects would arise right at the beginning: it would be the difficulty of knowing to which countries one should send the research team, or where to find a reliable pool of honest people or corpus of honest acts. Without a prior definition of *democracy* or *honesty*, the research could never get started.

Someone may object that, similarly, scientists would never have been able to be sure that the metal they were investigating really was gold without knowing in advance how to use the word *gold*. The objection itself epitomizes the confusion involved in putting the nomenclatorial cart before the empirical horse. The empirical discovery was the discovery of the existence of an element having a certain atomic number, relative atomic mass, etc.: what to call this element, once identified, was a quite separate question. The name *gold* was doubtless chosen because it was already traditionally in use to designate samples of the metal when found in a natural state in mineralogical deposits. But another name could have been chosen or invented. The question of how the scientists knew that this element 'really was' gold does not arise: it does not even make sense.

The case of democracy is quite different. Forms of democracy do not exist in a 'natural state', awaiting scientific investigation. Democracy is a type of government deliberately invented by human beings, and called by them *democracy* in order to distinguish it – in their own eyes – from other kinds of government, also invented by human beings. But they are also free to make their democracy work in a number of different ways and to incorporate different institutions into its workings. That is why a situation may easily arise in which a form of government called 'democracy' by those who live under it is not recognized as democratic at all by another community, which regards its own form of government as the model of democracy. There is no question of sending out research teams from Lagado to discover what democracy 'really is'. What they would find is a variety of forms of government all claiming the name *democracy* for reasons rejected by their rivals.

Honesty is a different case again. The reason why there is no question of discovering what honesty 'really is' is that it is intrinsically unclear – and always has been – whether the virtue that human beings think they recognize, and call *honesty*, is or is not the same as any of those which they also call by such names as *trustworthiness, truthfulness, probity, integrity*, and so on. Furthermore, what may count as instances or examples of this virtue or these virtues cannot be determined without taking into account details of the circumstances in which they are manifested and of the moral value-judgement being exercised by whoever applies the term in question. Here again there is no parallel with discovering the invariant features of a natural element such as gold.

Even those who think they are addressing the question of 'what *X* really is' as distinct from the question of 'how to define the word '*X*'' find it virtually impossible to avoid the latter question in cases like honesty. An example is A. C. Ewing on *The Definition of Good* (Ewing 1947). Ewing starts off by distinguishing between asking 'What is the definition of goodness?' and asking 'What things are good?', claiming that the former question is 'more fundamental' and declaring it to be the question with which he is concerned. But it is not long before he is discussing 'ethical terms' and their various 'senses', so that the discussion slides gradually into the realm of language. It is difficult to see how it could be otherwise, since it makes no sense to talk of *realia* as having various 'senses'. Tables and chairs do not have 'senses', and if goodness has senses then it belongs to a different ontological order altogether. Ewing often writes as if he thought goodness was neither a thing nor a word, but a concept. Even then, however, he cannot avoid the issue of verbal definition. He declares: 'A correct definition should give us what we mean by "good" or "ought" ' (Ewing 1947: 45). However this is to be interpreted (Who are 'we'? By what standards is a definition 'correct'?) it seems evident that the question addressed here is a question about *words. Ought* is neither a thing nor a concept, but a rather idiosyncratic English verbal form, having no exact counterpart in French, German or any other European language. In short, the problem with 'real definition' at this level is that there is no way of tackling it at all except via words and their uses in some particular language or languages. So however much a philosopher like Ewing may protest that what he is asking is 'not a question about what a term means' but a question about 'whether everything which has the defining property' in fact falls under the property which is the focus of his investigation, what he is actually doing all the time, willy-nilly, is arguing about the definitions of words.

* * *

All that has been said above about real definition may strike the reader as unremarkable and perhaps even as no more than common sense. Nevertheless, a pervasive conflation between real definition and the definition of words has been noticeable not only in philosophy but in certain schools of modern linguistics. The most blatant example is that of Bloomfieldian structuralism. According to Bloomfield, it is part of the task of the descriptive linguist to state accurately the meanings assigned to every form in the language under description. But in practice the possibilities of doing this are severely restricted, even when the language in question is well known. The reason for this is as follows:

> In order to give a scientifically accurate definition of meaning for every form of a language, we should have to have a scientifically accurate knowledge of everything in the speakers' world. The actual extent of human knowledge is very small, compared to this. We can define the meaning of a speech-form accurately when this meaning has to do with some matter of which we possess scientific knowledge. We can define the names of minerals, for example, in terms of chemistry and mineralogy, as when we say that the ordinary meaning of the English word *salt* is 'sodium chloride (NaCl),' and we can define the names of plants or animals by means of the technical terms of botany or zoology, but we have no precise way of defining words like *love* or *hate*, which concern situations that have not been accurately classified – and these latter are in the great majority. . . .
>
> The statement of meanings is therefore the weak point in language-study. and will remain so until human knowledge advances very far beyond its present state. (Bloomfield 1935: 139–40)

In the gamut of semantic theories available in modern linguistics, Bloomfield's is the most resolutely reocentric. For it is clear that what Bloomfield regards as an accurate definition of the word *salt* is nothing other than a real definition of salt. This, it should be noted, is treated by Bloomfield as capturing 'the ordinary meaning of the English word'; but this 'ordinary meaning' presumably differs from the technical meaning that the word might have for students of chemistry. Unless the technical meaning is assumed to be familiar also to millions of English speakers who have never studied chemistry. That seems unlikely. It becomes difficult at this point to follow Bloomfield's thinking. For if 'sodium chloride (NaCl)' is the ordinary meaning of *salt*, it would follow that many – perhaps the majority of – speakers of English do not know the meaning of one of the commonest English words. This picture of a linguistic community whose members are ignorant of the meanings of everyday words in their native language is one of the most bizarre that modern linguistics has to offer. But even more bizarre is the implicit conclusion that in order to define the word *salt* the linguist need not bother to consult native speakers and discover what they take it to mean: the linguist can safely ignore them and turn instead to a scientist who perhaps knows no English at all, but can say authoritatively what salt 'really' is.

* * *

At the opposite end of the linguistic spectrum from the semantics of Bloomfield one finds the semantics of Saussure. We are here talking about the Saussure of the *Cour de linguistique générale* which became the Bible of European structuralism, and not about the Saussure of the 'lost' notes, which were never published until nearly a century after Saussure's death (Bouquet and Engler 2002). Saussurean structuralism runs no risk of confusing the definition of a word with real definition. Far from it: the Saussurean linguistic sign is not a label attached to anything existing outside *la langue*. While Bloomfield treats meaning as what links a word to non-verbal reality, Saussure treats meaning as what links a sign to other signs within the same linguistic system. For Saussure, it is this internal network of similarities and differences of both form and meaning that structures the system, simultaneously identifying each individual sign and relating it to every other sign in the language. Saussure expressly rejects the idea that the meaning of the word *cheval* ('horse') is to be understood in terms of some kind of established connection between a certain sequence of French sounds and a certain species of animal (Saussure 1922: 97). For Saussure, the existence of horses in the world is no more required in order to account for the meaning of the word *cheval* than the existence of unicorns is required in order to account for the meaning of *unicorne*. The concept 'horse' is not the reflection of anyone's awareness of certain 'real' zoological facts, but the product of acquaintance with a certain linguistic system which structures the more general concept 'animal' in a certain way. In short, concepts, as far as Saussure is concerned, are not given independently of the linguistic signs by means of which they are expressed. In a much-quoted simile, the *Cours de linguistique générale* puts the point like this:

> In itself, thought is like a swirling cloud (*une nébuleuse*), where no shape is intrinsically determinate. No ideas are established in advance, and nothing is distinct, before the introduction of linguistic structure (*la langue*).
>
> (Saussure 1922: 155)

Thus mainstream linguistics in the twentieth century offered two radically divergent theoretical approaches to the problem of definition. One approach (Bloomfield's) sought to explicate linguistic knowledge by linking it up with scientific knowledge of non-linguistic reality. The other (Saussure's) postulated a psychological system with its own internal organization, not directly connected with or answerable to the external world at all.

Saussure's conception of this system was thoroughly holistic. Its units, both phonological (*signifiants*) and semantic (*signifiés*), are to be identified solely in terms of similarities with and differences from other units in the same system. Thus, strictly speaking, to define any given sign would require stating its relationships to every other sign. One could certainly not define *gold* by saying that it was the name given to a certain type of metal, since that would be to appeal to something outside the language. One could only proceed by comparing and contrasting the word *gold* with *silver*, *copper*, *zinc* and many other words, thus eventually pinning down with absolute precision its place in the total lexical structure of which it was part. In practice, Saussure never attempted to do this, although he gave schematic indications of how it might be done in principle (Saussure 1922: 175).

One relevant consequence of Saussurean holism is that any change in a single unit affects the entire system. Or rather, any change automatically brings a new system into being. So linguistic change proceeds, diachronically, by a succession of substitutions of later systems for earlier systems. (In practice, the changes may be so small as to pass unnoticed until they accumulate over a period of time; but this does not affect the theoretical explanation of the process.)

In effect, what the *Cours de linguistique générale* provides is as rigorous a theoretical justification as anyone has ever done for *both* components of the language myth. Its language systems not only operate as fixed codes, providing a single, unified set of signs for a single linguistic community (at one time and place), but explain in principle how it is possible to transfer thoughts between members of that community. The community in question, it need hardly be added, is envisaged as being what we referred to in Chapter 1 as being a 'completely homogeneous speech-community'. It is their very homogeneity that establishes what counts among them as common usage.

On the basis of the homogeneous model it is rather difficult to accommodate the phenomenon of stipulative definition, particularly in cases where it introduces a new word previously unknown. There seem to be two possible options. The less likely would be to admit that someone who introduces such a word by stipulative definition has *eo ipso* introduced a whole new system. The other would be to deny that anything has changed until the innovation proposed has received the collective ratification of the community. But neither option is very convincing. The first is awkward, given that those who introduce terms by stipulative definition are usually concerned with just one or two words, and rely implicitly on being able to stipulate without altering all the rest of the vocabulary in consequence. The second is awkward because it remains unexplained, at least within a Saussurean framework, how the rest of the community is in any position to understand the stipulation. If they *do*, however, then *pro tanto* the new term has already gained all the acceptance it needs to function as a linguistic sign. Whether it subsequently gains wider currency in general usage is quite a separate question.

Saussure, as far as is known, never indicated which of these theoretical options he might have preferred; nor did he devote any attention in lectures or notes to this particular problem. He was, however, quite clear that it is not within the power of any individual to alter a linguistic system already in place. We conclude that there is not much mileage to be gained by theorists of definition from adopting Saussurean semantics. It is true that meanings are thereby rescued from the vagaries of individuals and vested monolithically in the linguistic community as a whole; but this move leaves the apparent success of stipulative initiatives unaccounted for.

* * *

We have reserved until now any comment on what were traditionally regarded as the 'rules' of definition, such as always defining *per genus et differentiam*, never defining by means of synonyms, avoiding circular definitions, avoiding negative definitions, and so on. Robinson (1954: 140–8) lists and comments on these. We have not discussed them previously because we agree with Robinson that most of these 'rules' tacitly assume that definition is real definition (or confuse real definition with definition of words) and are in any case derived from Aristotle's *Topics.* Otherwise the so-called rules simply lay down general precepts conducive to clarity of exposition: they have nothing to do with definition as such.

The point may be illustrated by reference to the rule about avoiding synonyms. Under this rule, a definition such as '*sombre* means the same as *gloomy*', or just '*sombre* means "gloomy" ', would be condemned as merely substituting one synonym for another, but explaining the meaning of neither. What is the rationale of this condemnation? It can only be that if you do not know what *gloomy* means, you will have learnt nothing further from this definition about the meaning of *sombre,* except perhaps that it means the same as *gloomy.* But you might have known that already, and still be none the wiser about the meaning of either. And if you did not know that before, you will still be in the dark. So the condemnation of synonymous definitions is no more than a particular case of the more general condemnation of circularity. It is like criticizing a definition of the form '*gloomy* means the same as *gloomy*', on the ground that it tells you nothing new, even though doubtless correct.

This makes some kind of sense if one is dealing with real definition. That is to say, it advances knowledge and understanding not a jot to substitute one known synonym for another, if the objective is to learn more *about the thing designated.* But if the objective is to explain the meaning of a word to someone who is *ex hypothesi* ignorant of what it means, producing a synonym may well achieve the desired result. For it is possible that the learner may already be familiar with the synonym and what it means, although ignorant of the synonymity. In that case, the synonym will be a bridge to new understanding, and not just a circular return to square one.

This makes it difficult to agree with Locke when he denies that translations are definitions. For presumably an English speaker or writer who does not know what the French word *samedi* means can be enlightened (sufficiently for most purposes) by being told that it means the same as *Saturday.* A definition can only be as effective as the context allows it to be, and the context includes the situation of the person seeking to understand the meaning. The notion of a definition adequate to all occasions and all demands is a semantic *ignis fatuus.*

* * *

It seems appropriate at this point to say something about our view of definition in logic. Definition has been a thorn in the flesh of logic ever since Aristotle invented the syllogism in the fourth century BC. The problem is this. One cannot evaluate an argument without assigning a meaning to the words in which premises and conclusions are formulated. But it is not the business of the logician *qua* logician to tell anyone what words mean. On the other hand, the logician cannot proceed to conduct any analysis at all without assuming that definitions of words are already in place, or can be supplied when required.

Logic is the product of a literate society. This is evident from the way in which traditional logic presents its propositions as isolated, decontextualized statements ('All men are mortal') with no indication of the circumstances in which such statements are, were, or might be made. Only writing privileges such a reductive form of presentation, and only a literate mind would regard it as basic. It needs long acquaintance with the pedagogic use of the slate or the blackboard or the sand frame to treat such an *entrée en matière* as entirely 'natural'.

Aristotle, however, laboured under the disadvantage of trying to set up logic without having what would later come to be regarded as the full resources of a literate society. In particular, Aristotle's Greece had no dictionaries, and grammatical analysis was rudimentary. These lacunae left a profound mark on Aristotle's approach to his subject. It explains why he tried to detect patterns of argument operating at a level where the meanings of individual words could be largely ignored. He was the first to introduce another literate expository device – the use of letters of the alphabet as variables 'standing for' ordinary words. In this way he set logic on the path to becoming a kind of algebra of language. This path was to reach its ultimate destination only in the twentieth century with the publication of *Principia Mathematica*.

One sees Aristotle struggling with these handicaps in the awkward way he introduces the syllogism – that is, by giving the following stipulative definition:

> A syllogism is a form of words (*logos*) in which, when certain assumptions are made, something other than what has been assumed necessarily follows from the fact that the assumptions are such. By 'from the fact that they are such' I mean that it is because of them that the conclusion follows; and by this I mean that there is no need of any further term to render the conclusion necessary. (*Prior Analytics* 24b)

Nothing could be clearer than the fact that further definitions are required in order to make much sense of this at all. Without them, the pattern of connections which Aristotle sees as holding between premises and conclusion remains quite obscure, and the syllogism itself is left in a definitional limbo. Nor can the obscurity be removed by the simple expedient of citing examples. For instance, agreeing that if all men are mortal and Socrates is a man, then Socrates is mortal by no means elucidates the relationship obtaining between the three components ('all men are mortal', 'Socrates is a man', 'Socrates is mortal'). It is not even put beyond doubt whether the syllogism is supposed to be about connections between certain forms of words, or connections between thoughts, or connections between states of affairs. At the very least, one needs an explanation of how unstated 'assumptions' are to be detected and compared, why and in what respect one thing is held to 'follow from' another, to say nothing of how and why this 'following' is 'necessary' (*anagke*).

The only form of definition that Aristotle takes seriously is *per genus et differentiam*, and this is clearly best suited to real definition, where it provides a viable taxonomic tool for discussing plant and animal species. But when it comes to the meaning of words like *and*, or *not*, or *if*, – the 'logical words' *par excellence* – definition *per genus et differentiam* is useless. Aristotle, however, did not see definition *per genus et differentiam* as being just a useful classificatory device. Aristotle's logic, as Cassirer notes, is a 'true expression and mirror of the Aristotelian metaphysics.'

> The determination of the concept according to its next higher genus and its specific difference reproduces the process by which the real substance successively unfolds itself in its special forms of being. Thus it is this basic conception of *substance* to which the purely logical theories of Aristotle constantly have reference. (Cassirer 1910: 7)

To put much the same point in integrationist terms, Aristotle's syllogistic, while superficially 'abstract' in the way it compares and interrelates propositions, is actually pervaded at all levels by reocentric assumptions about meaning and definition.

Aristotle may be said to have invented not only the syllogism, but forged along with it the concept of logical necessity. He would later be taken to task for this. In *The Development of Logic*, Kneale and Kneale complain that he treats 'necessity' both (1) as characterizing the distinction between claiming that something is the case and claiming that it could not be otherwise, and (2) as marking what connects a premise and a conclusion. That is, he overlooks the difference between saying that 'every animal is necessarily mortal' and saying that what follows from the mortality of all animals and the fact that all men are animals, i.e. that every man is mortal, follows necessarily. This latter necessity has a different justification. It is justified 'not by any definitional connexion between the terms [sc. 'animal', 'man' and 'mortal'] but by the nature of the logical connexion signified by 'every . . . is' . . . . In other words we are dealing with a formal rather than a material necessity' (Kneale and Kneale 1988: 95). Kneale and Kneale think that Aristotle tacitly uses this latter distinction, but 'seems not to have reached the point of formulating it.'

What Kneale and Kneale do not call in question is whether definitional connections are a matter of necessity at all. Granted that all men are mortal and that Socrates is a man, it is by no means clear why the mortality of Socrates should be regarded as something separate that 'follows', rather than as a constituent part of the truth that has already been summarized in the generalization about all men. So there is an obvious case for saying that the conclusion, *pace* Aristotle, is not something *other than what has been assumed*. The generalization could hardly have been established if the case of Socrates had not been taken into account, along with many others, as part of the evidence. *That* is what is 'necessary', i.e. the necessity of subsuming all relevant instances under a generalization if the generalization is to hold. Had Socrates turned out, contrary to expectations, to be immortal, or at least still alive today, the choice would lie between revising the generalization or denying the humanity of Socrates. Either way (i.e. mortal or immortal) there is no necessity *de re* attaching to the status of Socrates or his relationship to the rest of the human race.

Nor is there any necessity if the connection is regarded as somehow inherent in the definition of terms such as 'man' and 'mortal'. For it is a contingent fact (at least, for those who accept the arbitrariness of the linguistic sign) that the terms in question have the meanings they do at any given time and place. The notion that the meaning of terms could not be otherwise (than they are or were) makes no linguistic sense. In dictionaries there is no ghostly form of the adverb *necessarily* positioned invisibly between the lemma and the definition of each entry.

So how did Aristotle come to perpetrate such a hopeless muddle in his attempt to systematize the syllogism? The answer, we suggest, is to be found in the assumptions Aristotle makes about language. If you believe (*De Interpretatione* 16a) that words are 'symbols' of 'affections of the soul', which in turn are direct images of actual things and events, then you can easily suppose, as Aristotle did, that a true statement is true in virtue of corresponding exactly to some state of affairs, this correspondence being guaranteed by the way semantics is underwritten by reality as all human beings perceive it. In short, the entire doctrine of 'necessity' in logic is rooted in Aristotle's reocentric view of meaning. It reflects a conviction (shared by Plato) that there must be some source of semantic invariance that explains and legitimizes human descriptions of the way things are. For Aristotle, unhappy with Plato's doctrine of transcendental Forms, reocentric definitions constitute that source. There is no 'beyond' to appeal to. The definition of 'man' rests on the unchanging nature of man, and the definition of 'mortal' on the unchanging condition of mortality.

If Aristotle had been concerned *qua* logician to analyse the basic semantics of the syllogism, he could hardly have overlooked such obvious facts as the following: that it needs to be understood that the Socrates who is said to be mortal is the same individual as the Socrates who is said to be a man (i.e. that the name *Socrates* does not identify two different people on different occasions of use), and that the term 'mortal' has the same meaning when predicated of a single man as when predicated of all men. So the syllogism cannot be reduced without further ado to the simple tripartite structure that Aristotle prefers. It would require some effort at more complex analysis, such as: 'if all creatures whom we call "men" are mortal, and if the term "men" is unambiguous, and if *Socrates* is the personal name of one of these creatures called "men", and if mortality is a condition that affects every mortal identically, and if the term "mortal" unambiguously designates all and only those affected by the said condition, then the individual just mentioned as having the name *Socrates* is subject to that condition in exactly the same way as any other creature in the class called "men".' The difference between this analysis and Aristotle's reveals what an integrationist might call 'the syllogistic gap': that is, the network of presuppositions that is being lost sight of when it is claimed as obvious that a certain conclusion about Socrates 'follows from' the premises stated.

Because Aristotle never bothers to spell any of this out, it was possible in the centuries that followed for logicians and other teachers to believe whatever they liked about the syllogism. As noted by Kneale and Kneale, some saw it as kind of higher-order grammatical analysis and classified it as an *ars sermocinalis*. Others saw it as a mechanism of thought underlying the psychology of reasoning.

> So long as men were content to take Aristotle's own works as their chief sources of logic, these differences of conception did not produce any great intellectual discomfort; by shifting their attention according to the part of the *Organon* with which they were concerned logicians could still think of logic as concerned alike with words, thoughts, and things. (Kneale and Kneale 1988: 738)

For the scholars of Port-Royal in the seventeenth century, logic was quite simply, as the subtitle of their treatise declares, 'the art of thought'. From the nineteenth century onward, however, the tendency has been to focus on logic as a system of formal patterns with its own symbolic structure, within which it is possible to offer deductive 'proofs' by the manipulation of signs in accordance with stipulative rules. This development, attractive mainly to mathematicians, may be seen as a reaction against a threatened takeover of logic by the newly emergent discipline of psychology. Certainly Aristotle could never have foreseen the day when Bertrand Russell could claim:

> logic has become more mathematical and mathematics has become more logical. The consequence is that it has now become wholly impossible to draw a line between the two; in fact, the two are one. (Russell 1919: 194)

Frege, one of the key figures in this merger, was a mathematician whose ruthless anti-psychologism drove him to resurrect a Platonistic metaphysics in which 'thoughts' exist in a timeless world of their own, immune both from human interference and the vagaries of language. According to Frege, it is a mistake 'to believe that logic deals with the mental process of thinking and with the psychological laws in accordance with which this takes place. That would be misunderstanding the task of logic . . .' (Frege 1918: 1).

Frege's position on definition is quite uncompromising: logic can operate only with terms precisely defined without any shadow of doubt:

> A definition of a concept (of a possible predicate) must be complete; it must unambiguously determine, as regards any object, whether or not it falls under the concept (whether or not the predicate is truly assertible of it). Thus there must not be any object as regards which the definition leaves in doubt whether it falls under the concept; though for us men, with our defective knowledge, the question may not always be decidable. We may express this metaphorically as follows: the concept must have a sharp boundary.
> (Frege 1893–1903: II.56)

Frege attacks his fellow mathematicians for their failure to recognize this requirement and keep to it. But its application, as far as he is concerned, does not stop at the boundaries of mathematics. He asks:

> would the sentence 'any square root of 9 is odd' have a comprehensible sense at all if *square root of 9* were not a concept with a sharp boundary? Has the question 'Are we still Christians?' really got a sense, if it is indeterminate whom the predicate 'Christian' can truly be asserted of, and who must be refused it?
> (Frege 1893–1903: II.56)

In Frege's day, logicians were also becoming keen to distance themselves from another newly emergent discipline, linguistics, which increasingly required engagement in empirical research into the social and physiological phenomena of human speech. A retreat into strict formalism thus provided a convenient way of maintaining the disciplinary independence of logic while at the same time dispensing logicians from donning white coats or doing 'field work'.

Definition, nevertheless, remained a residual problem. The most extreme formalist 'solution' consisted in announcing that to define a symbol was simply to specify that certain other symbols could be substituted for it in the right places in accordance with given rules. Perhaps the most notorious of these formalist definitions of definition was that of *Principia Mathematica,* where Whitehead and Russell dismissed definitions as 'mere typographical conveniences'. Less laconically, they described a definition as 'a declaration that a certain newly-introduced symbol or combination of symbols is to mean the same as a certain other combination of symbols of which the meaning is already known' (Whitehead and Russell 1910: 11). Here the Achilles heel of definition can still be seen peeping through a worn hole in the formalist sock: the appeal to symbols 'of which the meaning is already known' is a semantic postponement *sine die.*

As good formalists, Whitehead and Russell claim that for their purposes definitions are 'theoretically superfluous'. Nevertheless, they reluctantly concede a connection between manipulating symbols within the system and already familiar notions from outside. When what is defined is 'something already familiar, such as cardinal or ordinal numbers, the definition contains an analysis of a common idea, and may therefore express a notable advance' (Whitehead and Russell 1910: 12). In other words, they draw back from closing down their system of symbols from all contact with the outside world, since that would leave them vulnerable to the objection that their whole enterprise was of no more interest than formalizing the visible marks of a wallpaper pattern.

But this concession in turn left them vulnerable to charges of trying to have it all ways at once. Robinson accuses them of self-contradiction:

> In implying that the definiendum is an idea . . . they contradict their definition of 'definition', according to which the definiendum is a symbol. And in saying that the definiendum is often 'something already familiar', they

> contradict their previous doctrine that the definiendum is by definition 'newly introduced'. (Robinson 1954: 195)

Whether the author of a treatise on logic has been bitten by the formalist bug, or how badly, is often apparent on typographical inspection. In the 535 pages of John Dewey's *Logic* (1938), there is hardly a symbol in sight. Arthur Prior's *Formal Logic* (2nd edition 1962) is packed with page after page of labelled diagrams and unreadable formulae.

Those who followed closely in the logico-mathematical footsteps of *Principia Mathematica* may not have dismissed definition in quite as cavalier a manner as Whitehead and Russell, but they showed no greater enthusiasm for engaging with the problem. Wilfrid Hodges in his book *Logic* makes the understatement of the century when describing theory of definition as a 'corner of logic' that has been 'unjustly neglected' (Hodges 1977: 186). The fact is that logicians and mathematicians avoided it like the plague. Even Tarski, who tried to rescue it from the Siberia of metamathematics, admitted in his landmark paper 'On definable sets of real numbers' that

> Mathematicians, in general, do not like to operate with the notion of definability; their attitude towards this notion is one of distrust and reserve. (Tarski 1956: 110)

The reason, Tarski suggested, for this 'aversion' was that the meaning of the notion was 'not at all precise'. He set out to show that, nevertheless, the problem of 'making its meaning more precise' was not altogether intractable, even for mathematicians. What that meant, as far as he was concerned, was relativizing it to a suitable deductive system, chosen for the purpose. He was apparently unconcerned by the fact that this was not a solution at all but a simple evasion of everything that made the original problem problematic. (In other words, the evasion was justified if it enabled the rank and file of mathematicians to sleep soundly at night.) In a later paper on 'The establishment of scientific semantics', Tarski conceded that semantic concepts, such as 'truth' and 'definition', could be tackled only within the confines of 'formalized languages'. (Thus tackling them consisted of not allowing them to arise in the first place.) The trouble with what Tarski called 'colloquial language' was that 'this language is not something finished, closed, or bounded by clear limits' (Tarski 1956: 164). Or, to translate into the terminology we are using here, it was not a fixed code.

Philosophers less attracted to the austere beauties of formalism for formalism's sake have tried to maintain the more traditional position that logic has something to do with language and human ratiocinative process. But here the problem of definition returns to dog them in time-honoured fashion. According to Strawson (Strawson 1952), logic is all about the analysis of what he calls 'inconsistency', and this seems to be a psychological matter insofar as it involves 'accepting' definitions and linguistic 'rules'.

> We can deliberately fix the boundaries of some words in relation to those of other words. This is what we do when we *define* words or phrases. To introduce or to accept a definition is to announce or to agree that conjoining the defined (or defining) expression with the defining (or defined) expression by the words 'and' and 'not' in their standard use (or in any equivalent way), and referring this conjunction to one and the same situation, is to count as an inconsistency. Accepting a definition is agreeing to be bound by a rule of language of this kind. (Strawson 1952: 9)

In a footnote Strawson explains that this does not cover all uses of the words *define* and *definition*, but pleads in self-defence that he is using these words 'in a "strict" sense'. Where this strict sense comes from and what makes it strict are questions just as enigmatic as Strawson's bland appeal to the 'standard use' of the words *and* and *not*. What is actually happening here is that Strawson is putting forward a stipulative definition of his own for the key term in his theory; i.e. *inconsistency*.

Presumably when Strawson speaks somewhat arcanely of 'conjoining the defined (or defining) expression with the defining (or defined) expression by the words 'and' and 'not' in their standard use (or in any equivalent way), and referring this conjunction to one and the same situation' as an inconsistency, what this boils down to is a prohibition on claiming of any particular case that it is *a* but not *b* (where *a* is the definiendum and *b* the agreed or proposed definiens, or vice versa). But this will not work unless *a* and *b* both have exactly the same meaning – a definitional requirement that Strawson has not specified. There is no 'inconsistency' in saying of one's next-door neighbour that she grows flowers but is not a florist, even while accepting the dictionary definition of *florist* as 'person who deals in or grows flowers'. The definition is not an attempt to say how you *must* describe anyone; there may be all kinds of reasons why it would be inappropriate and misleading to describe one's flower-growing neighbour as a florist, even though the dictionary gives an informative and perfectly accurate account of what florists do.

But the first question that one is tempted to ask is whether what Strawson claims 'we' are doing in proposing or accepting a definition is a plausible account of the matter at all. Strawson himself seems to having nagging doubts about this, since he concedes (again in a footnote):

> We do not *generally* (in ordinary speech) draw up rules and make our practice conform to them; it is rather that we extract the rules from our practice, from noticing when we *correct* one another, when we are inclined to say that something is *inconsistent*, and so on. (Strawson 1952: 10. Italics in the original.)

How often, one wonders, do people catch themselves 'extracting rules' from their own practice and checking them by applying Strawson's 'and not' test? Is this a test that anyone has ever heard of being applied in 'correcting' the speech of another person? Or is the whole scenario a logician's fiction invented to support an otherwise obscure psychological explanation?

The reason why Strawson's 'and not' test falls down anyway becomes apparent when it is checked against a random sample of dictionary definitions. The snag is that definitions often refer explicitly only to a selection of the most typically relevant semantic features, so that when the word defined and the defining expression, conjoined by *and not*, are referred as Strawson requires, 'to one and the same situation', whether an inconsistency results will depend on the specifics of that particular situation. Particular situations do not always present the typical features mentioned in a dictionary definition. Thus, for example, it would be odd to deny that a game of cricket was in progress on the ground that it was not being played 'on a grass pitch', which is one of the definitional features cited in the *Concise Oxford Dictionary*'s definition of *cricket*; and absurd to convict anyone of 'inconsistency' who accepted the *COD* definition as a general guide to the usage of the term *cricket* but maintained that cricket could *also* be played on a matting wicket. Although it may grieve logicians, the fact is that definitions do not in practice constitute 'language rules' with firmly drawn limits of application that leave no room for context-sensitive deviations or improvements of any kind.

The most curious feature of Strawson's position is that towards the end of *Introduction to Logical Theory* he seems to have second thoughts about the doctrine of rules and definitions that he has been expounding hitherto. He admits:

> We do not judge our linguistic practice in the light of antecedently studied rules. We frame rules in the light of our study of our practice. Moreover, our practice is a very fluid affair. If we are to speak of rules at all, we ought to think of them as rules which everyone has a licence to violate if he can show a point in doing so. In the effort to describe our experience we are continually putting words to new uses, connected with, but not identical with, their familiar uses; applying them to states of affairs which are both like and unlike those to which the words are most familiarly applied. Hence we may give a meaning to sentences which, at first sight, seem self-contradictory. And hence, though some have incautiously spoken of the violation of type-rules as resulting in sentences which, though neither ungrammatical nor self-contradictory, are nonsense, it is in fact hard to frame a grammatical sentence to which it is impossible to imagine some sense being given; and given, not by arbitrary *fiat*, but by an intelligible, though probably figurative, extension of the familiar senses of the words and phrases concerned. (Strawson 1952: 230)

Here, in the space of a single paragraph, the left hand withdraws most of what the right hand has been laying down as the law throughout the previous chapters. The abrupt *volte-face* is revealing. What it seems to imply is broad agreement with Frege that logic can work properly only within the confines of an idealized, static language, and on the basis of definitions that set out 'sharp boundaries'. Clearly, 'ordinary language' is not like that. Strawson nevertheless believes that 'a realistic study of the logic of ordinary speech' is not 'impossible', but that such a study would be 'at best describing only the standard and typical uses of certain kinds of expression' (Strawson 1952: 231). But who is to judge what uses are 'standard and typical' Strawson's readers are never told. By this point they might reasonably feel reluctant to leave that judgement to a logician.

Chapter 4

Ostensive Definition and Linguistic Theory

Theories of definition tend to go hand in glove with theories about how languages are learnt. This is very evident in the case of Locke, who writes:

> if we will observe how children learn languages, we shall find that, to make them understand what the names of simple ideas or substances stand for, people ordinarily show them the thing whereof they would have them have the idea; and then repeat to them the name that stands for it; as *white, sweet, milk, sugar, cat, dog.* (Locke 1706: III.ix.9)

Locke here appeals to the teaching technique that later philosophers called 'ostensive definition'. The term seems to have be coined by the logician W. E. Johnson, but is variously defined by others. Robinson gives his own (stipulative) definition as follows: 'any method [sc. of teaching the meaning of a word] which does not rely on words alone, but also more or less directly uses the learner's experience of examples' (Robinson 1954: 119). That there must be some such method available is sometimes said to shown by the fact that we all begin life knowing the use of no words, and therefore 'our first instruction in them must occur without the aid of words' (Robinson 1954: 26). But this already makes at least one metaphysical assumption: namely, that our knowledge of words and meanings is not innate. Locke was evidently prepared to make that assumption.

A different method of learning, according to Locke, comes into play with the names of complex ideas:

> But as for mixed modes, especially the most material of them, *moral words*, the sounds are usually learned first; and then, to know what complex ideas they stand for, they [sc. children] are either beholden to the explication of others, or (which happens for the most part) are left to their own observation and industry; which being little laid out in the search of the true and precise meanings of names, these moral words are in most men's mouths little more than bare sounds; or when they have any, it is for the most part but a very loose and undetermined, and, consequently, obscure and confused signification.
> (Locke 1706: III.ix.9)

Locke never explains just how it is that merely repeating to a child the word *white* while showing examples of white things could ever bring about an understanding of the simple idea for which the word stands. But it is clear that there is a correlation between his account of language-learning and Locke's doctrine of definition; namely, that the words taught by ostensive procedures turn out to be those which are undefinable, whereas those which are definable are those that children cannot be taught ostensively. Although Locke does not insist on it, this *has* to be the case within the framework afforded by Lockean linguistic epistemology, because there is no way that just pointing to concrete examples (even where available) without further explanation could convey *which* combination of simple ideas the example represented.

In Bloomfield's linguistic theorizing there is a quite different correlation between the account of definition and the account of language-learning. According to Bloomfield:

> If someone did not know the meaning of the word *apple*, we could instruct him by handing him an apple or pointing at an apple, and continuing, as long as he made mistakes, to handle apples and point at them, until he used the word in the conventional way. This is essentially the process by which children learn the use of speech-forms. (Bloomfield 1935: 140)

Since Bloomfield does not admit 'ideas' as a valid theoretical concept, there is for him no question of explaining how ostensive teaching conveys the concept 'apple'; and since *a fortiori* he recognizes no category of 'simple ideas' he has no reason to restrict the role of ostensive teaching in the same way that Locke does. Moreover, his account is an improvement on Locke's in that he recognizes that an important part of language-learning involves learning what *not* to apply a word to: *apple* must not be applied to pears. Mistakes must be eradicated. Furthermore, his account does not suffer from the same kind of explanatory vacuity as Locke's. Since Bloomfield is a behaviourist, there is no question about *how* repeated pointing and handling in association with uttering the word *apple* manage to convey a meaning. The meaning *is* the habit. More exactly, learning the meaning is acquiring the right response to the right stimulus.

Bloomfield also proposes an alternative way of instructing someone who does not know the meaning of the word *apple*:

> If a questioner understood enough of our language, we could define the word *apple* for him by *circumlocution* – that is, in the manner of our dictionaries, by a roundabout speech which fitted the same situations as does the word *apple*, saying, for instance: 'The well-known, firm-fleshed, smooth-skinned round or oblong pome fruit of the trees of the genus Malus, varying greatly in size, shape, color, and degree of acidity.' (Bloomfield 1935: 140)

Unfortunately, this supplementary account brings Bloomfield into conflict not only with his earlier explanation of ostensive definition but also with his own behaviourist principles. As to the former, it is evident that merely pointing and handling would tell the learner nothing about such qualities as 'degree of acidity': it might not even be enough to make clear to the learner the difference between an apple and a wax ornament in the shape of an apple. From a behaviourist perspective, definition by circumlocution would be useless in teaching a child the meaning of the word *apple*, since producing a circumlocution does not have the required effect. *It does not teach the learner the habit.* Far from it: the learner might well understand the circumlocution, but be quite unable on that basis to identify examples of the fruit in question. Almost the only kind of 'situation' which could be 'fitted' both by the circumlocution and by the word *apple* would be one found within the covers of a dictionary. Reciting Bloomfield's proposed circumlocution to a shop assistant would not get the learner very far as a stimulus when trying to buy a pound of apples at the greengrocer's.

Locke's view that words that have to be taught by ostensive definition are not definable by means of other words turns up again in Bertrand Russell's *An Inquiry into Meaning and Truth* (Russell 1940). Here too we find the *a priori* argument that some such words (which Russell calls 'object-words' or sometimes 'primary words') must exist, because otherwise language could never get started. Russell holds that 'in the case of many object-words, it must be strictly impossible to *say* what they mean, except by a tautology, for it is with them that language begins' (Russell 1940: 24). Again: 'since the dictionary defines words by means of other words, there must be some words of which we know the meaning without a verbal definition' (Russell 1940: 63). This is the gap that ostensive definition allegedly bridges. For Russell, object-words are words whose 'meaning is learnt (or can be learnt) by confrontation with objects which are what they mean, or instances of what they mean' (Russell 1940: 23). This description leaves no room for doubt about the reocentric basis of Russell's semantics. The objects in question are not just things to which the words might be applied: the actual objects *are what they mean*, or instances of what they mean. The thing *is* the meaning of the word. In the learning process the word is juxtaposed to its own meaning, and it is in virtue of that juxtaposition that the learner finds out what the meaning is. The meaning is something visible or tangible or audible or detectable by one or a combination of the senses. It is certainly not an 'idea' in Locke's sense. Hence this explicit term *object-word*: 'the meaning of an object-word must be learnt in the presence of the object' (Russell 1940: 24). (In various places Russell seems to vacillate between saying that the meaning of an object-word (1) *is* learnt, or (2) *can be* learnt, or (3) *must be* learnt in the presence of the object; but these vacillations may be left on one side for present purposes.)

At all events, colours seem to count for Russell as 'objects'. And he seems to agree with Locke that you cannot learn the meaning of a colour-word unless you can see the colour. Nor can you indicate its meaning except by showing someone the colour.

> You can only explain (say) the word 'red' by pointing to something red. A child understands the heard word 'red' when an association has been established between the heard word and the colour red; he has mastered the

spoken word 'red' when, if he notices something red, he is able to say 'red' and has an impulse to do so. (Russell 1940: 24)

We are not far here from Bloomfield's patterns of stimulus and response. However, there is a problem. An integrationist might put it as follows. If learning means anything at all, it means integrating the new with the old. That integration can only take place on the basis of your own experience. In that respect, learning a word is on a par with learning anything else. You cannot learn by proxy. It follows that what the child learns as the meaning of the word *red* will depend on the child's colour vision. If colour vision varies from one child to another, different children will learn different meanings of the word *red*. To say that various children agree in calling, say, the colour of blood 'red' merely disguises the problem: for if their colour vision varies, they will be seeing different reds when looking at samples of blood.

Two conclusions follow. The first is that simple 'confrontation' with an object is not sufficient for learning the meaning of a word: the object must be perceived, and perceived in the right way. (Confronting a blind man with a red flag will result in no learning of the meaning of *red*.) The second is that even when the object is appropriately perceived (e.g. as a coloured object by someone who is not blind), that is no guarantee that training with the same objects will result in the same meanings being learnt. Therefore, either one must abandon the thesis that the meaning is the object, or else concede that, at least in some types of case, different learners acquire different meanings of 'the same word'. But abandoning Russell's reocentric semantics in favour of Locke's psychocentric semantics does not help: it will lead to the same conclusion, i.e. that different learners may attach different 'ideas' to the same word. And this will happen *even in the case of what Locke calls names of 'simple ideas'* unless the deliverances of the senses are the same for all learners. But where does this guarantee come from? We seem to be taken back once again to something like Aristotle's assumption that the world is the same for all observers (*De Interpretatione* 16a), an assumption that appears for purely physiological reasons to be false.

According to Russell, a language might consist entirely of object-words. He calls this an 'object-language'. This is the lowest in a hierarchy of languages: it does not include words like *is*, or *or*, or *all*, or *believe*. In Russell's hierarchy each language contains all its predecessors, i.e. any lower-order languages. So all languages have an object-language as an intrinsic component. In his chapter entitled 'The Object-Language' he provides a more exact account of what object-words are: they are 'defined, logically, as words having meaning in isolation, and, psychologically, as words which have been learnt without its being necessary to have previously learnt any other words' (Russell 1940: 62). He notes that the two parts of this definition 'are not strictly equivalent', but stipulates that 'where they conflict the logical definition is to be preferred'. This presumably means that if a word *had* been learnt without the previous learning of any other words, it would still not qualify as an object-word unless it had 'meaning in isolation'.

With this addition of this proviso, however, Russell's definition becomes totally obscure. In isolation *from what?* From anything else? From the learning process itself? Could there be a language with just one word? Russell provides no answers to these questions. Nevertheless, he proceeds to identify four factors that need to be considered in the learning of an object-word. These are: the understanding of the heard word in the presence of the object, understanding it in the absence of the object, speaking it in the presence of the object, and speaking it in the absence of the object. He adds that 'roughly speaking, this is the order in which a child acquires these four capacities' (Russell 1940: 63). This puzzling remark sounds like an empirical observation of language-learning in the nursery, but it can hardly be quite that. There is no 'roughly speaking' about the order. If Russell's account of ostensive learning is right, there can be no question of understanding the word in the absence of the object *before* understanding it the presence of the object. No object: no meaning. Similarly, there can be no question of speaking the word in the absence of the object without it having already been spoken in its presence, unless uttering a sound that happens fortuitously to resemble the word in question counts as 'speaking' it. Might it be the case that the capacity for speaking the word in the presence of the object was acquired before the capacity for understanding the word in the absence of the object? There is a problem with that; namely, whether it is reasonable to say the child is speaking the word if it has so far failed to grasp what difference the presence or absence of the object makes.

These questions point to a deeper flaw in Russell's entire scenario. There is no way of cashing the term *understanding*. What the child needs to grasp, precisely, is that the sound is not just a noise but a word; and specifically the name of a certain object. If the child already knows in general what it is for a sound to be the name of something, it might be supposed that it can apply this knowledge to any novel sound when presented in the right circumstances. But how this could be grasped in the case of the child's *first* word remains unexplained. Certainly it cannot be explained just by invoking a litany of repetitions.

Russell attempts to finesse the difficulty by giving a pseudo-Pavlovian description of teaching a dog what its name is:

> The process consists of calling him, rewarding him when he comes, and punishing him when he does not. We may imagine that, to the dog, his name means: 'either I shall be rewarded because I approach my master, or I shall be punished because I do not'. Which alternative is considered the more probable is shown by the tail. (Russell 1940: 63)

But, *pace* Russell, if Rover thinks that that is what 'Rover!' means, then the dog does not yet understand that *Rover* is his name, and to call that an example of a dog knowing its own name begs the whole question. This is not explanation but anthropomorphism. The comparison between dog and child limps badly in any case. Rover never learns to speak his own name, or learns about its use in his absence. Indeed, the case of learning one's own name presents something of a problem for Russell's account, since it is impossible for a child to hear its own name *in absentia*. It would seem to follow that, however we learn our own names, it cannot be by the programme Russell describes. They cannot be object-words in his sense. And this seems odd, since a child is usually introduced to its own name at a very early stage in the word-learning process.

Russell was by no means the only twentieth-century philosopher to get stuck in the quagmire of ostensive definition. His protégé Wittgenstein took a position that, in his later work, was quite different from Russell's. Glock summarizes Wittgenstein's scattered comments as follows:

> For the logical positivists, ostensive definitions were a means of injecting empirical content into a formal, uninterpreted calculus. . . . Wittgenstein moved in the opposite direction. Commenting on Waismann's attempts to summarize the *Tractatus*, he denied that an ostensive definition (*hinweisende Erklärung*) provides a 'connection between language and reality', and later claimed that for this reason 'language remains self-contained and autonomous'. . . . This is a startling claim. But Wittgenstein does not deny that we, for the most part, talk about language-independent things; he denies only that the latter constitute the meanings of our words, and hence that there are *semantic* connections between language and world. Empirical propositions refer to language-independent items and are verified or falsified by the way things are. But this distinguishes them from ostensive definitions. One must distinguish the use of a sentence of the form 'This is *A*' to make an empirical statement from its employment in giving an ostensive definition. . . . The latter does not 'describe' the object pointed at as *A*, either truly or falsely, but defines what counts as being *A*.
>
> (Glock 1996: 275. Omitting the bibliographical references given by Glock.)

If this is an accurate summary, it would seem that lurking behind Wittgenstein's view one can glimpse a survival of the old doctrine that stipulative definitions have no truth value. But is teaching the meaning of a word (whether ostensively or otherwise) intrinsically stipulative? Glock elaborates by means of a comparison: 'An ostensive definition cannot simultaneously be a description, just as the juxtaposition of a ruler with a rod cannot simultaneously constitute a measurement of the rod and a calibration of the ruler.' Wittgenstein does indeed say in *Philosophical Investigations*:

> There is *one* thing of which one can say neither that it is one metre long, nor that it is not one metre long, and that is the standard metre in Paris.
>
> (Wittgenstein 2001: §50)

But history has caught Wittgenstein out here. It turns out that the standard metre in Paris is short. (For discussion, see Harris 2005: 145–50.) To say this is not to make the self-stultifying claim that the standard metre bar in Paris is not the length that it is, but the historical observation that those who determined the length of the bar got it wrong. This is in no way nullified by the other historical observation that for centuries no one noticed the error. What is obvious, simply, is that one cannot measure any metre bar against itself. For measurement, there have to be at least two *comparanda.* But, *pace* Wittgenstein, it does not follow that ostensive definitions are neither true nor false. On the contrary, a teacher who tries to teach a child the meaning of the word *apple* by pointing to an apple and saying 'This is an apple' does so, presumably, in the belief that that is the truth. If the demonstration were challenged by someone who asked 'Is that true?', it would be odd for the teacher to reply 'Oh no, of course not'. The teacher is explaining what the object in question is usually called, and *for that reason* recommending that usage to the learner. But there is no internal conflict between the assertion and the recommendation. They are not separate linguistic acts that have to be done one at a time. It makes no sense to ask your teacher: 'Are you *telling* me that's an apple, or just trying to define the word?' (as if the two were mutually exclusive).

* * *

We turn now to a discussion of the integrationist position on definition. We start from the unexciting lay observation that in familiarizing someone with the use of any sign for purposes of communication it may often be helpful either to point to examples ('This is an apple', etc.) or to give a verbal account ('An apple is the fruit of a tree of the genus Malus', or '*Apple* is what we call the fruit of a tree of the genus Malus', etc.) Such procedures can be applied both to linguistic signs and to non-linguistic signs. Whether both types of procedure deserve to be called *definition* does not seem to us to matter much: both have been so called in the past and it seems to lead to no confusion apart from one we have already commented on: that is, a potential conflation between real definition and definition of words. Whether what is allegedly given or identified by a definition is to be called the *meaning* of the sign also seems to us not to matter a great deal. Again, with the proviso that the term *meaning* does not serve to obscure or conflate differences that should be recognized and kept in mind.

A more controversial integrationist tenet is the following: that no form of definition can render the meaning of a sign determinate, i.e. can guarantee that those who have either formulated or understood the definition have thereby grasped the same meaning. Definition, in short, *always* allows room for semantic divergence and hence misunderstanding. It may, depending on the circumstances, *reduce uncertainty* but cannot *eliminate* it.

A very similar position to this has sometimes been advanced in philosophy of language, notably by Quine; but for reasons quite different from ours. Quine's position has its basis in behaviourism and in certain assumptions about the continuity between philosophy and science: ours does not.

Quine has his own version of the primitive uses of language, not unlike Wittgenstein's hypothetical 'language games'. One of them runs as follows:

> 'Ouch!' is a one-word sentence which a man may volunteer from time to time by way of laconic comment on the passing show. The correct occasions of its use are those attended by painful stimulation. Such use of the word, like the correct use of language generally, is inculcated in the individual by training on the part of society; and society achieves this despite not sharing the individual's pain. Society's method is in principle that of rewarding the utterance of 'Ouch' when the speaker shows some further evidence of sudden discomfort, say a wince, or is actually seen to suffer violence, and of penalizing the utterance of 'Ouch' when the speaker is visibly untouched and his countenance unruffled.
>
> For the man who has learnt his language lesson, some of the stimuli evocative of 'Ouch' may be publicly visible blows and slashes, while others are hidden from the public eye in the depths of his bowels. Society, acting solely on overt manifestations, has been able to train the individual to say the socially proper thing in response even to socially undetectable stimulations. The trick has depended on prior concomitances between covert stimulation and overt behavior, notably the wincing instinct.
>
> We can imagine a primitive use of 'Red' as a one-word sentence somewhat on a par with 'Ouch'. Just as 'Ouch' is the appropriate remark on the occasion of painful stimulation, so 'Red', under the usage which I am now imagining, is the appropriate remark on the occasion of those distinctive photochemical effects which are wrought in one's retina by the impact of red light. This time society's method of training consists in rewarding the utterance of 'Red' when the individual is seen looking at something red, and penalizing it when he is seen looking at something else. (Quine 1960: 5–6)

Quine concedes that in practice 'the uses of "Red" are less simple.' But this is nevertheless the basic model of language-learning that he wishes to establish for purposes of his argument. The integrationist has no such story to tell or model to establish. If an integrationist wished for some reason to find out how 'Ouch' was learnt, the recommended method would be to engage in some linguistic field-work. But it is difficult to believe that Quine's account has any such basis. It bears all the hallmarks of a fiction invented to illustrate certain propositions that Quine in fact takes as given. The story of 'rewards' and 'punishments' for utterances of 'Ouch' comes, like similar stories in Russell and others, straight from simplified popular accounts of what Pavlov's dogs did. No attempt is made to supply any plausible reason why the man's peers should take it upon themselves to reward or punish him, depending on whether or not he seemed to utter 'Ouch' in the right circumstances. And presumably on the many occasions when the poor fellow in pain uttered 'Ouch' in private, society had no means of exercising any control over his behaviour anyway.

The next step in Quine's story is the deliberate assimilation of the case of 'Ouch' to the case of 'Red'. Whether there is any research to support this we are never told. Again, it seems improbable. But now Quine's story begins to encounter its first problems.

> The critic, society's agent, approves the subject's utterance of 'Red' by observing the subject and his viewed object and finding the latter red. In part, therefore, the critic's cue is red irradiation of his own retina. (Quine 1960: 6)

But this is puzzling, since as yet Quine's reader has been given no explanation of how the critic has learnt to do this, i.e. to give the subject a reward in response to the dual stimulus provided by (1) the activity in the critic's own retina and (2) the subject's utterance of 'Red'. There is no behavioural basis for proceeding thus, since *ex hypothesi* the subject's utterance is not a response to the stimulation of the critic's retina, but to what is happening in his own. Quine offers the lame rationale that 'a partial symmetry obtains between the subject's cue for utterance and the critic's cue for approval'. But this 'symmetry' is another figment of Quine's fairy-tale: no one knows for sure whether what the subject sees is what the critic sees. At the very least, the critic would have to conjecture that such a symmetry obtained, to imagine himself in the subject's shoes, or something similar. But these are mental feats or assumptions not easily explained in terms of stimuli and responses, and in any case rebarbative to the whole spirit of behaviourist reductionism.

Quine, in short, wants to have his behaviourist cake and eat it. His story about 'Red' involves an agent (the critic) whose actions can only be rationalized by supposing that he is *not* acting just on the basis of verbal habits already acquired in the manner he seems bent on inculcating in the learner.

Quine now makes a further move. He posits that in a case like 'Red' a 'nearly uniform stimulatory condition is shared by simultaneous observers' (Quine 1960: 7). This cagey formulation leaves it unclear whether the 'stimulatory condition' is (1) whatever they are looking at or (2) the 'photochemical effects' of their looking. This is only partly clarified by Quine's statement that 'all the assembled retinas are irradiated by substantially the same red light'. But whichever it is, the concessions 'nearly uniform' and 'substantially the same' grant that it is not actually uniform or exactly the same. So if it is not uniform or exactly the same there must be differences. What this boils down to, therefore, is that different stimulatory conditions presented to simultaneous observers somehow produce an identical verbal response, for reasons not yet satisfactorily elucidated. Nevertheless, for Quine this is a relatively straightforward case. He admits that a more difficult case is one where 'each of a party of observers glances at a tile from his own vantage point and calls it square', despite the fact that 'each of them has, as his retinal projection of the tile, a scalene quadrilateral which is geometrically dissimilar to everyone else's' (Quine 1960: 7).

But this does not bother Quine unduly either. They have somehow managed to acquire the habit of calling the tile 'square' even when no square projection stimulates their retinas. How? All Quine tells us is that 'the learner of "square" has to take his chances with the rest of society, and he ends up using the word to suit'. This shifts the burden of responsibility from learner to teacher, i.e. to the rest of society: all the learner has to do is conform. What Quine does volunteer, however, is a statement of necessary conditions:

> In general, if a term is to be learned by induction from observed instances where it is applied, the instances have to resemble one another in two ways: they have to be enough alike from the learner's point of view, from occasion to occasion, to afford him a basis of similarity to generalize upon, and they have to be enough alike from simultaneous distinct points of view to enable the teacher and learner to share the appropriate occasions. A term restricted to squares normal to the line of sight would meet the first requirement only; a term applying to physical squares in all their scalene projections meets both. And it meets both in the same way, in that the points of view available to the learner from occasion to occasion are likewise the points of view available to teacher and learner on simultaneous occasions. Such is the way with terms for observable physical objects generally; and thus it is that such objects are focal to reference and thought. (Quine 1960: 7)

This portentous way of peeling a very small psychological onion would already be comic if it were not dressed up as theoretical explanation. Those additional frills transform it from the comic into the absurd. The fact is that Quine's example of the term *square* and its mismatch with retinal images is a complete red herring. It has nothing to do with teaching and learning or pressures to conform. Or even to do with human society. For all primates are in the same evolutionary boat here. They are neurophysiologically adapted to track sequences of sense impressions as being causally connected to single objects in the external world, and inability to manage that kind of on-line analysis would have led to their extinction millions of years ago. Looking at square tiles from various angles is no different from looking at anything else from different angles. It would be both confusing and counterproductive to have separate words for all the possible visual impressions that changes in perspective bring. It has nothing to do with choosing 'a basis of similarity to generalize upon'. Nor with imposing any arbitrary collective decision to make do with a single word instead of having dozens of different words corresponding to different appearances of a square tile. What *is* arbitrary – and here Quine has failed to learn the 'language lesson' illustrated by his own example – is the particular way *square* is defined by lexicographers. Quinean semantics is shackled by its subservience to behaviourist epistemology.

Integrationist semantics does not suffer from this handicap. Integrationists start from the assumption that communication depends on signs. But these signs are not already established in advance of the act of communication. The making of signs is part of the act itself. However many prior examples have been provided ostensively in the learning process, there still remains work for the speaker to do. For the initial series of examples will have been finite in number – a finite number of apples and non-apples, say. But every apple differs in some respect from every other. When each 'new' specimen comes along, it is the speaker who must *decide* whether to call it 'apple' or not. That decision is the speaker's contribution to the sign-making process and to the communication situation.

The making of signs may indeed be modelled on previous signs: but that is a merely contingent aspect of the process, not a determining factor, much less a predetermining factor. For the process itself is open-ended. Consequently, as Saussure observed in his 'lost' notes (Bouquet and Engler 2002: 88), since the number of these signs and their reciprocal and relative aspects may change from one moment to the next, the upshot of this activity may also change from one moment to the next. That Saussurean description corresponds exactly – we would claim – to the experience of taking part in everyday conversation, where all understanding of what is said depends from one moment to the next on context. It appears to be less so when reading a written text, but that is because most written signs obey different communicational constraints and the parameters of context are artificially restricted. The sign itself (i.e. its physical manifestation) appears static and fixed.

Once these factors are recognized and given their due, there is no more need for postulating invariant collective codes that allegedly make it possible for one individual to exchange thoughts with another. Nor arcane accounts of stimulus-and-response learning processes that allegedly explain how the individual is socially coerced into acquiring the collective code. Communication in all its forms is permanently at the mercy of circumstances and human reactions that are, in the final analysis, unpredictable. Which amounts to saying that the serious student of human communication cannot expect that study to be a 'science'.

Where does that leave the vexed question of definition? We have already argued that the established practice of stipulative definition reveals the Achilles heel of fixed-code semantics as applied to the linguistic community in general. It remains for us to explain how that practice is possible. How can one individual defy 'common usage' and successfully impose idiosyncratic semantic interpretations on an audience?

We shall first comment on some potential answers that we do *not* subscribe to. A fixed-code theorist might be tempted to say that stipulative definition can only be successful in virtue of the fact that common usage already supplies a fixed code for the stipulator to use. Moreover, he might add, the definition has only a temporary application and has no effect on the code itself. In short, to put it in Saussurean terms, these are matters of *parole*, not of *langue*.

This sounds plausible in certain types of case. It sounds plausible when stipulative definition is used to avoid ambiguities ('By *insensible* I mean *imperceptible*, not *unconscious*', 'By *Everest* I mean the double-glazing company, not the mountain', etc.). It sounds plausible when stipulative definition is used to avoid tedious repetitions or circumlocutions ('By *partner* I mean *person of either sex regularly co-habiting with the individual in question*', 'By *local* I mean *within a radius of about fifty miles*', etc.). The plausibility might even extend to cases where the proposed definition is outlandish or seems to lack serious motivation. The creator of Humpty Dumpty wrote in his *Symbolic Logic:*

> If I find an author saying at the beginning of his book, 'Let it be understood that by the word "*black*" I shall always mean "*white*", and that by the word

"*white*" I shall always mean "*black*",' I meekly accept his ruling, however injudicious I may think it. (Carroll 1896: 166)

But the more perverse the stipulation the less convincing the claim that the stipulator is still operating within the confines of common usage. For although the terms of the definition may themselves be drawn from the vocabulary of common usage, what is being proposed patently turns common usage topsy-turvy. Here it is apposite to recall Alice's objection to Humpty Dumpty: it is all very well declaring that by *glory* you mean 'a nice knock-down argument', but *can* you make words mean so many different things? At this point the fixed-code theorist faces a dilemma. For if Humpty Dumpty *can*, then this is tantamount to an admission that common usage is not a fixed code after all. But if Humpty Dumpty *cannot*, then his stipulative definition was never legitimate in the first place. The horns of this dilemma might be described in much greater detail; but here we leave it for the fixed-code theorist to sort out, and rest content with stating our conviction that the fixed-code theorist will find it impossible.

This is not because we wish to evade a discussion of the issue, but because we wish to focus on an even greater dilemma for the fixed-code theorist to face. It arises from the fact that stipulative definition is not in any case confined to the types of case considered immediately above. That is, it is not restricted to operating with terms drawn from an inventory already known. Stipulative definition can also be used to introduce expressions which have no previous *locus standi* in common usage, and consequently trespass outside the boundaries of the hypothesized fixed code altogether. Furthermore, this linguistic possibility is of immense value and importance. Without it, the technical languages of mathematics, physics and many other branches of human inquiry could never have been established.

It will not do for the fixed-code theorist to protest that these technical languages are themselves fixed codes. For they are constantly being expanded by further processes of stipulative definition, as the history of the subjects in question clearly shows. But, more importantly, even if these technical languages remained static for long periods of time, that would not explain how they arose in the first place. Where technical languages are concerned, there is no miraculous process of virgin birth. Nor can a fixed code from within itself procreate other fixed codes. If it has genetic potential it is not a fixed code.

The integrationist answer to Wittgenstein's sceptical question 'Can I say "bububu" and mean "If it doesn't rain I shall go for a walk"?' (Wittgenstein 2001: 16fn) is: 'Yes, you can; but it would be better and avoid a lot of confusion if you made this clear in advance by means of a stipulative definition.' Wittgenstein's reply to his own question is: 'It is only in a language that I can mean something by something'. To which an integrationist would add: 'And you already have that language to hand.'

The integrationist position can be summed up as follows. An individual can defy common usage and successfully impose idiosyncratic semantic interpretations on an audience precisely because words are *not* signs whose meanings are circumscribed by the 'rules' of fixed codes or imposed by collective authority, whether overt or tacit. They are free creations of the human mind.

* * *

Should we have any readers who still hanker for this position to be stated in technical terms drawn from modern linguistic theory, let us try to oblige. The nearest approximation we can think of would be to say that what we are maintaining is that stipulative definitions function as performatives – in something like the Austinian sense of *performative* (Austin 1962). We have to say 'something like' because, as will become apparent below, integrationists cannot accept the standard Austinian account.

Austin drew everyone's attention to the way in which saying 'I apologize' or 'I promise' in the appropriate circumstances, is interpreted as being not just a statement *about* some linguistic act, but as itself *constituting* an act of the kind designated by the verb in question; namely, as an apology or a promise. You apologize by *saying*, in the appropriate circumstances, 'I apologize', and promise by *saying*, in the appropriate circumstances, 'I promise'. This makes *apologize* and *promise* verbs of a different kind from, say, *die*. You cannot die by *saying*, in the appropriate circumstances, 'I die'. Austin used this kind of example to drive a theoretical wedge between 'performatives' and what he called 'constatives'.

Although the distinction seems clear enough on first inspection, it led both Austin and his critics into a maze of difficulties which are not our present concern (Fann 1969). But what makes it *prima facie* tempting to assimilate stipulative definitions to Austinian performative utterances is that in grammatical form both can look like statements, but these 'statements' are often held to have no truth value. Austin later seems to have doubts about this in the case of performatives, but he starts off with very forthright assertions on this score. Having given initially a few examples of performatives, he declares:

> None of the utterances cited is either true or false: I assert this as obvious and do not argue it. It needs argument no more than that 'damn' is not true or false.
> (Austin 1962: 6)

Another reason for proposing the assimilation is that one of Austin's stock examples of a performative is 'I name this ship the *Queen Elizabeth*' 'as uttered when smashing the bottle against the stem' (Austin 1962: 5); and this, although perhaps not a stipulative definition, seems very close to introducing by fiat a designation not previously accepted. At the very least it has certain similarities to saying, for instance, 'I call this new plastic *carbolene*', or, as in Kelvin's case, 'I call this unit of conductivity *mho*'.

If stipulative definitions are to be included in the category of performatives, they must presumably be subject to the kinds of Austinian 'felicity conditions' that performatives in general are subject to. What these might be in the case of stipulative definitions has never been specified in detail, but it seems they would have to go further than Robinson's fifteen 'rules' for stipulative definition (Robinson 1954: 80ff.). These include cautions against stipulating more than is necessary, against stipulating that different words have the same meaning, and so on. But they do not lay down what, in general, *has* to be the case in order for a stipulative definition to succeed. In particular, there is nothing corresponding to what Austin takes to be the first 'rule' for felicitous performatives; namely, that 'there must exist an accepted conventional procedure having a certain conventional effect, that procedure to include the uttering of certain words by certain persons in certain circumstances' (Austin 1962: 14).

We suggest that Austin's first 'rule' can be satisfied by treating any utterance of the form 'I define *f* as *m*', in the right circumstances, as filling this role; that is, as functioning in the same way as 'I apologize' in the case of apologies and 'I promise' in the case of promises. The stipulator, therefore, is to be seen as invoking this verbal procedure insofar as his stipulation relies on a form of words understood as announcing that he hereby defines *f* as *m*.

Austin never explains how a given verbal formula comes to have the particular performative function that it does, but Searle, developing Austin's theory of speech acts, addresses the question explicitly. The trouble is that Searle is a fixed-code theorist, and his answer appeals to 'the semantical rules' of the language to which the verbal formula belongs (Searle 1969). (Thus e.g. 'I apologize' allegedly acquires its performative role in virtue of the semantical rules determining the meaning of the verb *apologize* in English.) By making this move Searle in effect hands over the definition of performative verbs to be settled by 'common usage'. But where the verb *define* itself is concerned (in 'I define *f* as *m*') this would be tantamount to an evasion of the issue. For what the stipulator is doing in many cases will conflict with common usage: to make that clear is often the whole point of the definition. So appealing to common usage in order to settle whether *define* is a performative verb leads straight to a theoretical dead end.

Thus for an integrationist it would be quite inadequate to abandon the analysis at this juncture by appealing to something as nebulous as semantical rules and general English usage. The so-called semantical rules of English are inventions of grammarians and the meaning of the verb *define* is no more determinate than that of any other verb. Rather, the performative function of 'I define *f* as *m*' is to be understood as an attempt to reduce potential misunderstanding by *narrowing down* – for a certain range of contexts – certain possibilities for the interpretation of *f*. It succeeds only insofar as an audience is led to interpret *f* accordingly (Austin's 'uptake'). But the uptake is down to every individual member of that audience. Each of them must reach their own decision about how best to do that: this is something that the stipulator cannot do on their behalf. And that interpretational process is their own (creative) contribution to communication.

When seen from this angle, the difference between stipulative definition and dictionary definition is not as great as was traditionally assumed. We propose that the lexicographer may also be read as employing the performative formula 'I define *f* as *m*', but leaving open the range of contexts to which the stipulation applies. This manifestly increases the burden placed upon the readers, who must decide for themselves which contexts the definition fits and which it does not.

What that amounts to in particular cases can only be revealed by examining some of the tacit assumptions underlying the cases in question, and this we propose to do in the following chapters.

II. Definition and the Dictionary

Chapter 5

The Lexicographer's Task

Definitions, in modern literate societies, are commonly thought to be found in dictionaries; but a dictionary is not just *any* list of words and meanings. The lexicographer's treatment and arrangement of materials differs entirely from the glossographer's. The glossographer's point of departure is a given text, and the aim is to elucidate the meanings of words as and where they occur in that text. The lexicographer has no such fixed starting point. Very occasionally, some lexicographers claim that their starting point is not a single text but a finite collection of texts (such as all books printed in Ruritania during the sixteenth century). But as soon as they present their lexicon in alphabetical order, they have already attempted to impose a predetermined arrangement on this material. Lexicography is not multiple glossography. *Nor could it ever be, even in principle.* For the construction of a dictionary requires decisions about what to include and what to omit. It also requires decisions about how to classify and subdivide across the range of materials included. The glossographer encounters none of these problems, but must simply decide which words in a text require explanation, and how best to explain them *in that context.*

It is sometimes said that, chronologically, lexicography developed out of glossography. This impression may be strengthened by the common practice in major dictionaries of supplying copious quotations from particular texts. But it needs to be established straight away that the lexicographer's task and the glossographer's are entirely different. What the glossographer is called upon to supply is not a definition of the word in the lexicographer's sense: it has no implication of generality.

In this and the next two chapters we shall be mainly concerned with what are nowadays called 'general' (as opposed to 'specialized') dictionaries; that is, dictionaries 'intended to provide a comprehensive description of the whole language, with special attention to vocabulary' (Hartmann and James 1998: 61). A dictionary such as the one from which this definition is quoted, Hartmann and James' *Dictionary of Lexicography*, would count as 'specialized'.

General lexicography underwent a major change in the nineteenth century with the introduction of what were called 'historical principles'. As regards definition, this resulted in making what were already confused issues even more confused. The irony is that these 'historical' lexicographers almost certainly believed that their work was a signal contribution to clarifying questions of definition and not, as it turned out to be, another source of obfuscation.

The explanation for this can be traced directly, as we shall attempt to show, to their lack of any adequate semantic theory on which to base their treatment of the materials they studied. The unfortunate legacy of their efforts is still apparent today, since their successors continue to make mistakes that are instantly recognizable as those typical of nineteenth-century lexicography. Since the quasi-religious awe with which dictionary definitions are often regarded by the general public shows no sign of diminishing, it is important to understand the difference between what the 'historical' lexicographers were actually doing in their dictionaries and what they *thought* they were doing.

Where lexical definition is concerned, any appeal to history is bound to be misleading, and the reason can be very concisely stated. To borrow Saussurean terminology, it invites conflation between synchrony and diachrony. What a word means for any given user or group of users is a question that cannot be settled by bringing into consideration the language of their ancestors. That can only obscure matters and divert inquiry along semantically irrelevant lines. One can no more analyse present linguistic usage on the basis of past linguistic usage than a cartographer can draw a reliable street map of London today on the basis of information about the city in Georgian or medieval times. That would not only be foolish but confusing for current road-users.

In lexicography the appeal to history commonly takes two forms. The earlier and cruder consists in treating the definition of a word as something authoritatively established by a previous generation. The later, less crude, but no less deeply mistaken, consists in treating the definition of a word as a cumulative historical process.

* * *

> When I took the first survey of my undertaking, I found our speech copious without order, and energetick without rules: wherever I turned my view, there was perplexity to be disentangled, and confusion to be regulated; choice was to be made out of boundless variety, without any established principle of selection; adulterations were to be detected, without a settled test of purity; and modes of expression to be rejected or received, without the suffrages of any writers of classical reputation or acknowledged authority.
>
> (Johnson 1755)

This paragraph from the Preface to Johnson's *Dictionary of the English Language* is worth quoting in full because it illustrates a point which is fundamental to our treatment of definition. A lexicographical definition, we shall argue, does not in most cases identifiy a meaning independently existing in actual usage and *discovered* there by the lexicographer: it is deliberately *constructed* and *allocated* by the lexicographer on the basis of materials selected for study, and its allocation will depend on the viewpoint the lexicographer has chosen to adopt. We shall try to demonstrate this by reference to the work of two of the foremost lexicographers of English: Samuel Johnson and James

Murray, the latter being in charge of the *New English Dictionary* (later called the *Oxford English Dictionary*) from 1879 until his death in 1915.

It has become almost a ritual for general lexicographers to disavow any intention of *passing judgement* on usage, and to claim that their dictionaries merely record it. Both Johnson and Murray duly follow this ritual, but their own practice belies it. The passage from Johnson cited above is enough to discredit the notion that the task of the lexicographer is simply to take note of and register the facts. As is evident from Johnson's brief survey of the difficulties confronting him, actual usage in its totality is chaos. No lexicographer in the world ever undertook to document chaos. The lexicographer's aim is to reduce chaos to order.

Johnson distinguishes two senses of *Definition.* In logic, he tells us, it is 'the explication of a thing by its kind and difference'. More generally, it is 'a short description of a thing by its properties'. Both of these are manifestly real definitions. Neither fits the sense in which a definition is what the lexicographer supplies for each and every word in his dictionary, whether or not the word is the name of a 'thing'. This Johnson calls not a 'definition' but an 'explanation'. The Explanation, he says in his Preface, is 'that part of my work on which I expect malignity most frequently to fasten'. Here he speaks for most lexicographers.

> To interpret a language by itself is very difficult; many words cannot be explained by synonimes, because the idea signified by them has not more than one appellation; nor by paraphrase, because simple ideas cannot be described. When the nature of things is unknown, or the notion unsettled and indefinite, and various in various minds, the words by which such notions are conveyed, or such things denoted, will be ambiguous and perplexed. And such is the fate of hapless lexicography, that not only darkness, but light, impedes and distresses it; things may be not only too little, but too much known, to be happily illustrated. (Johnson 1755)

Johnson's complaints repay attention, because they throw more light on his conception of the lexicographer's task than any positive statement he ever makes.

1. *Synonyms.* In the passage quoted above, Johnson seems to imply that giving explanations would be easier if English synonyms were more abundant than they are. This suggests that if the lexicographer can find an exact synonym, the task of 'explanation' is done. In quite a number of cases Johnson does give a one-word explanation (e.g. he explains *ballad* as 'A song' and *bard* as 'A poet'); so presumably in these cases the reader is to understand that the two terms thus equated are synonymous, since Johnson makes no attempt to explain what kind of song a ballad is, or what kind of poet a bard is.

This will seem odd to anyone who finds it strange to describe church hymns as 'ballads', or Virgil as a Roman 'bard'. But there is something even odder to be accounted for. By mentioning synonyms at the start, Johnson seems to be implying that if a word lacks a synonym, the lexicographer must fall back on other expedients (such as paraphrase) which are less precise. But suppose there were a language in which every word had an exact synonym. Would an ideal dictionary then consist simply of an alphabetical list of synonyms? And in that dictionary would there be a matching entry for each pair of words, with the terms reversed (e.g. *bard* defined as 'poet' and *poet* defined as 'bard')? The obvious objection that someone might raise would be that although this dictionary provided a comprehensive list of synonym pairs for the language in question, the lexicographer had failed to explain what any of these pairs meant. But circularity in itself Johnson does not see as problematic: there is nothing wrong, he thinks, with explaining *hind* as 'the female of the stag' and *stag* as 'the male of the hind'.

Johnson makes no attempt to say how it is possible to determine whether two words are synonyms or not. As far as he is concerned, it would appear, synonymy – on the rare occasions when it occurs – is just a brute linguistic fact: the lexicographer recognizes it, and welcomes it for purposes of definition, but does not need to account for it (just as, for example, the botanist might note that sometimes two species of flower are identical in colour, but feel under no obligation to explain that similarity). There is nothing that corresponds to *justifying* the recognition of synonymy (as one might, for instance, justify the intuitive judgement that two distances were equal by taking the trouble to measure them).

2. *Paraphrase.* This alternative to finding synonyms will not work, according to Johnson, in the case of 'simple' ideas. He seems to have taken the notion that simple ideas are undefinable straight from Locke's *Essay* (Locke 1706: III.iv.7), and makes no attempt to produce any supporting argument of his own. Locke's influence on Johnson has been examined in detail (McLaverty 1986), and the number of quotations from Locke in the *Dictionary* (more than 3,000) speaks for itself. But although Johnson was fond of citing Locke, it is far from clear that Johnson always understood what Locke was arguing. In particular, he does not seem to have understood what Locke counts as simple ideas. According to Locke our idea of the colour green is a simple idea; but Johnson has no difficulty in defining the relevant sense of *green* ('having a colour formed commonly by compounding blue and yellow, of the colour of the leaves of trees or herbs'). This explanation might suggest that, for Johnson, the fact that the colour can in practice be made artificially by mixing other colours suffices to establish that we are not dealing with a simple idea (even though it is by no means apparent just from inspecting the leaves of trees or herbs). This does not apply, however, to *yellow*, which Johnson explains as 'being of a bright glowing colour, as gold'.

On similar reasoning, the idea of any substance that cannot be made by compounding others would have to count as a simple idea. But Johnson is not inhibited from giving his readers a long and detailed explanation of *diamond* ('the most valuable and hardest of all the gems, is, when pure, perfectly clear and pellucid as the purest water; and is eminently distinguished from all other substances by its vivid splendour, and the brightness of its reflexions . . .', etc.). In short, there seems to be some confusion in Johnson's mind between simple 'ideas' and simple 'things', as well as an inconsistency in practice over providing paraphrase explanations for their names.

3. *Unknown things.* Johnson sees a problem with words designating things of which the nature is unknown. This suggests he is embroiled in a confusion of which it is impossible to accuse Locke: i.e. between explaining what the thing is and explaining what the word means. A reader who had understood Locke's *Essay* could never have conflated the two. There may be endless things to which names are given, but of which the nature is not understood. The name may even be based on quite mistaken assumptions about the thing (as Locke knew and Socrates had pointed out centuries before Locke), but that lesson seems to have escaped Johnson. In some instances he provides just a long description of the thing, as if that automatically supplied the meaning of the word. Thus, for example, his entry under *crocodile* begins: 'An amphibious voracious animal, in shape resembling a lizard, and found in Egypt and the Indies.' Did Johnson suppose that a geographical location of the creature's habitat was part of the meaning of the word *crocodile*? The answer is that he evidently does not distinguish between information about the animal and information about the designation *crocodile*. In short, he falls into the ancient trap of conflating lexical definition with real definition.

It is relevant to compare this with Murray's definition, which reads:

> A large amphibious saurian reptile of the genus *Crocodilus* or other allied genera. The name belongs originally and properly to the crocodile of the Nile (*C. niloticus* or *vulgaris*); but it is extended to other species of the same or allied genera, and sometimes to the whole of the *Crocodilia*, including the Alligators of America and the Gavial or 'crocodile' of the Ganges.

The comparison is all the more interesting in that Murray makes a point of insisting on the distinction between real definition and lexical definition:

> a Dictionary of the English Language is not a Cyclopaedia: the Cyclopaedia *describes things*, the Dictionary *explains words*, and deals with the description of things only so far as is necessary in order to fix the exact signification and use of words. This involves, however, some acquaintance with the things to which words refer. The meaning of technical words, for example, or of words used in Natural History, cannot be clearly apprehended or explained by one who is wholly unacquainted with the processes, or has never seen the objects, which they describe. (Murray 1884. Italics in the original.)

But this is a baffling claim in various respects. Does the reader actually need to 'have some acquaintance with' a crocodile in the flesh (live or dead) in order to understand a dictionary definition of *crocodile*? Murray evidently thinks so; but he supplies no reasons for this odd belief. If we compare Murray's entry with the article *Crocodile* written by his contemporary the Cambridge zoologist H. F. Gadow for the eleventh edition of the *Encyclopaedia Britannica*, it become clear that Murray has certainly decided that there are many things that people do *not* need to know about crocodiles in order to grasp the meaning of the word. He does not explain what distinguishes crocodiles from alligators, or what different species of crocodile there are. (He does not mention, for instance, the 'marsh crocodile', *C. palustris.*) It is odd that in some ways Gadow's 'cyclopaedic' article supplies more linguistic information than Murray's about what these various reptiles are called. Gadow gives the Greek, Egyptian and Arabic names, and observes that 'Australians are in the habit of calling their crocodiles alligators'. (Presumably Murray did not know this, or regarded Australian English as falling outside his remit.) Murray's statement that the name 'belongs originally and properly to the crocodile of the Nile' is also curious: 'originally', doubtless because those were at one time the only crocodiles known, but why 'properly'? What did those who first used the word *crocodile* (or one of its ancestral forms) know about crocodiles? And in what respect, by calling it *crocodile,* could they have given the creature its 'proper' designation?

It will be necessary to return to Murray's doctrine of linguistic 'propriety' below, but for the moment let us simply note this: here, as in many other cases, Murray, like Johnson, seems to have no rational or non-arbitrary way of drawing the distinction between semantically relevant and semantically irrelevant information. Nor is this surprising. For no careful examination of the thing, or the word, or both together, spontaneously yields an itemization of what has to be known about the thing in order to grasp the meaning of the word.

If Murray is right about this, he has set the general lexicographer (i.e. himself) an impossible task; for there is no context-neutral solution to this problem. It may be feasible to state what needs to be known (or assumed) about the thing in order to grasp how the word in being used *in a particular instance.* But that will vary according to what *else* is assumed to be known or taken for granted in that particular episode of communication. If generalization is required – we shall argue – the lexicographer needs a quite different concept of lexical meaning from Murray's.

4. *Indefinite notions.* Johnson seems ready to entertain the possibility that even when the nature of the thing is known, the corresponding idea may still be uncertain because it is 'various in various minds'. It is not entirely clear what is worrying him here. It may be that different people have different opinions of the nature of the thing, and these differences are reflected in their differing uses of the word. But if that is the problem, this is a case which calls for the lexicographer to distinguish between different meanings. On the other hand, it may be that what Johnson finds problematic is the vagueness with which the supposed authorities apply the term. This seems to be the case with *gas.* Johnson tells us that the word is 'used by Van Helmont, and seems designed to signify, in general, a spirit not capable of being coagulated'. Then he adds: 'but he uses it loosely in many senses, and very unintelligibly and inconsistently'. It becomes difficult to distinguish cases where there appears to be uncertainty about the idea from those in which there is uncertainty about the nature of the thing. Is Van Helmont himself not sure what a gas is? Or is it Johnson who is having

trouble understanding Van Helmont's idea. We touch here on a question concerning which Johnson *qua* lexicographer is quite frank; namely, the question of the general lexicographer's personal competence with respect to matters that he knows little about. There is a famous anecdote told by Boswell of how Johnson, when asked by a lady how he came to define *pastern* as 'the knee of an horse', replied 'Ignorance, Madam, pure ignorance.' In his Preface he candidly admits that there are some words 'which I cannot explain, because I do not understand them'. That is an example of honesty which later lexicographers were slow to follow.

5. *Things too well known.* This seems at first sight to be the opposite of the complaint that often too little is known. But how could a lexicographer have *too much* information at his disposal? Here we see Johnson uneasily catching sight of the fact that not everything about the thing is necessarily relevant to explaining the meaning. And perhaps even catching sight of the fact – although this is less certain – that the same thing might have equally apposite designations with different meanings. But he has not yet got as far as Murray's distinction between Dictionary and Cyclopedia.

These five initial complaints by no means exhaust Johnson's list. He continues:

> To explain, requires the use of terms less abstruse than that which is to be explained, and such terms cannot always be found; for as nothing can be proved but by supposing something intuitively known, and evident without proof, so nothing can be defined but by the use of words too plain to admit a definition. (Johnson 1755)

This is the first time he has used the term *definition* in discussing his project, and perhaps he is using it here in the sense of 'explication of a thing by its kind and difference' – in which case this complaint is no more than a repetition of his point about paraphrase. But it may be that Johnson's 'plain' words are just words so familiar in everyday speech that the very attempt to explain what they mean takes on a certain air of absurdity. It is relevant to recall in this connection that earlier lexicographers such as Cawdray and Cockeram had seen it as one of their principal objectives to explain 'hard' words – these being obscure or learned terms with which the average general reader was not likely to be acquainted. From the perspective of this tradition, which Johnson has not entirely abandoned, it must have seemed obvious that one did not need the services of a lexicographer to explain what was already common linguistic knowledge, any more than one needed the services of a lawyer to explain that theft was a criminal act. In this respect there was still, for scholars of Johnson's generation, a considerable difference between a bilingual dictionary and a monolingual dictionary. The former assumed total lack of familiarity with the language being described, whereas the latter did not.

* * *

Three classes of word are recognized by Johnson as posing intractable problems for lexicographical 'explanation'. One class is 'expletives'. These, he says, are words 'of which the sense is too subtle and evanescent to be fixed in a paraphrase'. In dead languages, they 'are suffered to pass for empty sounds, of no other use than to fill a verse, or to modulate a period'. But in living languages they have 'power and emphasis, though it be sometimes such as no other form of expression can convey'. Another class is 'particles', which are 'among all nations applied with so great latitude, that they are not easily reducible under any regular scheme of explication'. A third class is one 'too frequent in the English language': verbs

> of which the signification is so loose and general, the use so vague and indeterminate, and the senses detorted so widely from the first idea, that it is hard to trace them through the maze of variation, to catch them on the brink of utter inanity, to circumscribe them by any limitations, or interpret them by any words of distinct and settled meaning. (Johnson 1755)

Examples of this last class that he singles out for mention in his Preface are the verbs *bear, break, come, cast, full, get, give, do, put, set, go, run, make, take, turn* and *throw.* (With some, nevertheless, he made a valiant effort: the entry for *take* lists 113 different senses, including combinations like *take up* and *take on.*) This leads him on to discuss a more general problem: that a living language is 'variable by the caprice of every one that speaks it'. The point is reminiscent of Locke. But Johnson presses it harder. It means that some words

> are hourly shifting their relations, and can no more be ascertained in a dictionary, than a grove, in the agitation of a storm, can be accurately delineated from its picture in the water. (Johnson 1755)

The comparison is an odd one, if indeed human 'caprice' is the sole cause of variation in usage. The storm simile suggests, rather, the action of powerful external forces. But in the mid-eighteenth century there was no linguistic theory available to Johnson that would have suggested what social forces might be working against semantic stability, or why some words seemed more susceptible to variation than others.

Murray is noticeably silent in public on the problem of individual 'variability', although he evidently recognized it in private. He told one correspondent:

> it is a free country, and a man may call a *vase* a *vawse,* a *vahse,* a *vaze,* or a *vase,* as he pleases. And why should he not? We do not all think alike, walk alike, dress alike, write alike or dine alike; why should we not use our liberty in speech also, so long as the purpose of speech, to be intelligible, and its grace, are not interfered with? (Murray 1977: 189)

This is in effect a reiteration of Johnson's point about 'caprice' and it presumably applies to meanings no less than to pronunciations. How could it be otherwise? It is Murray at his most Lockean, invoking that principle of 'inviolable liberty' of language that Locke insists on in his *Essay Concerning Human Understanding* (Locke 1706: III.ii.8). But if he recognized the problem, Murray did not consider how to solve it, other than by an *ex cathedra* allocation to the lexicographer of the right to ignore individual usages not deemed to be worth taking into account. He justified this by declaring that the English language had no determinable limits, and resorting to a striking analogy in the General Explanations introducing the first fascicule of his dictionary:

> That vast aggregate of words and phrases which constitutes the Vocabulary of English-speaking men presents, to the mind that endeavours to grasp it as a definite whole, the aspect of one of those nebulous masses familiar to the astronomer, in which a clear and unmistakable nucleus shades off on all sides, through zones of decreasing brightness, to a dim marginal film that seems to end nowhere, but to lose itself imperceptibly in the surrounding darkness. (Murray 1884)

Although memorable, the parallel is inexact. The reason for the astronomer's problem is the great distance of the nebula from the terrestrial point of observation: it is not the limitless character of the nebula itself.

Both Johnson and Murray seem to be groping for – but never quite grasping – a theoretical distinction that would not be readily available to linguists before Saussure formulated his celebrated dichotomy between *langue* and *parole*. Murray's successors still had not grasped it by 1933, when the complete version of the *Oxford English Dictionary* was at last published.

* * *

Johnson calls the various different meanings a word may have its 'senses'. These, he complains, it is often difficult to disentangle one from another:

> When the radical idea branches out into parallel ramifications, how can a consecutive series be formed of senses in their nature collateral? The shades of meaning sometimes pass imperceptibly into each other; so that though on one side they apparently differ, yet it is impossible to mark the point of contact. (Johnson 1755)

Here at last we come to a complaint that has nothing to do with external factors, or the limitations of the material available, but is intrinsic to the lexicographical enterprise. What Johnson is lamenting, although he does not himself see it that way, is the lack of any coherent, systematic approach to semantic analysis. He speaks of having developed a lexicographical 'method', based on 'experience and analogy': but in fact he had none.

To what extent was Murray's lexicography an improvement in this respect? Murray certainly had a different concept of lexicography, but nevertheless one in direct line of descent from Johnson's. An important difference between the two men was that, unlike Johnson, Murray was not a man of letters. He preferred to regard himself, he said, as a 'man of science' (Murray 1977: 292), although he had no scientific qualifications. He also – on the title page of the first edition of the *NED* – made a point of describing his collaborators as 'scholars and men of science'. But, as a man of science, he was sufficiently in awe of the world of letters to confine himself, like Johnson, to words that could be found in published sources. Although he was perfectly well aware that there was a living English that existed outside the covers of any book, the portion of the English language captured in his dictionary was primarily printed English. He boasts of including typical quotations 'from all the great English writers of all ages'. He was also willing to accept examples from daily newspapers (and insisted on this against the opposition of the Delegates of the University Press). But, like Johnson before him, he never seems to have been convinced that lexicography required putting the investigation of spoken usage (including that of illiterate speakers) on a par with the investigation of written usage; nor to have reflected that the development of English would have been quite different over the centuries if it had been left in the hands of the literate classes.

In Murray's view a dictionary entry was first and foremost an account of the history of the word. But his policy of giving priority to published texts in effect put the the lexicographer in basically the same position as a political historian who confines his attention exclusively to documentary sources. The lexicographer, like the historian, cannot claim to speak from personal knowledge of a past long since gone, while his account of present-day facts holds no special authority unless his access to information is in some way superior to that of his contemporaries. For a man of science, Murray adopted an approach to editing his dictionary that would hardly have passed for 'scientific' in the late nineteenth century in any other 'science' than philology: that is, collecting second-hand information from a self-selected army of volunteers.

Murray complained in a letter to Henry Sweet in 1882: 'I shall have to do the best I can at defining probably 80,000 words that I never *knew* or *used* or *saw* before' (Murray 1977: 190–1). But his routine procedure for arriving at the definition of such words was simply to write and inquire of people whom he assumed *did* know. He wrote to, among others, the Director of the Royal Botanic Gardens at Kew, to the Secretary of the Astronomical Society, to the Librarian of Cambridge University Library, and to the editor of *The Times*. He wrote to reputable authors with queries about the meaning of words they had used in their published works, but it would doubtless have struck him as preposterous to ask his own domestic servants for their views about words current in colloquial speech. In brief, his view of 'the English language' was, in practice, no less class-bound than that of Johnson a century and a half earlier.

But there was another factor at work. Murray's years as a teacher had imbued him with a didacticism that never left him. His granddaughter, in her biography, speaks of a certain 'inability to throw off the schoolmaster' (Murray 1977: 287). Thus although Murray, like Johnson before him, protested that his task was to record usage, not to pass judgement on it, both of them passed judgement on it all the time. Murray did not hesitate to indicate which usages – even if well attested – he regarded as unacceptable or suspect. He revived the practice introduced by earlier English lexicographers of marking disapproved or dubious cases by a special symbol in the dictionary (Murray chose the so-called 'blind P' or 'reversed P'), as a kind of warning sign to the reader. Thus, on his own initiative, he created a lexicographical category of 'incorrect' English, standing in opposition to the 'correct' English that the majority of his entries dealt with. This dichotomy, formally marked, immediately gave his work the prescriptive dimension that it might otherwise have lacked.

How exactly did Murray conceive this category of disapproved usage? He explained the 'blind P' as indicating 'catachrestic and erroneous uses, confusions, and the like'. The word *catachrestic* is particularly worthy of note: it was one of the 'inkhorn' terms of which Johnson was so fond. *Catachresis*, according to Murray's own entry, means 'improper use of words'. What is ironic here is that Murray himself may not have realized what catachresis 'properly' is; namely, a type of trope in Classical rhetoric. Johnson evidently did not know that, as his own entry reveals: 'It is, in rhetorick, the abuse of a trope. . . .' But it isn't. It is the form of trope in which an expression is extended to cover cases which have no customary designation of their own. Quintilian gives the following example (*Inst. Orat.* 8.2.6): in Latin there is no verb meaning 'to throw a ball', but the verb *iaculari* is used to describe such cases, even though *iaculari* strictly means 'to throw a javelin' (*iaculum*).

What probably misled Johnson (and doubtless others) was the fact that Greek *katachresis* was often translated into Latin as *abusio* (as, for instance, by Cicero in *Orator* 27.94). But this is not in the English sense of 'abuse' but (with a different meaning of the prefix *ab-*) of 'further use' or 'extension': it is an extended application of the original word. It differs from metaphor, as Quintilian explains, in that metaphor replaces another word, whereas in catachresis there is no other word to replace. Murray in turn was misled by Johnson, from whom he copied his definition of *catachresis*. So Murray's characterization of these cases of 'improper' usage in English is a lexicographical muddle from start to finish.

That such uses may not have been regarded as 'improper' by their users does not seem to have worried Murray in the least. Nor did he always accept that that distinguished authors must be right about their own usage. He complained pedantically of Browning that he 'constantly used words without regard to their proper meaning' and so had 'added greatly to the difficulties of the Dictionary' (Murray 1977: 235).

* * *

Thus between 1755 and the eventual publication of the complete *Oxford English Dictionary* in 1933, the theory of lexical definition had made little visible progress. This makes it easier in some ways to see what the unchanging assumptions about word meanings had been throughout that period. They amount to three.

1. It was believed that, in spite of innumerable variations and changes, each English word at any given period had its own proper or canonical meaning(s).
2. The meaning(s) in question must be known to at least some well-informed persons, but not necessarily known to all who used the word in question.
3. In most instances, the meaning(s) in question could be stated or described, at least approximately, by using other English words.

From this trio of assumptions the task of the lexicographer follows. The lexicographer, if ignorant of the proper meaning(s) of any word, must either find out by inquiry from some person or persons in possession of this knowledge, or else infer the meaning(s) from available evidence, and then define the meaning(s) in question by using other English words. But this apparently straightforward programme begs a series of questions.

* * *

In the first place, by what objective tests does the lexicographer judge his *own* understanding of what a word means? *Ex hypothesi*, it cannot be taken for granted that the lexicographer, even if a native speaker of the language, already knows the proper meaning(s) of a word. As Murray points out in the letter to Sweet quoted above, we are not *born* with this knowledge: 'my conceptions are alike acquired, artificial, personally-warped and garbled.' In other words, the lexicographer's own grasp of the language is as much an object for investigation and critical assessment as anyone else's.

This is an inescapable conclusion if one accepts Locke's view of meaning; and Murray's talk of his own conceptions being 'acquired', 'artificial' and 'personally-warped' seems at first to conform to that view. But there is a problem. On Locke's view, there is no such thing as the 'proper' meaning of a word in Murray's sense: Smith and Jones may ascribe conflicting meanings to the word *democracy*, but there is no question of one being the 'proper' meaning and the other not. For both Smith and Jones, according to Locke, have the inalienable liberty to associate any combination of ideas with any word they please. That is precisely why Locke advocates defining one's terms for purposes of any serious discussion: it is the only way to reduce the risk of misunderstanding. He nowhere suggests that misunderstanding can be avoided altogether if everyone keeps to the 'proper' meaning of the word.

Locke does indeed have a doctrine of 'propriety', but neither Johnson (who also speaks of 'propriety') nor Murray follows Locke in this. When Johnson accuses 'illiterate writers' of forgetting 'propriety', those he is classifying as 'illiterate' are those incapable of producing literary works worthy of serious attention, even though – he says – they may achieve a certain 'renown' as the result of 'publick infatuation'. Johnson ascribes the neglect of 'propriety' by these writers to their 'not knowing the original import of words'; in other words, to their ignorance of etymology. So it seems that to Johnson's mind the 'propriety' of a word's use depends on its etymological meaning.

This is far removed from what Locke understands by 'propriety', which applies only to the 'civil' use of words:

> By their *civil* use, I mean such a communication of thoughts and ideas by words, as may serve for the upholding common conversation and commerce, about the ordinary affairs and conveniences of civil life, in the societies of men, one amongst the other. (Locke 1706: III.ix.2)

Given this restriction, 'the rule of propriety' is, for Locke, simply 'common use'. But, as if realizing that the expression *rule of propriety* verges on the oxymoronic, Locke adds immediately that this 'rule' is 'nowhere established'. On the contrary, 'it is often matter of dispute, whether this or that way of using a word be propriety of speech or no' (Locke 1706: III.ix.8). This is patently not what either Johnson or Murray had in mind. For if, as lexicographers, they gave priority to identifying undisputed definitions of words used in 'common conversation', their constant appeal to the usage found in literary works would be an irrelevance. In any case, the records of 'common conversation' for earlier periods are scanty, to say the least.

The lexicographical notion that words have 'proper' meanings is therefore an awkward superimposition on Lockean semantics. What is its source? In Johnson's case, that source is the deep respect of a 'man of letters' for reputable English authors – those whom he refers to as 'writers of classical reputation or acknowledged authority', or sometimes as 'good writers', or 'the best writers'. Johnson's dictionary is commonly regarded as 'the only English dictionary ever compiled by a writer of the first rank' (Burchfield 1985: 87). In the concluding section of his Preface, Johnson modestly raises the question of whether 'I shall add any thing by my own writings to the reputation of English literature' and says that this 'must be left to time'. But he could hardly come closer to suggesting that one of his qualifications as a lexicographer is that he himself ranks – or will be ranked by posterity – among the writers of excellence in that tradition.

Murray's claim can hardly be that, since Murray denies that he is a man of letters, and appears to accept that even reputable English authors do not always use words in accordance with their proper meaning. The difference between Johnson and Murray on this issue is a significant one. Whereas Johnson thinks that writers of classical reputation or acknowledged authority, especially those writing before the Restoration, *establish* the proper meaning of a word, Murray sees the usage of any writer as being open to criticism according to whether or not it *conforms to* the proper meanings of the words used. So in his case the question remains of where the criteria of propriety come from.

The answer seems to be that Murray's schoolmasterly didacticism inclines him to believe that knowing how to use words 'properly' is what one learns from a 'proper' education, just as knowing how to add and subtract is what one learns from competent instruction in mathematics. He once responded to Henry

Sweet, who thought a Scotsman was at a disadvantage in dealing with English pronunciation, that, on the contrary, he had the advantage of having had 'to learn a standard pronunciation in order to teach English' (Murray 1977: 190). Evidently for Murray the proper pronunciation was the one he had been taught. The notion of proper meanings is the counterpart in semantics of proper pronunciation in phonetics. These things, for Murray, were what one had learnt if one had had a good education. But this simplistic assumption supplies only a circular answer to the wider question of correct usage: i.e. that a usage is correct because it is what is taught as correct. For Murray the schoolmaster, that is a sufficient answer. But Murray the lexicographer and 'man of science' is once again faced with a theoretical problem that he cannot resolve.

* * *

When it comes to ascertaining the meaning of a word from those deemed to know it, the problems begin to mount. If you do not know the meaning of a word yourself, how are you to judge whether someone else knows it? Murray evidently relies on the collectivity of 'scholars and men of science'. But this solution will not work if the scholars and men of science are not of one accord; for then the lexicographer will be called upon to adjudicate a dispute which is quite outside his zone of expertise. The only way forward for the lexicographer seems to be to acknowledge *both* – or, if there are more than two – *all* views. But there is something manifestly paradoxical about this compromise. If conflicting definitions of a word are accepted, albeit reluctantly, by the lexicographer, because experts disagree, that automatically undermines the notion of there being one 'proper' meaning.

With the next item on the agenda, difficulties multiply. For here the lexicographer has to make an inference on the basis of evidence – the evidence being the totality of examples under scrutiny. But if *ex hypothesi* the lexicographer does not already know the meaning of the word in question, it is hard to see how to determine whether example *A* exemplifies the same meaning as example *B*, or a different meaning. We shall examine some practical examples of this conundrum later.

Finally, having determined what the meaning is, the lexicographer has to state it in some alternative verbal formulation. That requirement seems obligatory, under pain of reducing lexicography to absurdity. No one wants a dictionary where the meaning of *elephant* is given simply as 'elephant'. But it is a requirement that poses the most acute theoretical problem of all. For it is by no means obvious that a language like English is structured in such a way as to make it always possible to provide an alternative English formulation that accurately states the meaning in question. Johnson, well in advance of Murray, realized this:

> The rigour of interpretative lexicography requires that *the explanation, and the word explained, should be always reciprocal*; this I have always endeavoured, but

could not always attain. Words are seldom exactly synonimous; a new term was not introduced, but because the former was thought inadequate: names, therefore, have often many ideas, but few ideas have many names. It was then necessary to use the proximate word, for the deficiency of single terms can very seldom be supplied by circumlocution.

(Johnson 1755. Italics in the original.)

So, by a circuitous route, one is brought back again to the thorny problem of synonymy. It was a problem that would continue to worry philosophers and semantic theorists well into the twentieth century, and we shall comment on it in more detail in the following chapter.

* * *

We now come to the most contentious part of our thesis concerning lexicography. So far, nothing has been said about the socio-political aspects of the lexicographer's task. That lacuna must now be filled. We wish to claim that the definitions offered by general lexicographers such as Johnson and Murray are stipulative definitions, in spite of their historical garb.

This is not to deny that such dictionaries may contain much historical information, and to the extent that they do they are interesting and valuable. Nevertheless, it would be naive to suppose that this is a case of history for history's sake. The information about the past has been carefully selected to support a further aim relating to the present. This aim emerges as soon as the lexicographer appeals to any doctrine of 'proper' usage. All definitions purporting to capture orthodox or 'good' linguistic practice are inherently stipulative: in effect, they instruct the reader 'This is how the word *should* be used and understood'. They are stipulative in just the same respect as the *Highway Code* is stipulative. It tells one how people *should* behave on the road, not how they actually do behave. It proposes a model to be followed, just as a dictionary does.

The dictionary as a model or lexical rule-book is a post-Renaissance phenomenon in the Western tradition. It reflects the emergence of societies in which it is of importance to be able to demonstrate familiarity with and conformity to approved modes of linguistic behaviour, usually those adopted by some privileged sector of the community, and the corresponding ability to distance oneself from linguistic practices thought to be characteristic of the lower orders. It is no coincidence that Johnson indicates the social status of many of the words he registers: 'bad', 'barbarous', 'cant', 'country', 'low', 'rustick'. His readers wanted to know what to avoid.

General dictionaries also reflect the nationalism which promoted, and was promoted by, the political formation and consolidation of the modern states of Europe. From this perspective it became important to establish the existence of a national language, with its own identity and its own forms of excellence. The foundation of the Académie Française in the early seventeenth century by order of the king of France was the first official recognition of such a need, and its dictionary eventually appeared in 1694.

It is in this context that the appeal to history becomes of such importance in lexicography. It is imperative to present contemporary approved usage as descended in direct line of continuity from the national past, or what is retrospectively declared to be such. This is manifest again in the case of Johnson, who sees a connection between propriety of usage and the 'purity' of the language: he goes so far as to equate the two in his *Plan of a Dictionary of the English Language* (Johnson 1747). He does not disguise his admiration for the English writers of the time before the Restoration, 'whose works I regard as *the wells of English undefiled*, as the pure sources of genuine diction' (Johnson 1755). Occasionally one sees Johnson's patriotic fervour bordering on xenophobia: he rails against translators for introducing foreign idioms, and complains that, unless restrained, they will 'reduce us to babble a dialect of France' (Johnson 1755).

In the case of Murray, the whole project of the *New English Dictionary* was presented from the start as a patriotic endeavour. The work was eventually approved by and dedicated to Queen Victoria herself, gaining its editor a knighthood in the process (the first but not the last lexicographical knighthood). Murray claimed that the nucleus of his dictionary consisted of words whose 'Anglicity' (i.e. Englishness) was unquestioned. Along with the *NED* came a new sociolinguistic fiction; that of so-called 'standard English'. The prescriptive implications of that term are overtly paraded in the definition given in the 1933 *Supplement*, where *standard* is said to be 'applied to the variety of the speech of a country which, by reason of its cultural status and currency, is held to represent the best form of that speech'. Murray's personal alignment with that myth is evident in his revised article for the eleventh edition of the *Encyclopaedia Britannica*, where he substitutes 'Standard English' for what, in the ninth edition, he had called English '*par excellence*' (Murray 1911).

Linguistic 'standardization' is an inherently prescriptive notion. Murray's dictionary, as he must have realized, would become not only a monument to but a powerful instrument of that ideal. He was shaping the English language of the future. His definitions would become 'standard' definitions, cited as authoritative everywhere, from the Houses of Parliament to the village school, when guidance on English usage was sought. His failure, as a 'man of science', to resolve any of the theoretical problems of lexicographical definition thus became an irrelevance. His public did not seek theoretical solutions: they simply wanted reassurance about what was 'right'. And that was what his definitions gave them.

* * *

One of Murray's Oxford successors in the late twentieth century, Robert Burchfield, a firm believer in the existence of 'standard English', is on record as declaring that there is 'no clear boundary' between prescriptive and descriptive lexicography: it is 'much more an attitude of mind' (Burchfield 1985: 91).

Our view, *pace* Burchfield, is that in general lexicography there are no descriptive definitions: there are only degrees of prescriptivism.

Burchfield's confusion on this issue is illustrated when he cites the following example:

> Thankyou everso much for the Bangles they are a very plesent contributon for my megar Collection. Christmas here was a bit of a bore (not ment to say that but its' true) We had no family or friends to enjoy it with (I'm telling you this Because it becomes very Boreing telling people what a Lovley Christmas we had when infact it was incredibly boreing) (Burchfield 1985: 91)

This is an excerpt from a letter written in 1982 by 'a well-brought-up fifteen-year old'. According to Burchfield 'the obvious inadequacies of such writing' are not dealt with 'in standard dictionaries and grammars', *whether of the prescriptive or the descriptive variety.* Moreover, they 'could hardly be, given that the patterns (if such they are) of spelling, grammar and punctuation are' – he says – 'not easily predictable'. The explanation is revealing. The notion that grammarians and lexicographers can only be expected to deal with what is 'predictable' (either predictable conformities or predictable deviations) is itself blatantly prescriptive. But the example cited is bizarre as an illustration of Burchfield's claim, since no competent schoolteacher would have the slightest hesitation in 'correcting' the 'mistakes' of English in this child's letter.

If Burchfield is right about 'attitudes of mind', then Murray's attitude of mind in any case puts him clearly in the prescriptivist camp. It was an attitude very much in line with public expectations of the general lexicographer's task in Murray's day. A so-called 'Society for Pure English' was established in 1913, whose members included Murray and two of his co-editors, Henry Bradley and W. A. Craigie. The Society obviously felt, like Johnson, that the 'purity' of English was important and needed defending. Public attitudes to 'correct' usage have not altered greatly since. When the third edition of Webster's *New International Dictionary* was published in America in 1961, reviewers immediately complained that it was too permissive and failed to offer sufficient guidance as to what was 'standard'. (The *New York Times* accused it of being likely to accelerate the 'deterioration' already apparent in the English of college students.) The lexicographers working for Oxford University Press were more conservative: when the *Supplement* to the *OED* was published in the 1970s and 1980s, Murray's successors were still using his original warning symbol to proscribe new English usages, such as the verb *refute* in the sense of 'deny, repudiate'. (Why this should be regarded as 'wrong' remained, it goes without saying, magisterially unexplained.)

This is all the more remarkable in that by 1934 even members of the Society for Pure English were beginning to have doubts about 'standard English', and their faith needed to be strengthened. This can be seen in *Tract No XXXIX* which the Society published in that year under the title *The Best English.* Its author, H. C. Wyld, then Merton Professor of English Language and Literature at

Oxford, claimed that it used to be thought (mistakenly) that standard English was a 'perfectly uniform' language 'spoken by every one who did not speak a provincial dialect' (Wyld 1934: 604). But this was 'remote from the truth'. On the contrary, 'the actual fact' was that 'thousands of persons' spoke what the author proposed to called 'Modified Standard'. This recently identified form of English was, he held, 'the result of an attempt to speak the "best" or "standard" English by those who have not had the advantage of hearing and speaking it from childhood up' (Wyld 1934: 604–5). 'Modified Standard' was thus standard 'gone wrong' (Wyld 1934: 605). In fact, it was not standard at all, because there were many different varieties of it. Nevertheless, as opposed to these different varieties, there also existed what he called a 'Received Standard'. This was 'a kind of English which is neither provincial nor vulgar, a type which most people would willingly speak if they could, and desire to speak if they do not' (Wyld 1934: 605).

Thus purists invented a new myth to replace the old myth: 'Standard English' gave way to 'Received Standard English' – a linguistic ideal to which, allegedly, all or most of the English-speaking population in the 1930s aspired. Where was this ideal English to be observed in practice? It was the English 'spoken by members of the great Public Schools, and by those classes in society which normally frequent these' (Wyld 1934: 605). Wyld's contemporaries who were concerned with the cause of 'pure English' took all this myth-making in their stride. As if to clear up any lingering doubt about the matter, Wyld went on to claim that his newly recognized Received Standard English was superior to all other kinds in existence:

> this is the best kind of English, not only because it is spoken by those often very properly called 'the best people', but because it has two great advantages that make it intrinsically superior to every other type of English speech – the extent to which it is current throughout the country, and the marked distinctiveness and clarity in its sounds. (Wyld 1934: 605)

The phrases *very properly called* and *intrinsically superior* are particularly worthy of note.

In retrospect it is clear that Murray's example paved the way not only for this unashamed linguistic snobbery but for the no less overt prescriptivism of linguistic martinets like the Fowler brothers, who also worked as lexicographers for Oxford University Press and were members of the Society for Pure English. Some grammarians, moreover, were willing to argue that distinguishing between 'good' and 'bad' English was part of the linguist's function in the modern world. Sidney Greenbaum maintained in his book *Good English and the Grammarian* that 'a descriptive grammar is incomplete if it fails to take account of prescriptions' and urged that 'grammarians have a responsibility to prescribe, because they are equipped to do so' (Greenbaum 1988: 36). What goes for grammarians presumably goes, *mutatis mutandis*, for lexicographers. So here one sees a forthright, albeit belated, defence of something very like Murray's policy.

It raises a basic question, however, about the linguists' alleged expertise: what is it that 'equips them' (in Greenbaum's words) to prescribe about questions of usage? Does that 'equipment' actually make their own prescriptions and proscriptions more impartial or valuable than anyone else's? An instructive case is Murray's refusal to accept the legitimacy of the word *absolete*. Although it is attested in 'good' seventeenth-century writers, Murray claimed it to be a confusion between *absolute* and *obsolete*. But when Shakespeare apparently perpetrates a similar confusion between *gaze* and *glare*, producing a previously unattested verb *glaze* meaning 'to stare', he escapes censure. It is not difficult to see what considerations probably weighed in the balance here: (1) reverence for Shakespeare, (2) the tenuous survival of *glaze* as a dialect word, and (3) the failure of *absolete* to survive at all. In short, the condemnation of *absolete* is based on hindsight. There is no evidence to indicate that in the seventeenth century *absolete* was regarded as any less genuine an English word than *glaze*: its relegation to the limbo of 'confusions' is a reflexion of the lexicographer's historical perspective.

A no less instructive case is the way Greenbaum himself deals with the widely criticized use of *hopefully* as a disjunct (i.e. meaning 'it is to be hoped'). He first runs through the objections to it:

> It has been condemned as a foreign importation, a loan translation from the German, although there is no evidence for this. In Britain it is suspect as doubly foreign, an American infiltration from a German source. Some have argued that it is wrong because adverbs should modify verbs and be related to the subject of the sentence. (Greenbaum 1988: 11–12)

Then he delivers his own verdict *qua* grammarian:

> But it is normal in English for adverbs to convey the speaker's comment. . . . The rage against the disjunct use of *hopefully* has therefore no grammatical justification. (Greenbaum 1988: 12)

The use of 'therefore' in this judgement is the first point to note. In other words, the grammarian's verdict is presented as a rational conclusion, based on expert knowledge of the structure of English. In fact, it is based on a *non sequitur* – a fallacy that any undergraduate could point out. The argument that Greenbaum presents goes as follows: since one can say e.g. *Happily, the war will soon be ended*, or *Fortunately, the war will soon be ended*, or *Obviously, the war will soon be ended*, there can be nothing wrong with saying *Hopefully, the war will soon be ended*. This, however, is manifestly an argument from analogy, and – as Quintilian pointed out centuries ago (*Inst. Orat.* I.vi.16) – where language is concerned, arguments from analogy are question-begging. One might as well argue that *gooder* is the correct comparative of the adjective *good*, on the ground that *shorter* is the comparative of *short* and *longer* of *long*. Languages abound in incomplete analogical patterns at all levels – phonological, morphological, syntactic and semantic. But it does not matter how well exemplified the analogy may be: there is no valid inference from 'This fits an analogy' to 'This is correct'. To suppose that what makes *shorter* the 'correct' comparative of *short* is conformity to the analogy of *longer, harder, weaker,* etc. would be just as obtuse as arguing that what makes '21' the correct answer to the question 'What is the sum of 20 plus 1?' is the analogy between '20+1=21' and '30+1=31', '40+1=41', etc.

Perhaps there are better arguments available than Greenbaum's for regarding prescription as part of the linguist's task. But if so, they must be lurking in some very obscure corners. The alleged 'expertise' that makes the linguist professionally competent to prescribe and proscribe usage turns out on inspection to be only as impressive as the logic deployed in reaching the linguist's conclusions. And that is often not very impressive.

Be that as it may, the upshot of the new perspective on general lexicography adopted by Murray and his successors is not in doubt: they introduced a new purist concept of definition as the statement of the historically *correct* meaning(s) of a word (which might or might not coincide with the meaning(s) attributed to a word by its users).

Chapter 6

Definitions and History

One of the other unfortunate consequences of the adoption of so-called 'historical principles' in nineteenth-century lexicography was to perpetuate a confusion about meaning that had been commonplace in the Western tradition ever since the linguistic speculations of the Greeks and Romans; namely, that the 'true' or 'proper' definition of a word is revealed by its etymology. Murray's insistence on tracing every word back to its supposed etymon made it virtually impossible in practice to separate questions of etymology from questions of semantics. It casts the etymologist in the role of high priest, and the lexicographer as his acolyte. This hierarchy runs counter to the commonsense assumption that it is possible to know the meaning of a word while knowing nothing at all about its etymology. (This situation, as Saussure argued, is one that obtains generally for linguistic communities.) Tracing an etymology, on the other hand, is impossible without knowing the meaning of the word in question.

Neither Johnson nor Murray seem to have realized the methodological implications of this, and the way they tackled problems of definition would in retrospect inevitably seem naive from the perspective of modern linguistics. A lexicographer lacking any grasp of the theoretical distinction between *langue* and *parole* would be bound to conflate the two. Asking 'What did *arma* mean in Classical Latin?' would be construed as asking a composite question which could be broken down into asking such questions as 'What does *arma* mean in the first line of Virgil's *Aeneid*?'. But once the distinction between *langue* and *parole* is in place, these would separated as belonging to different orders of inquiry. Virgil's use of the word in a particular text would be a question of *parole*, not a question of *langue*. As for 'Does Classical Latin *arma* mean the same as modern English *arms*?', where the units are identified at the level of *langue*, but there are two different *langues* involved, that would belong to a different order of inquiry again.

From this later linguistic perspective, the reason why the lexicographer has to be concerned with such questions is that in all three types of case the semantic relations are different. But Murray shows no signs of realizing this. He will happily give a quotation from Chaucer as illustrative 'evidence' for a meaning defined in Victorian English. What Murray does realize is that there is no possibility of constructing a dictionary of any kind unless the lexicographer can at least tell whether one expression has or has not the same meaning as another; for *every* entry demands an answer to that question. Every entry characterizes a word as either differing or not differing semantically from some other word or words within a certain linguistic domain. It does not have to be assumed that difference of form entails difference of meaning: nevertheless – and this is a quite different point – one reads a dictionary entry under the standing assumption that the word is to be understood as *differing* in meaning from any other word not explicitly mentioned. (For instance, when Johnson explains the word *bard* as meaning 'poet', the reader must assume that it somehow differs in meaning from, say, *cabbage.* For if *bard* meant 'cabbage' *as well as* 'poet', Johnson would have failed in his duty as a lexicographer by not pointing this out. But no one, for obvious reasons, expected Johnson to point out explicitly under *bard* the fact that it differs in meaning from *cabbage.*)

Questions about sameness and difference of meaning also arise when the same form occurs on different occasions of use (for instance, on different pages of the same text, or even twice in the same sentence). So identifying sameness of meaning is fundamental to the whole enterprise of lexicography. It might be thought that sameness of meaning cannot be determined until it is known independently what the meaning is of each of the items being compared. But this is not so. In practice, determining the meaning of *X* is inextricably bound up with determining whether or not it differs in meaning from *Y.* There will be cases where the lexicographer can produce plausible evidence that *X* and *Y* do *not* have the same meaning, but without being able to state exactly what either means. These cases may even be far commoner than lexicographers like to suppose.

* * *

Some modern authorities claim that cases of synonymy never occur; that there are no pairs of words that show no semantic differences at all. Thus according to Hartmann and James, 'complete' ('absolute', 'strict' or 'total') synonymy 'is impossible' (Hartmann and James 1998: 135).

This would be news to biologists, for whom 'absolute synonyms' are simply alternative names for the same species, and are common. Thus *Alogostrephus nattereri* and *Spirostreptus cultratus* are 'absolute synonyms' (Winston 1999: 135), and lists of such synonyms are frequently given in papers discussing species. Hartmann and James would presumably protest that this use of *synonym* involves a conflation of denotation with connotation. Having two or more names for the same species is no assurance that the names have the same meaning, since although the species may be identical denotatively the features alluded to in their names may well – and often do – differ. (Cf. Frege's famous example of *Evening Star* and *Morning Star.* It is not necessary to know whether these names denote the same star in order to conclude that they are not identical in meaning.)

Hartmann and James give as their reason for denying the possibility of absolute synonymy that 'no two words ever have exactly the same sense in terms of denotation, connotation, formality or currency'. But this is far from convincing. Why all four criteria have to be satisfied simultaneously they do not explain, and why frequency of occurrence should be regarded as a semantic criterion at all is a mystery.

Murray would not have accepted this curious doctrine, and nor do we. (The *NED* even draws attention to cases of synonymy and marks them with an equivalence sign (=).) Nevertheless, an adequate explication of synonymy demands certain theoretical requirements about which Murray is silent. In Murray's pre-Saussurean semantics, virtually the only theoretical tool available was the distinction between denotation and connotation, revived by Mill just before work started in earnest on the *NED*. Murray was clearly aware of Mill's distinction, as his entries for *denotation* and *connotation* show. But whether he accepted Mill's distinction is another matter. In his 'General Explanations' prefaced to the first fascicule of the dictionary, Murray mentions proper names and why they fall 'outside the province of lexicography'. He describes them as 'merely denotative', even though – he claims – proper names, and especially adjectives and verbs derived from them, 'acquire more or less of connotative value' (Murray 1884).

This is patently in conflict with Mill's doctrine of proper names, as expounded in his *System of Logic* (1st ed. 1843, 8th ed. 1884). For there Mill states categorically:

> Proper names are not connotative: they denote the individuals who are called by them; but they do not indicate or imply any attributes as belonging to those individuals. (Mill 1884: I.ii.5)

According to Mill, a connotative term is 'one which denotes a subject and implies an attribute'. Thus all 'concrete general names' are connotative.

> The word *man*, for example, denotes Peter, Jane, John, and an indefinite number of other individuals, of whom, taken as a class, it is the name. But it is applied to them, because they possess, and to signify that they possess, certain attributes. (Mill 1884: I.ii.5)

From this it follows that if the word *man* had a synonym, that word would have to denote the same indefinite number of individuals, but also connote exactly the same set of attributes. If it fulfilled the first condition but not the second, it would not be a synonym. This has obvious implications for defining both terms.

Did Murray see that? The way he treats class names is instructive. As noted in our previous discussion of his definition of *crocodile*, there are certain known attributes of this class of animals that he omits from his definition. But his decision to include some features and exclude others seems entirely arbitrary. There is no indication that he ever seriously addressed the question of how to determine the connotation of a class name, or realized that a name may have a denotation that would be agreed by everyone in the linguistic community, but connotations varying from one group of users to another. (For instance, it would be possible to define *crocodile* as 'reptile with a four-chambered heart', which would cover all and only animals denoted by that term. But it is unlikely that this would correspond to the connotation of the word for speakers other than students of zoology.)

So what does Murray's definition of *crocodile* actually capture? Manifestly, the denotation of the term as determined by biologists of Murray's own day. What is absurd about it is that Murray gives the earliest example of the use of the word in this sense as dating from the early fourteenth century, when all biological classification was pre-Linnaean and the 'genus *Crocodilus*' (the key term in Murray's *definiens*) had not yet been recognized. But this is typical of Murray's semantics. What he regularly does is formulate a definition that corresponds to nineteenth-century usage and retroject it as far back as possible into the past.

In other words, Murray's first 'historical principle' (although it is never overtly stated as such) seems to be the following: *always assume that today's meaning is the same as the original meaning, unless there is textual evidence to the contrary*. Thus, in the ideal case where no change intervenes, a word today will have exactly the same meaning or meanings that it first had on entering the language. It will neither have acquired new meanings, nor lost any. Let us call this Murray's historical principle of 'semantic inertia'. It underlies the whole treatment and classification of meanings throughout his lexicographical work. It follows from this principle that only when there is clear evidence of a past *departure* from current usage does the lexicographer have to take notice. It also follows from the same principle that the number of different meanings recognized for the surviving modern form of the word will be equivalent to the number of semantic *changes* that have occurred throughout its history (assuming that none of the meanings has become obsolete). Thus *ab initio* the recognition of semantic differences between uses of the word at any given point in time is made subservient to what has happened, or is believed to have happened, in its previous history. The sheer anachronism of this approach never seems to have struck Murray, convinced as he was that mere inspection of examples could tell the trained lexicographer whether or not a word attested in an earlier text was being used in its modern sense or not.

Something similar seems to be the assumption of the current Oxford school of lexicography. Thus we are told (Silva 2000: 78) that in the preparation of the new third edition of the *OED*, there will be a strict 'methodological separation of etymology and semantics'. Each existing entry, minus the etymology, will be scrutinized by a 'general reviser', who 'incorporates relevant new data and either confirms or emends the definitions and sense ordering'. But how the reviser is supposed to carry out this task, other than by inspecting the examples in the 'data base', is not explained. Nevertheless, when completed, the revised entry is next 'reconsidered by an etymologist'. The latter revises the etymology, 'frequently with considerable amendment', and also 'checks that there is a logical development of the senses flowing out of the new etymology', and that the 'existing sense-ordering holds'. Again, no clarification is forthcoming as to how the etymologist is to carry out the checking without reference to the semantic hypotheses already incorporated in the entry. Patently, this is only a very superficial 'separation of etymology and semantics', if it can be called 'separation' at all. It is a return to the old nineteenth-century assumption that somehow the etymology has to 'explain' the semantics, barely disguised by the appeal to a 'logical development of the senses'. What tacit logical principles are being invoked here, and where do they come from? In practice, as in Murray's case, the assumption seems to be that, when the examples are collected together and arranged in the right groups, the 'facts of usage' will somehow 'speak for themselves' and dictate the appropriate definition or definitions.

The trouble with lexicography 'on historical principles' is that it actually gets in the way of answering basic semantic questions. It is an obstacle to the study of meaning, not a contribution. Let us take a very straightforward case – straightforward, at least, in the way it would have appeared to a Victorian philologist of Murray's generation. In the fourteenth century, at a time when French was still spoken to some extent in England (as by the prioress of Chaucer's *Canterbury Tales*) the French noun *liberté* was borrowed into English as *libertee*. There was already a native English word *freodom*, and both words survive side by side to the present day (*liberty*, *freedom*). Their etymologies are quite distinct, *freedom* being of Germanic origin. But are their meanings different? Were they different in meaning in Chaucer's day? Have they developed different meanings since? These are questions to which one might expect Murray's dictionary 'on historical principles' to supply the answers.

In the case of the *NED* entries for the words *liberty* and *freedom*, the principle of semantic inertia has clearly been applied. (Both entries were drafted, as it happens, in sections of the dictionary edited by Bradley, so any discrepancies between them could hardly be attributed to different hands.) In the case of *liberty*, ten different meanings or types of usage are distinguished and numbered, some of these being subdivided. Of these ten, three are represented as having remained unchanged since the fourteenth century. In the case of *freedom*, fifteen different meanings or types of usage are distinguished and numbered, of which again some are subdivided. Four of the fifteen are represented as having remained unchanged since the fourteenth century or earlier. But in only one case is a meaning of *liberty* explicitly equated with any meaning of *freedom*. This is meaning 3b of *liberty*, where the definition is followed by the unequivocal note '= FREEDOM 5'.

The definition Bradley gives for *liberty* 3b reads: '*Philos.* The condition of being free from the control of fate or necessity'. However, the reader who looks up the definition given for *freedom* 5 finds something considerably more complex: 'The quality of being free from the control of fate or necessity: the power of self determination attributed to the will.' It is difficult to know whether or not the later entry is intended to be a correction to the earlier one. The introduction of '*Philos.*' suggests that this usage of the word *freedom* is confined to philosophical writing, and the substitution of 'condition' for 'quality' seems significant. But the most obvious difference is the omission from *liberty* 3b of 'the power of self determination attributed to the will'. The two halves of the definition previously given for *freedom* 5 never sat happily together in any case, since they seem on the face of it to present quite different meanings, rather than complementary facets of a single meaning. Bradley has also added under *liberty* 3b the following observation: 'Now chiefly in expressed antithesis to *necessity*; the phrase *liberty of the will* occurs, but *freedom* is more common in this connexion.'

It seems highly likely that Bradley has been influenced here by reading Locke on the subject (see below); but where he gets the notion that *liberty* means freedom 'from the control of fate' remains an enigma. Another puzzle about Bradley's entry for *liberty* is why any distinction of meaning at all is drawn between *liberty* 1 and *liberty* 2. The first of these is defined as: 'exemption or release from captivity, bondage or slavery'. There follow examples ranging from the *Canterbury Tales* down to *Uncle Tom's Cabin*. Then a separate group of examples, corresponding to what the *NED*'s metalinguistic terminology calls a 'subdivision of the sense', is listed under 'b': 'In religious use: Freedom from the bondage of sin, or of the law.'

This arrangement clearly invites one to see the 'religious' meaning as a metaphorical extension from the previously listed 'secular' meaning. But in fact the earliest example of the 'religious' meaning (from Wycliffe) antedates the earliest example of the 'secular' meaning. Now according to Murray's statement in the prefatory 'General Explanations', 'that sense is placed first which was actually earliest in the language', and although it may not be first attested, there is usually enough evidence 'to enable us to infer the actual order'. But it is difficult in this case to see what that evidence is, and no less difficult to see why the examples grouped under 'b' have to be regarded as representing a subsequent metaphorical extension at all. One suspects here the operation of another tacit 'historical principle', which assumes that 'concrete' meanings always come first, and subsequently 'give rise to' corresponding 'abstract' meanings. Where the concept of liberty is concerned, that would be a particularly unconvincing piece of armchair psychology; i.e. that it is physical release from some form of servitude that underlies the notion of being under no mental or moral or spiritual obligation.

This brings us to the curious term *exemption* that features so prominently in Bradley's 'secular' definition. Bradley has clearly copied it straight from Johnson, who defines the primary meaning of *freedom* as 'Liberty; exemption from servitude; independence'. But being exempt from something implies that an exception has been made: where there is no compulsion of any kind, there can be no exemption. To define *liberty* as meaning 'exemption' is to presuppose that non-liberty is the general rule.

Here problems with Bradley's entry begin to multiply. In defining the 'religious' meaning of *liberty* he uses the term *freedom* as part of the explanation. But which of the various senses of *freedom* is – or are – apposite here? Readers are left to work that out for themselves: Bradley offers no clue. Similarly, when he uses the term *liberty* in defining the listed senses of *freedom*, a parallel problem arises about the various senses of *liberty*, and likewise remains unresolved.

Turning now to Bradley's definition of *liberty* 2, one finds the term *exemption* brought into play again, this time alongside *freedom*: 'exemption or freedom from arbitrary, despotic or autocratic rule or control'. The first *or* in this definition is ambiguous. Does it imply that *exemption* and *freedom* are to be taken as synonymous here? Or are exemption and freedom distinct alternative possibilities? The answer has obvious implications for the interpretation of *exemption* in the case of *liberty* 1; but again readers are left to puzzle it out for themselves. Is there a difference between *exemption* and *freedom* here or not? If so, what is it? If not, why are both words needed for purposes of definition?

The only difference between the definitions of *liberty* 2 and the 'secular' meaning of *liberty* 1 seems to be the emphasis placed in *liberty* 2 on the 'arbitrary, despotic or autocratic' nature of the constraints from which liberty exempts or frees those subjected to them. But this is by no means apparent from the examples cited: most of the quotations given under *liberty* 2 might with equal plausibility have been grouped under the 'secular' meaning of *liberty* 1, and vice versa. In any case, what reason is there for supposing that the meaning of the word *liberty* alters according to how severe or obnoxious the constraint is? That would be like supposing that the meaning of the word *preference* alters depending on whether it is a question of preferring tea to coffee, or football to cricket, or sea travel to air travel.

Bradley's entries supply no clear answer to the question of whether *liberty* and *freedom* were ever, in any of their uses, synonymous terms or not. On the contrary, the definitions themselves repeatedly raise such questions and leave them dangling.

* * *

The general problem with interpreting linguistic material from the past is that there is no way of interrogating dead speakers or writers about their own usage. It is clear that any lexicographer operating on Murray's 'historical principles' will be driven to assume that the meaning of a word remains unchanged *unless there is evidence to the contrary*. For the majority of attested examples of a word are likely to prove uninformative, given that writers tend to assume that their readers already understand the meanings of most of the words used.

If Peter Punctilious writing in the middle of the eighteenth century (let us suppose him to have been an exact contemporary of Johnson) declares, for example, 'Liberty is indeed a noble cause', that vouchsafes *eo ipso* very little indeed about what Punctilious's readers are expected to understand by the word *liberty*. Noble causes come in endless profusion and are extremely diverse in character. All that is clear is that, according to Punctilious, liberty is one among them. But if he declares 'Liberty is indeed a noble cause and freedom is another' he at least gives his readers to understand that, as far as he is concerned, liberty and freedom are not the same thing. And *that* is information which is potentially of some use to the lexicographer attempting to construct a semantic characterization of the relationship between *liberty* and *freedom* holding at the period in question.

The unfortunate fact – unfortunate for the lexicographer – is that the mass of semantically uninformative attestations of a word will far outweigh the few informative attestations. When one looks at the illustrative quotations supplied in the *OED*, it becomes evident that the great majority of them fall into the semantically uninformative category. In many cases, they *might* have the meaning attributed to them by the editors, but there is no clear indication that they *do*. The reader has to take that on trust.

How about the semantically informative cases? These are most likely to occur in texts devoted to explicit discussion of a relevant topic or topics, where a premium is placed on careful exposition, analysis and avoidance of ambiguity. But the way the *OED* treats such cases 'historically' can actually obscure the relevance of the semantic evidence they do contain, as we shall now try to show.

Of the texts which promise a rich harvest of informative uses of the words *liberty* and *freedom*, we shall focus attention on two. The earlier of the two is the long chapter 'On Power' in Book II of Locke's *Essay Concerning Human Understanding*. The other is Mill's *On Liberty*, an essay published in 1859, which rapidly achieved the status of a classic on the subject. Both authors, in our view, write English prose with exemplary lucidity in the expository style of their respective times, and are keenly attentive to the meanings of the words they use. Locke revised 'On Power' several times in successive editions in order to deal with various criticisms. We shall examine the final version, which presumably represents the philosopher's most mature reflections on the complex issues involved. Mill in his *Autobiography* declared that every sentence in *On Liberty* had been 'gone through' several times by himself and his wife to make sure that it expressed exactly what was intended. Both these texts, in our view, give important information about the meaning of the word *liberty*, but none of this appears in the *OED*. We shall argue that in the case of Locke there is no evidence to show that the terms *liberty* and *freedom* differ in meaning, at least in this chapter, whereas in the case of Mill's essay this is far more doubtful.

1. *Locke*. Locke uses the word *liberty* 72 times in this chapter (on 27 occasions in the phrase *at liberty*) and *freedom* 22 times. He describes his own discussion as 'this inquiry into human liberty' (§73) and says that 'true notions concerning the nature and extent of liberty are of so great importance, that I hope I shall be pardoned this digression' (§74). It is not in fact a digression, since Locke needs the notion of liberty *and a specific interpretation of that notion* in order to ground his psychocentric theory of language, which is central to the whole *Essay*, and will be elaborated in Book III. (That is why the 'digression' is placed at this point.)

Locke does not assert bluntly that liberty *is* freedom, nor does he link the two expressions conjunctively (e.g. 'Liberty, or freedom, is . . . '); but he nevertheless makes exactly parallel statements using both terms. For instance: 'Liberty . . . is the power a man has to do or forbear doing any particular action according as its doing or forbearance has the actual preference in the mind' (§15) is almost immediately followed by: 'If freedom can with any propriety of speech be applied to power, it may be attributed to the power that is in a man to produce, or forbear producing, motion in parts of his body, by choice or preference' (§16). Or again: 'freedom consisting in a power of acting or not acting'

(§23) is followed in the same paragraph by: 'liberty consisting in a power to act or not to act'; and a few pages later by: 'In this, then, consists freedom, viz. in our being able to act or not to act, according as we shall choose or will' (§27).

Throughout the chapter, the use of the words *liberty* and *freedom* is linked by the use of the adjective *free* (43 examples in all) in connection with both. Particularly relevant is Locke's use of the expression *free agent* (6 examples); an *agent* being one who or that which acts, and a *free agent* being one 'at liberty' to act (or not to act). Thus, according to Locke, a tennis ball 'is not taken by any one to be a free agent' (§9). The ball has no 'preference of motion to rest, or *vice versa*; and therefore has not liberty, is not a free agent' (§9). Again, the circulation of the blood is something which a man finds 'not in his power by any thought or volition to stop; and therefore in respect of these motions, where rest depends not on his choice, nor would follow the determination of his mind, if it should prefer it, he is not a free agent' (§11).

Locke objects strenuously to the notion that the will is free, or may be considered a free agent. It is people who are free, not their wills: 'liberty, which is but a power, belongs only to agents, and cannot be an attribute or modification of the will, which is also but a power' (§14). The question of whether a man's will is free is 'unintelligible' and 'altogether improper': 'it is as insignificant to ask whether a man's will be free, as to ask whether his sleep be swift, or his virtue square' (§14). In short, it is what later philosophers would dismiss as a 'category mistake'.

Reference was made above to Locke's need for a particular interpretation of the notion of liberty, and this is the point at which to elaborate that remark. What Locke accomplishes in this chapter is something that no English philosopher had previously attempted. He presents a carefully argued case for regarding liberty as a *psychological* matter. That is the point of treating liberty as a 'power' – 'power' being for Locke one of our 'simple ideas'. The whole argument hinges on this, and would collapse if 'power' were a complex idea. Liberty, for Locke, is a mental construct. It arises internally from 'the consideration of this extent of the power of the mind over the actions of the man', and it is something that 'everyone finds in himself'. If this is right, there is no question of the primary meaning of *liberty* being derived from opposition to social constraints such as slavery. A person who had never heard of slavery would still know what liberty was, since the idea arises from the mind's reflections on its own activities.

By this strategy Locke is able to present the meaning of the word *liberty* as a single idea, standing in opposition primarily to *necessity*, and implying that the agent is a thinking creature. This is the core of Locke's psychological doctrine of liberty, and he is quite explicit about it: 'liberty cannot be where there is no thought, no volition, no will' (§8). (It is worth noting in passing that Locke disagrees absolutely with Hobbes on this point. For Hobbes, the concept of liberty 'may be applyed no less to Irrationall, and Inanimate creatures, than to Rationall' (Hobbes 1651: Ch.21). Presumably by the same token Hobbes would have no objection to speaking of the liberty of a tennis ball to follow a certain trajectory, since all Hobbes takes *liberty* to mean is the absence of 'external Impediments of motion'.)

According to Locke, the reason why a man confined in a room cannot be said to be 'at liberty' is that he cannot get out even if he wanted to. Whether he actually *does* want to is neither here nor there. 'So that liberty is not an idea belonging to volition, or preferring; but to the person having the power of doing, or forbearing to do, according as the mind shall choose or direct. Our idea of liberty reaches as far as that power, and no farther' (§10). It follows, for Locke, that the prisoner is not at liberty to stay either, even if he willingly would: he has no choice in the matter. So what he wills is beside the point.

If our interpretation of Locke's claim is right (or even plausible), it is evident that determining whether *liberty* and *freedom* are synonymous *in this chapter* is not a matter of staring at the many examples, or listing them, but of *following and analysing* Locke's discussion. Now whether the lexicographer *qua* lexicographer is qualified to do this is another question: it certainly cannot be done by casual inspection of the text. For the relevant context of these uses is not just the individual sentences in which the words happen to occur, but the whole train of argument in Locke's *Essay*. And this raises contentious issues at every turn.

The more complex these issues become for the student of philosophy, the more problems mount up for the lexicographer. For the lexicographer then has to decide whether the semantic relations that Locke assumes, for purposes of his argument, to hold between the words *liberty* and *freedom* are those which his contemporaries would likewise assume to hold. Or is Locke here engaged in what is sometimes called 'persuasive definition' (that is, trying to bolster his argument by making question-begging assumptions about the meanings of the terms in which he has chosen to present it)? We suspect the latter. But whether our suspicion is right or not does not let the lexicographer off the hook of having to go into the matter in much more detail than might seem at first sight to be required.

What we think is going on in Locke's case is roughly this. Locke is committed to a psychocentric theory of language. His basic contention (contrary to Aristotle's) is that words are not names of things but names of ideas. Ideas are private: they are not open to inspection. Ideas, for Locke, fall into two categories: simple and complex. Complex ideas are not 'given' in Nature. They are internal creations of the human mind. It is this notion of 'creating' ideas that gives Locke so much difficulty. How is it possible? In order to answer the question he has to attribute to the mind a certain capacity – which he calls *liberty* – to combine simple ideas into complex ideas. Here it is relevant to make a point about the English of Locke's day: there was – and still is, as it happens – no English adjective from *liberty* that corresponds to the noun in the way in which, in French, there is *libre* corresponding to *liberté*. So Locke 'borrows' for this purpose the adjective *free*. If he had to forgo the use of the adjective *free*, it would be well nigh impossible for him to state his case. But by constantly using *free* as the adjective corresponding to *liberty*, he is able by cumulative repetition to persuade the reader that, just as it is tautological – and so needs no argument – to assert that whoever is 'free' enjoys 'freedom', so the assertion that whoever is 'free' enjoys 'liberty' is equally tautological. By the end of the chapter these associations are so securely in place that the equivalence seems to call for no further demonstration. Whatever can be said about freedom, or by using the word *freedom*, can be said just as well about liberty, or by using the word *liberty*. In short, the synonymy of *liberty* and *freedom* is an unstated premise of Locke's argument.

Is there anything question-begging about this equivalence? The weak point hinges on the opposition to *necessity*. Locke wants to define *liberty* in terms of opposition to *necessity*. But there is ample room for various kinds of 'necessity'. The exceptionless regularity by which all physical bodies (including those of human beings) are subject to the laws of Nature seems to belong to quite a different order of 'necessity' from the way in which constraints are imposed on human beings by other human beings. Locke's critic might well argue that it is a semantic fudge to call both cases 'necessity': the first is perhaps better described as 'inevitability'. To take two of Locke's own examples, not being able to get out of a locked room has very little in common with not being able to resist the force of gravity when falling from a bridge – except that wishing it were otherwise will make no difference. But that is precisely the similarity that Locke has fastened on in order to treat both as cases of 'necessity'. Locke's case would have been stronger had he been able to point to examples where *free* is customarily used to describe actions carried out under the (hypothetical or imaginary) suspension of natural laws; but he cites no such cases. And even if, *per impossibile*, the physical laws determining that the falling man will inevitably end up in the water were temporarily suspended, there is no good reason for supposing that he could decide to reverse his fall in mid-air without further ado, any more than from the removal of all physical impediments to swimming there follows automatically the ability to swim.

In short, the case against Locke's semantics would be that where natural laws operate, it is not that freedom to do otherwise is somehow *prevented*, but that the question of freedom or non-freedom simply *does not arise*. So when, for instance, Locke describes the man falling into the water as 'not a free agent' (§9), he is already misdescribing the situation in a way that suits his own conclusions. The man falling into the water is neither free nor unfree but in no position to exercise a 'power' of any kind. To say that he is not free to stop falling is just as absurd as to describe a dead man as not being hungry. But that is precisely how Locke wants to define *free agent*, because that is what his argument requires.

The formidable problem for the lexicographer is how to capture all this semantically pertinent information within the confines of one lexical entry. Whatever the answer, it cannot be done by listing, as the *OED* does, a truncated quotation from 'On Power' under *liberty* 3, with a definition that is in part copied from that same quotation, but minus all the important qualifications that Locke adds. That is completely misleading.

2. *Mill*. Does Mill treat *liberty* as having the same meaning as Locke? Mill's discussion takes off from quite a different starting point and follows quite a different direction. Mill moves the whole discussion of the subject into the moral sphere. It is not just a question of whether you *can* do what you want but whether

it would be desirable or right to do it. Unlike Locke, Mill is not at all interested in what he dismisses in his opening sentence as 'the misnamed doctrine of philosophical necessity', but in the relations between the individual and society. We think there is a reason why Mill chose to entitle his essay *On Liberty*, rather than *On Freedom*. Liberty, for Mill, is a matter of rights and responsibilities. It is only indirectly connected with the mind's recognition of its own powers, or the adventitious absence of external constraints.

A comparison between Mill's use of the terms *liberty* and *freedom* is interesting. Of the noun *liberty* there are 90 examples in the essay, including five in the plural. The noun *freedom* occurs 49 times, but never in the plural. So Mill speaks of *liberties*, but never of *freedoms*. The adjective *free* occurs 41 times and the adverb *freely* five times. Unlike Locke, Mill never uses the expression *free agent*, or the phrase *at liberty*. This latter feature could be a question of idiosyncratic stylistic preference, but we think there is more to it than that.

The first important difference from Locke is that, for Mill, the word *liberty* designates not just a power or capacity, but the successful *execution* of a desired course of action (or non-action). Thus he goes much further than Locke when he writes: 'liberty consists in doing what one desires' (Mill 1859: Ch.5). This is not just a matter of being *able* to do something, but of actually *doing* it. He never says that freedom consists in doing what one desires. That suggests that Mill recognizes an important semantic difference between the words *liberty* and *freedom*: namely *freedom* means only 'absence of impediments or constraints', as opposed to the practical implementation of one's wishes. That would be perfectly consistent with Mill's argument throughout the essay. He does not like talking about people being 'at liberty' because that suggests that liberty is a state of affairs, not an action (cf. *at rest, at peace, at war*).

However, like Locke, Mill is working within the resources of an English which offers him only *free* as the adjective corresponding to *liberty*. That makes it difficult to maintain a consistent and perspicuous differentiation. There is a great deal of collocational overlap. In the essay, we have one example of *religious liberty* (p.66), and one of *religious freedom* (p.67); two of the phrase *principle of liberty* (pp.175, 180), and one of *principle of freedom* (p.173); four of *liberty of the individual* (pp.113, 119, 152, 172), one of *freedom of the individual* (p.179); one of *liberty of the press* (p.75), one of *freedom of the press* (p.182); three of *human liberty* (pp.71, 134, 160), one of *human freedom* (p.185); one of *political liberties* (p.60), one of *political freedom* (p.181); one of *liberty of action* (p.68), two of *freedom of action* (pp.165, 175); three of *freedom of opinion* (pp.71, 115, 116), but none of *liberty of opinion*. This amount of collocational overlap might seem to indicate that the words *liberty* and *freedom* are interchangeable, but it is difficult to rule out the possibility that for every liberty Mill envisages a corresponding freedom, liberty always involving action (or inaction) as desired, as against mere lack of hindrance or opposition. (Thus, for instance, *freedom of the press* would be apposite in describing a state of affairs in which there was no censorship or official control of publications, regardless of whether editors took advantage of this to publish controversial material. But only if they did take such action would they be demonstrating the *liberty of the press.*) Under this conceptual schema, it would be possible to have freedom without progressing to liberty.

The next important difference between Mill and Locke concerns Locke's contention that doing what you want to do does not *eo ipso* constitute liberty. It follows from this that, in theory, an individual might go through life without ever being forced to do anything contrary to his own wishes, *but never be at liberty.* We might call this 'Locke's paradox'. For Mill, this paradox would be a self-contradiction, because liberty just *is* doing what one desires.

A third difference relates to the will and hence to the notion of choice. Locke sees no problem here: as far as he is concerned, an act of will determines what you want to do and the only question then is whether you have the power to do it. Not so for Mill. The will is not the supreme arbiter. What is desirable, according to Mill, is not a matter of what you think you would like to do, but of what actually is, objectively, in your best interests, as you would see if you were in full possession of the facts. Thus he argues there would be no 'real infringement' of liberty if a person were stopped from crossing a bridge by someone who knew that the bridge was unsafe. Why is there no infringement of liberty here? Because no one in their right mind desires to fall off the bridge into the river. In other words, it is possible, on Mill's view, that you do not always know what you desire, and someone else may have a better appreciation of your true interests than you do yourself. This feature of Mill's doctrine, as critics have pointed out, seems to leave the theoretical door open for all kinds of interventions by a nanny state, compelling citizens to do what the state judges to be good for them.

So, again, what a writer means by the word *liberty* turns out to be much more complicated than one might at first sight expect. We have chosen to focus on these examples because we think that the two texts examined here represent important moments in what the *NED* definitions claim to be recording; namely, the semantic history of the word *liberty* in English. It is clear, it seems to us, that there are major differences between Locke's definition of *liberty* and Mill's. Locke's chapter and Mill's essay are both, in effect, elaborate stipulative redefinitions of the term. But this is not reflected in the *NED* entries. Either Bradley did not spot the differences, or else he found it impossible to articulate them within the semantic confines imposed upon him by the 'historical principle' of semantic inertia, which required him to recognize as few changes of meaning as possible. Lack of observation, or misguided methodology? Probably both. Thus he ends up listing Locke's definition of *liberty* under exactly the same meaning as he gives for Chaucer's use of the word: and that, whatever else it may be, is to perpetrate a piece of historical nonsense and an injustice to great English philosopher into the bargain. As for Mill, no quotation from *On Liberty* appears under any of Bradley's meanings for the word: and that simply defies comment.

* * *

What conclusions do we draw from all this? It is not just that Bradley made a poor fist of defining the word *liberty* through failure to examine the available evidence with sufficient care. Nor is it just that Bradley is trapped in a lexicographical method that makes it extremely difficult to recognize semantic distinctions when they manifest any degree of complexity. Both these criticisms are valid. But what we also hope to have shown is that the basic enterprise of constructing a comprehensive 'historical' definition – one which supposedly embraces diachronically the work of different writers working at different periods under different assumptions – is theoretically incoherent. It sets up a metalinguistic unit (a 'meaning' of *X* in 'English' over some vaguely identified time-span) which answers to no demonstrable set of first-order linguistic facts at all. In short, it is a reification derived from the very parameters that the lexicographer has chosen to adopt for the purpose of compiling a dictionary.

Chapter 7

Types and Problems of Definition

It is commonplace in the discussion of dictionaries to distinguish between various types of definition. Here, for purposes of exposition, we shall follow the typology suggested in Robinson 1954, although – as will become apparent below – we have serious reservations about its theoretical basis.

1. *Synonymous definition.* This has already been encountered in discussing the lexicographical work of Johnson and Murray, neither of whom explains in any lucid way the rationale tacitly underlying synonymous definition. Robinson probes the question further. He sees the 'synonymous method of word-thing definition' as one which 'consists in giving the learner a synonym with which he is already familiar'. By this means, the learner is informed 'that the word being defined means the same as some other word whose meaning he already knows' (Robinson 1954: 94–5). This is a risky method, because it assumes that what the learner takes the 'familiar' word to mean is what the lexicographer hopes the learner will take it to mean. Depending on whether this expectation is fulfilled, the synonymous method is as likely to misinform dictionary-users as to enlighten them. The 'explanation' of meaning consists in no more than reporting or asserting a word-to-word synonymic equivalence.

Robinson notes that dictionaries often seek to remedy the 'defectiveness' of the synonymous method by giving more than one partial synonym 'in the hope that the false in each will be cancelled by the others' (Robinson 1954: 95). This, Robinson points out, 'demands much more previous knowledge of language from the learner than does the pure method of synonyms'. Furthermore, if the word to be defined has any 'pecularity' of meaning, one cannot 'give this peculiarity to the learner merely by removing all wrong suggestions' (Robinson 1954: 95).

It seems to us, however, that there is a more fundamental problem with the accumulation of 'partial synonyms'. It is often far from clear how the total is to be interpreted. The potential ambiguities are obvious. Thus, to take Robinson's example, one may find *catalogue* defined in a dictionary as 'list, register, or complete enumeration'. But does this mean that lists, registers and complete enumerations are typical *examples* of catalogues? In other words, is *catalogue* a class name for a class which includes lists, registers and complete enumerations? Or does it mean that *catalogue* is a term meaning whatever it is that lists, registers and complete enumerations *have in common*? These would be two very different definitions of the word *catalogue.*

Robinson includes the synonymous method under his more general category of 'word-thing' definitions, but pauses to consider the objection that it is actually a 'word-word' method. He concedes that supplying a synonym by way of definition 'at the least implies a word-word definition or suggests how one might be formed'. But this – in our view – misses the point: the objection is that synonymous definition does not *imply* any 'word-word' definition but actually *is* 'word-word' definition and nothing else. *It defines one word by reference to another* (as distinct from drawing a diagram, or pointing to an object, or engaging in any other form of non-verbal activity). Robinson pleads that

> sometimes when a man says that 'valour' means courage his purpose is, not to state the word-word fact that the word 'valour' is equivalent to the word 'courage', but to state the word-thing fact that the word 'valour' means the thing courage. (Robinson 1954: 96)

Doubtless sometimes 'a man' does act in the way Robinson describes, and with the purpose that Robinson attributes to him. But that does not in any way alter the fact that in uttering or writing the word *courage* to explain the word *valour* he uses one word in order to explain another.

2. *Analytic definition.* Robinson distinguishes synonymous definition from 'the method of analysis' (Robinson 1954: 96–8). This requires the employment of 'a phrase that gives the analysis of the thing' (i.e. of the thing designated by the word to be defined). Thus *octagon* may be defined as 'polygon having eight sides'.

Robinson regards this as another example of 'word-thing' definition; but since it would be tedious to keep reiterating our objections to this view, we here give notice that, for reasons indicated above, we regard Robinson's whole classification of 'word-thing' definitions as misguided. To produce the words 'polygon having eight sides' as a definition of *octagon* is, we maintain, another example of 'word-word' definition. Where it differs from so-called synonymous definition is in deploying a phrase rather than a single word as the *definiens* expression.

It also differs consequentially in other ways. The use of a phrase to define a single word allows the lexicographer to give what Robinson construes as 'an analysis of the thing'. But whether it has to be construed in this way is an open question. Aristotle's method of definition by genus and differentia is, for Robinson, a classic example of analytic definition when applied to the definition of words. We do not rush to endorse this example, because it seems to us to beg some important questions, for reasons that we shall now try to elucidate.

According to Robinson, the theory underlying Aristotelian analytic definition can be put very simply like this:

> To indicate what specific object a word means, name a bigger class within which that object falls, and then name something that distinguishes it from the rest of that class. (Robinson 1954: 96)

If this is right, it requires a theory of names to be already in place, in order to supply a rationale for the procedure of analytic definition. We think this puts the cart before the horse. To construct a viable theory of names and naming, one first needs to be able to make sense of the kind of predication involved in analytic definitions. Robinson's account starts in the wrong place: what it says is that the *name* of the 'bigger class' (e.g. *animal*), together with the *name* of the distinguishing feature (e.g. *rational*), conjointly identify a smaller class, of which the name is *man*. But how would anyone recognize – or question, or verify – the viability of this kind of generalization unless they already grasped what it means to say of any particular man that he is a rational animal (or – before that – a loving husband, a good father, or an egregious rogue)? And does one have to be sure that *no* other animals are rational before defining *man* in this way? Could Aristotle have been sure that there were no rational apes living somewhere in the forests of Africa?

In the second place, we think that Robinson himself is guilty here of confusing lexical definition with real definition. Aristotle's method was originally applied to real definition: to suppose that it can be applied *mutatis mutandis* to the definition of words immediately invites the conflation of denotation with connotation. Let us suppose, for the sake of argument, that it is true that all and only those creatures designated by the term *man* are both animals and rational. Then what has been achieved by a definition of *man* as 'rational animal' is, certainly, the identification of a certain class of creatures. But this takes us no further than the denotation of the term (i.e. the class comprising what Mill calls 'Peter, Jane, John and an indefinite number of other individuals').

Connotation, for Mill, is a matter of 'implying attributes'. 'A connotative term is one which denotes a subject, and implies an attribute' (Mill 1884: I.ii.5). The term *man* denotes all the individuals in the class thus named, but it is applied to them 'because they possess, and to signify that they possess, certain attributes'. This raises the whole question of how to determine which attributes are implied. Mill proposes, in the case of *man*, that these 'seem to be corporeity, animal life, rationality, and a certain external form, which for distinction we call the human.'

> Every existing thing, which possessed all these attributes, would be called a man; and anything which possessed none of them, or only one, or two, or even three of them without the fourth, would not be so called. (Mill 1884: I.ii.5)

If this is so, the definition of *man* as 'rational animal' cannot be right, because that would allow, say, the possibility of men who had the bodies of horses. Why Mill thinks that such a possibility has to be ruled out he does not say. He does not actually claim that his four attributes are the only attributes contributing to the connotation of *man*. But nor does he explain how one would set about determining the definitive set of such attributes.

This seems to leave the lexicographer in a connotational quagmire. For it is perfectly possible – and commonly the case in everyday communication – that by applying the term *man* either to an individual or to a class of creatures one is taken to be implying attributes other than just the four Mill mentions. Indeed, the attributes Mill identifies may often be of relatively little importance in the communicational context in which the word is used. To say 'John is a man' may be taken to imply not just that John, like everyone else, has corporeity, animal life, rationality and a human form but, for instance, that he is no longer a boy, that he is adult, physically mature, or even that he is no weakling, will stand up for what he thinks are his rights, and so on.

All this leaves it very uncertain what counts as an analytic definition. Some lexicographers, as Robinson notes, rest content with naming the 'bigger class', and do not always identify the relevant differentia(e). Thus the *OED* defines *golland* as 'a name given to various species of *Ranunculus*, *Caltha*, and *Trollius*', making no attempt to say *which* species are so called. 'This is very common,' says Robinson tolerantly, 'because many words are such that we require much space and labour to give and receive a specific account of their meaning, while a merely general account satisfies most of our needs.' That may be so, but it seems somewhat arbitrary to suppose that 'most of our needs' do not include knowing anything as obscure as which species are called *golland*. A more serious problem is that it seems questionable whether merely naming 'the bigger class' deserves to be called a definition at all. Otherwise the door would be open to analytic definitions such as '*lion*: animal of some kind'. It could be argued that even this tells the ignorant inquirer *something* about the meaning of *lion*. But whether it tells anyone enough to be of any value is obviously doubtful, since exactly the same definition would be applicable to *elephant*, *kangaroo*, *squirrel*, and thousands of other English words. There must presumably come a point at which the lexicographer realizes that failing to distinguish between words manifestly differing in meaning must bring lexicography into disrepute.

It is interesting that Murray was always complaining that his collaborators were making *too many* semantic distinctions. (This was because he was under pressure to reduce the number of column inches per entry.) We should like to propose a lexicographical rule of thumb about semantic differentiation. It requires that the definitions given must at least make it possible to distinguish between any two words in the dictionary that *differ* in meaning. This automatically rules out vague or loose definitions of the type '*lion*: animal of some kind' (assuming that the dictionary includes names of other animals). Whether this criterion disqualifies the *OED* definition of *golland* will then depend on whether there exist different English names for other species of Ranunculus, Caltha and Trollius. We do not know whether this is the case; but for our present purposes it suffices to point out that, whether there are or not, this criterion at least has the merit of providing a principled linguistic justification for the *omission* of differentiae: which is quite a different matter from offering feeble excuses about lack of space and the amount of lexicographical labour required. (Murray did not even get this far in elaborating a consistent lexicographical methodology.)

The notion of analytic definition lies at the centre of a problem known to philosophers as the 'paradox of analysis' (Langford 1952; Moore 1952). The problem may be stated in its simplest form as follows. If it is correct to give, say, 'male sibling' as the analysis of the concept 'brother', and correct to state the analysis in that form, it seems necessary that the expression *male sibling* should have the same meaning as the word *brother*. For if it did not, the analysis as stated would be incorrect, or at least incomplete. But if *male sibling* and *brother* do have the same meaning, either may be substituted for the other without altering what is being asserted; and the analysis given then appears to be just as uninformative as saying that *brother* means 'brother'. The argument carries over to any analysis of a form in which *bc* is proposed as the explication of *a*. This reduction to triviality seems to strike at the heart of the philosophical programme of conceptual elucidation that was proposed in so-called 'analytic' philosophy of the twentieth century, of which Moore and Russell at Cambridge were leading exponents.

Although some insisted that philosophical analysis was concerned with concepts, not with words, that hardly dealt with the problem, since presumably the results of conceptual analysis needed to be stated verbally at some point; and at that point the paradox would re-emerge. That is to say, the philosopher would need to show that the chosen way of stating the analysis was both correct and non-trivial. (The alternative would have been for analytic philosophers to resign themselves to producing analyses that could never be expressed verbally at all, and that, even if a safe option, was not an especially attractive one.)

It has also been claimed that analyses of the type which equates *a* with *bc* are informative, even for those who already know what *a* means and what *bc* means, insofar as the analysis may make *explicit* what was previously no more than *tacit* knowledge. That is, the analysis may draw attention to what may not have been consciously realized before. Thus according to Stebbing, it may 'enable us to see what it was we were *meaning* when we used the expression that is now defined' (Stebbing 1930: 441). This explanation verges on self-contradiction: for if *bc* somehow reveals to the user for the first time what was previously meant by *a*, then *a* must originally have been used in ignorance or confusion, in which case *bc* was *not* what the user meant. (It would be like supposing that only when Mrs Jones belatedly realizes that a hundred pence make one pound does she at last understand what she has been paying the greengrocer for a pound's worth of potatoes.) Furthermore this curious retrospective justification of the semantic equation between *a* and *bc* still does not seem to dispose of the original objection, for it is tantamount to conceding that the analysis in the form proposed reveals no new information (although anyone who had never taken the trouble to think about what *brother* meant might regard it as revealing to be told that it meant 'male sibling', just as anyone who had never taken the trouble to work out the square root of 49 might be surprised to learn that it was 7). In these cases, being 'informative' is a matter of the psychology of the individual, not a property of the analysis or its formulation.

Analytic definitions, according to Hempel, are what dictionaries attempt to provide. An analytic definition is 'true or false according as its analysans is, or is not, synonymous with its analysandum'. The problem, in Hempel's view, is that this 'presupposes a language whose expressions have precisely determined meanings', and this condition 'is not generally satisfied by natural languages' (Hempel 1952: 9). It is impossible, according to Hempel, to specify a precise meaning for a word such as *hat*, because it lacks both determinacy of usage and uniformity of usage. It lacks determinacy of usage because 'various kinds of objects can be described or actually produced in regard to which one would be undecided whether to apply the term or not' (Hempel 1952: 10). *Hat* lacks uniformity of usage because different users will differ in judging whether certain objects are 'hats', and 'even the same user at different times will pass different judgments' (Hempel 1952: 10). Hempel concludes that the notion of a true analytic definition 'rests on an untenable assumption'.

We shall have more to say about the problem of semantic indeterminacy later (Chapter 10). Here it suffices to point out that Hempel's sceptical argument is weak. He offers no reason for supposing that it would be impossible to find *some* hats that all members of a linguistic community could agree 'were hats'. Indeed, if no such agreement were possible, it is hard to see how the community could have institutionalized such a word as *hat* in the first place. So what remains obscure is not the meaning of the word *hat*, but why Hempel should suppose that the existence of problem cases makes it impossible to produce an analytic definition at all. (This is rather like supposing that the fact that some ships sink renders travel by sea out of the question.) Furthermore, it never becomes clear what Hempel takes the requirement of synonymy to entail. In his exposition of analyticity, the notions of truth and semantic equivalence chase each other round in a never-ending dance.

In considering the paradox of analysis, G. E. Moore was eventually driven to conclude, with remarkable candour, that he now realized he did not know 'at all clearly' what he meant by saying that '*x* is a brother' is identical with '*x* is a male sibling', while denying that '*x* is a cube' is identical with '*x* is a cube with twelve edges' (Moore 1952: 667). We suspect that many lexicographers, if similarly honest, would have to admit that they do not know 'at all clearly' what they mean by the analytic definitions they put in their dictionaries. And many philosophers would have to admit that they do not know 'at all clearly' what they mean by declaring such definitions untenable.

Does it matter? It depends on the use to which the definition is put. It may not matter a great deal to the average dictionary-user. But it may matter much more if, say, the interpretation of a contract or the settlement of a legal dispute depends upon it. In any case, it matters to anyone who is trying to construct a general theory of definition.

3. *Synthetic definition.* Robinson distinguishes between analytic definition and what he terms, not altogether felicitously, the 'synthetic' method (Robinson 1954: 98–106). His justification for this terminology is that 'whereas the analytic method indicates the thing meant by showing it as a whole of parts, the synthetic does so by showing it as part of a whole.' He also suggests two alternative terms; *relational* and *locant.* The latter is borrowed from Ogden and Richards (*The Meaning of Meaning*, 1923), while the former reflects the idea that this method

'indicates the thing meant by mentioning its relation to some other known things'.

We doubt whether this is a viable or a useful distinction. For analytic definitions too are definitions which relate their *definienda* to 'other known things'; for instance, defining *man* as 'rational animal' relates the class of men to the class of animals, and thereby shows it also to be 'part of a whole'. Robinson himself concedes that in some cases it may not be clear whether a definition is analytic or synthetic, and this is certainly true of his own definition of *synthetic.*

What seems to lie behind Robinson's category of synthetic definition, to judge by his own examples, is the conviction that there are some things (NB *things*, i.e. *realia*, not words) that cannot be, or have not so far been, analysed. This sounds like a repeat of Johnson's mistake on the same subject (see Chapter 5). Robinson claims that it was impossible to give an analytic definition of the word *water* before the analysis of water (the liquid) was known. (By the analysis of water he seems to mean its chemical composition.) But this is quite unconvincing. It would have been possible to give an analytic definition of *water* long before the results of chemical research were known, or even before research was begun: e.g. 'liquid which, in its pure state, is colourless, odourless, transparent and potable'. This might not be a very good definition, but it is just as analytic as '*man*: rational animal'.

Robinson says that there is no possibility of giving an analytic definition of *blue*, because 'the tint itself' has not been analysed and 'does not look like being so'. So he does not count an 'analysis' of colour as consisting in correlation with light of a known wavelength, and presumably would deny that any 'optical analysis' of light is rightly so called. Colour, we think, is an interesting example where taking a prior philosophical or scientific position on the question of what colour 'really is' influences what will count as defining the meaning of colour terms. Basicially, there are only two positions available. One is that colours are in the eye of the beholder. The other is that colours are properties of material objects. Both views were acknowledged by Thomas Reid in the eighteenth century: 'Philosophers affirm that colour is not in bodies but in the mind; and the vulgar affirm that colour is not in the mind, but a quality of bodies' (Reid 1764: VI.v.179).

Murray's *NED* entry made a valiant attempt to compromise, by defining *colour* as 'the quality or attribute in virtue of which objects present different appearances to the eye when considered with regard only to the kind of light reflected from their surfaces'. Whether this definition makes sense at all is a moot point that we shall not pursue here; but in any case it manifestly fails to represent what *colour* means or has meant for most lay English speakers. No one seriously thinks that the Union Flag is red, white and blue only in the daytime, but changes its colour when the sun goes down.

Another odd feature of Robinson's position on analytic definition is that the definition of *21* as 'successor of 20' turns out to be analytic, even though it manifestly relates that numeral to its position in a series of other numerals. One wonders what kind of analysis has been carried out on the 'thing' to justify treating 'successor of 20' as analytic. A couple of pages later, however, he cites, apparently with approval, Russell's contention that all mathematical definitions are synthetic, consisting in 'pointing out a fixed relation to a fixed term'. It seems that by this stage Robinson has become bemused by his own distinction and is unsure how to apply it.

4. *Descriptive definition.* Robinson treats this as being in part a subcategory of synthetic definition (Robinson 1954: 104–5). The term 'definition by description' is proposed by C. I. Lewis. According to Robinson, descriptive definition 'proceeds by referring to some character of the thing that is non-essential but uniformly present in all known cases of it and absent in all other known cases.' (Does the term *non-essential* unwittingly betray Robinson's residual belief in 'real essences'?) An obvious example would be defining *man* as 'animal that laughs'. According to Lewis, descriptive definition is restricted to cases where the features picked out by the definition are ascertained inductively, not deductively.

5. *Implicative definition.* It is so called, according to Robinson, because it 'provides a sentence which implies that the word means so and so' (Robinson 1954: 106–8); but it might also be termed 'contextual' definition, because 'it puts the word in a context which determines its sense'. An example is: 'A square has two diagonals, and each of them divides the square into two rightangled isosceles triangles.'

This corresponds in certain respects, although not exactly, to what Mautner also calls 'contextual' definition, where 'the expression to be defined is mentioned not in isolation but in its characteristic context' (Mautner 1997: 111). Thus to define *divided by*, one might explain 'a divided by b' as 'the number x such that $bx=a$'.

According to Robinson, the main distinctive characteristic of implicative definition is that it 'uses' the word being defined, but does not 'mention' it. Robinson here accepts the usual philosophical doctrine of use-and-mention (according to which saying '*Life* is a short word' is a case of mentioning the word, whereas saying 'Life is short' is a case of using it). This is central to Carnap's notion of translating between the 'material' and the 'formal' modes of expression, which he held to be the key to solving many philosophical puzzles (Carnap 1937), and likewise to Quine's concept of 'semantic ascent' (e.g. shifting from talk about whether miles exist to talk about the word *mile* and how it is used: Quine 1960: 272).

Since we do not accept the doctrine of use-and-mention (for reasons set out in detail in Harris 1996), we are inclined to think that recognizing implicative definition as a distinct type of definition is likely to introduce more perplexity than enlightenment. In our view, there are indefinitely many instances in which words might be considered to be both 'used' and 'mentioned' at the same time, and Robinson's 'A square has two diagonals . . .' could be one. (That would depend on the communicational context. The question cannot be answered by looking at the grammar of the sentence or whether the word is placed in inverted commas.) Perhaps a clearer example would be Bentham's definition of *duty*:

> That is my *duty* to do, which I am liable to be *punished*, according to law, if I do not do: this is the original, ordinary, and proper sense of the word *duty*.
> (Bentham 1776: V. 7)

– which is presented both as a statement of what one's duty actually is and as an exposition of what the word *duty* means.

According to the standard philosophical doctrine, when a lexicographer gives a definition such as '*man*: rational animal', this is a paradigm case of 'mentioning' the word *man*. But that, we would say, is already imposing a philosophical interpretation on the dictionary, and one which has little in the way of common sense to recommend it. What the lexicographer is doing, in our view, is using the orthographic form *man* to identify (refer to) the lexical item which is the subject of the entry. Counting that as a 'mention' of anything is a metalinguistic red herring. It does not belong to a different order of use from listing the orthographic form *Smith* in a telephone directory. (It would court absurdity to claim that in a telephone directory Smith's name is not used. Patently, the name is used to identify the subscriber.)

Furthermore, we do not agree that the sentence Robinson cites as an example of the implicative definition of the word *square*, can be regarded as one which, in isolation, 'puts the word [i.e. *square*] in a context which determines its sense'. If it is so regarded, then again we have a case of simultaneous use and mention. Consider the following expanded version: 'A square, in the geometrical sense of the term, has two diagonals . . .'.

In any case, the meaning of the word is no more *determined* by the rest of the sentence than that of any other word in the sentence. Robinson is here confusing the meaning of the word *square* with what might be inferred about squares if it were assumed *that this expresses a true statement*. But looking hard at the rest of the sentence does not tell anyone whether it is true or not. That would in any case depend on how, for instance, one interpreted the word *diagonal*.

6. *Denotative definition*. This 'consists in mentioning examples of what the word applies to' (Robinson 1954: 108). Here we find Robinson explicitly invoking 'the well known doctrine of denotation and connotation' (presumably Mill's), but nevertheless declining 'to define how I am going to use the words 'connotation' and 'denotation', or to confine myself to a single rigid usage'. It is difficult to know what to make of this: what at first appeared to be on offer is so speedily withdrawn again.

According to Robinson 'it is usually impossible to recite the whole of the denotation' in a definition. 'We do not have names for all birds or for all sorts of birds.' This is true; but no one ever supposed that defining *bird* involved naming every bird in existence, or every species of bird. What Robinson seems to think *is* possible is 'mentioning some part of the denotation', and that this itself constitutes an independent method of definition.

But does it? One reason for doubt is that even if, *per impossibile*, names for every existing bird were available, just memorizing the list of names does not get anyone very far in understanding what *bird* means. For it would still be possible for someone who had a faultless grasp of the denotation of that term, someone who could recognize and call every bird by its name, not to know what *bird* meant (other than 'creature with its name on this list'.) Mill realized this, and that is why he added to his account of connotative names the proviso that one must understand *why* the name was applied to the individuals or classes thereby denoted.

This is where we disagree with Mill. That is: we think it is question-begging to say that the word *man* is applied to certain creatures 'because they possess, *and to signify that they possess*, certain attributes' (our italics). The purpose for which a word exists is not something permanently attached to it, or any inherent feature that can be discerned by scrutiny of a sufficient number of uses. The boot is on the other foot. Given the denotation of the word *man*, different users will use it to 'signify . . . certain attributes' that may vary according to the context, and depend on implicit or explicit contrasts with other words or even non-verbal signs that might be relevant in that context. In short, Mill made the error of supposing that denotation and connotation were in some way intrinsically connected at a context-neutral level (i.e. at what Saussure would have called the level of *langue*). But he never produced any explicit arguments for that connection. Why he made the assumption is nevertheless clear enough: his doctrine of denotation and connotation is introduced as one of the foundations for his general account of logic. Traditional Western logic cannot afford the luxury of a semantics in which connotation is allowed to float free of denotation. That would immediately call into question the validity of the Aristotelian syllogism and the whole subsequent development of the discipline of logic based upon it.

We see no reason why the lexicographer (as distinct from the logician or the philosopher) has to respect Mill's doctrine, much less frame definitions in accordance with it.

7. *Ostensive definition.* We have already discussed this in some detail in Chapter 4. Robinson produces the usual argument designed to show that there must be *some* non-verbal method or methods of defining the meanings of words, since newborn babies do not arrive in the world with an innate stock of words. What is being begged here is the question of whether introducing an infant to the way a word is used is *eo ipso* a form of definition. There is an obvious case for saying that definition belongs to a much later stage of language acquisition. There is also a case for saying that it makes no sense to talk of ostensive definition unless and until the learner has already progressed to a stage where non-ostensive definition is already familiar.

Robinson concedes that teaching a learner anything about language is impossible unless the learner has already 'acquired the general idea of symbolization'. This, he thinks, has to be done 'only once in a lifetime' (Robinson 1954: 118). But once it is done, the subsequent increase in the learner's stock of words and meanings presents no great problem. The trouble with this simplistic account is that Robinson thinks that grasping 'the general idea of symbolization' is a matter of 'learning that this word is a symbol of that thing' (Robinson 1954:

118). This observation shows unmistakably to what extent Robinson's entire discussion of definition is based on reocentric assumptions.

Since, as integrationists, we reject reocentric theories of language lock, stock and barrel, it will come as no surprise to the reader that we reject Robinson's account of language-learning. We do not propose to set out an alternative account here; for that would go far beyond the scope of this book. It will have to suffice to say that, in an integrationist account, acquiring the concept of a 'word', in the sense in which lexicography is concerned with words, emerges as a complex and sophisticated process. The breakthrough to 'symbolization' does not take place 'only once in a lifetime', on the basis of some 'Eureka!' experience, as Robinson suggests when he cites Helen Keller's autobiography for a first-hand account of such an experience. Furthermore, we would wish to argue that in literate societies understanding what a word is will always be based on familiarity with a particular writing system, the introduction of which plays no part at all in Robinson's developmental narrative.

So we do not think that there is anything corresponding to what Robinson calls 'that first great definition', which supposedly takes place at some time in childhood. This momentous event is a philosopher's illusion conjured up by a flawed semantic theory.

Some lexicographers have developed what amounts to their own version of ostensive definition. This is found in so-called 'illustrated' dictionaries, where pictorial aids are provided to supplement lexical entries. According to Hartmann and James (1998: 71), this practice dates back to the fifteenth century, and may be regarded as an intermediate stage in the progress towards the 'visual dictionary' and the 'electronic dictionary'. The latter nowadays offers the possibility of film and sound recordings to accompany the entries included. These technological developments pose an interesting question. Where does definition stop?

According to the editors of *The Oxford Illustrated Dictionary* (2nd ed. 1975), their work 'attempts to combine in a form that can be handled conveniently the essential features of dictionary and encyclopaedia'. This still leaves room for doubt as to whether the illustrations are part of the definitions. But when they go on to say that 'each is intended to show the meaning of a word or indicate the character of the thing for which the word stands' and that 'the subjects chosen for illustration are those that can be defined more clearly by this means than verbally', it seems that a definitional function is certainly being assigned to the illustration. Unfortunately, they then go on to theorize about 'drawing' as follows: 'a drawing has to be of a particular thing, and therefore gives an example of the particular use of the word rather than a generalized statement'. This is semiological gobbledegook. (The *therefore* is particularly arresting.) We cannot see any reason for supposing that a drawing *has* to be of a particular thing. In fact, most of the illustrations in *The Oxford Illustrated Dictionary* are manifestly not of 'particular things', but of generalizations as visually interpreted by the illustrator (e.g. 'a horse', 'a nerve-cell or neuron').

What is more interesting (but it does not apply to the *OID*) is that a photograph of, say, the Eiffel tower, might conceivably be supplied to illustrate the lexical entry for *tower*. Here there is no doubt that the photograph is of one particular tower. Does it constitute part of the definition of the word in the dictionary? Mill would say that the tower itself is certainly part of the denotation; but not the photograph of the tower. (That would be part of the denotation of the expression *photograph of a tower*.) However, the Eiffel tower, although famous, is hardly a typical tower. And here one seems to be brought back again to the problem of connotation. Has the word *tower* changed its meaning since – and as a consequence of – the building of the Eiffel tower? Does *tower* mean something different for people who have never heard of – or seen, or seen images of – the Eiffel tower? Or is the user of an illustrated dictionary supposed to ignore the physical eccentricities of the Eiffel tower, while nevertheless treating the illustration as part of the definition of *tower*?

The point about these questions is not that they cannot be discussed, but that discussion yields no unequivocal answers; and that fact itself, in our view, reveals something about the semantic no man's land in which the general lexicographer is perpetually condemned to wander. Whatever advances in computer technology may make it possible for the dictionary-maker to recruit and deploy in the way of 'information' (visual, audible, or in any other sensory modality) to incorporate into lexical entries, that will not solve the problem of where to draw the line between linguistic and non-linguistic facts. That there is such a line to be drawn, however uncertainly, is one of the standing myths of modern lexicography. Since its powerful endorsement by Murray, it has continued to haunt lexicographical theory. (For a recent version, see the entries *encyclopedia* and *encyclopedic dictionary* in Hartmann and James 1998.)

8. *Definition by rule*. Robinson recognizes one other type of definition, in order to cover a ragbag of cases that cannot plausibly be explained by relating a word to some language-independent 'thing'. In these cases the method recommended is 'simply to state the rule of their employment' (Robinson 1954: 130). Thus his rule for the personal pronoun *I* is that 'it is to be used by each utterer to indicate himself'. The rule-giving method has obvious applications to awkward cases like defining the meaning of *if*, *although* and *not*, which are words used primarily to articulate relations internal to sentences. But it also might be regarded as a category under which all the other types of definition could be subsumed. That is to say, one could regard an analytic definition such as '*man*: rational animal' as giving the rule for the use of the word *man*. And so on for all the other types of definition Robinson distinguishes: they could all be formulated as 'rules'.

The question that this raises is: what constitutes a 'rule'? If definition is 'rule-governed', as Robinson appears to imply, it is important to know in what sense, and where the relevant rules come from. His rule for the pronoun *I*, cited above, suggests that rules are prescriptive: the rule says that the word is 'to be used' in such-and-such a way. But who lays down this prescription is not divulged. Elsewhere, however, as far as we can see from Robinson's brief discussion of definition by rule, it seems that he is conflating the notion of a rule with that of a regularity. In which case, the appeal to rules is explanatorily vacuous: all it does is insist that the uses described do regularly occur.

* * *

Any lexicographer, on examining Robinson's typology, would doubtless point out that the same basic problems crop up repeatedly in slightly different forms in different modes of definition. Here we shall focus on two of these problems. One is a problem of semantic differentiation, and the other a problem of scope, but they overlap. The problem of scope is epitomized in the question we raised above: 'Where do definitions stop?'

Neither in Murray's day nor since has anyone come up with an objective way of deciding how many different meanings, or shades of meaning, a word has. (By 'objective' is to be understood here a procedure that does not just rely on the lexicographer's own intuition.) The complexity of the issue is illustrated by a famous dispute between lexicographers over the definition of the word *mahogany*. In 1940 an article appeared in the journal *Language*, at that time one of the leading publications in the field of linguistic theory, taking the editors of the 3rd edition of *Webster's* dictionary to task for inadequacies in their account of this word. The author of the article, Kemp Malone, alleged that the editors of *Webster* had failed altogether to identify the main meaning of *mahogany* in contemporary American usage (Malone 1940). Since the word was abundantly attested in written sources, this was, as Malone said, 'a very serious criticism indeed'. It was, indeed, more than that: in effect, it was an indictment of mainstream lexicographical methodology.

Webster listed seven meanings for *mahogany*. The first two (for present purposes we shall ignore the other five) read:

> 1. The valuable hardwood of a tree, the traditional mahogany (sense 2), used extensively for furniture and cabinetwork. It varies in color from a deep reddish brown to brownish yelllow, and is susceptible of a high polish.
> 2. A tropical American tree (Swietenia mahagoni), largely confined to the West Indies, yielding mahogany (sense 1).

Malone proposes to correct this to:

> 1. A more or less hard and heavy wood derived from various related and unrelated tropical trees; the wood usually has interlocked or cross grain, varies in color between reddish brown and brownish yellow, seasons well, and takes a high polish; it is much used for fine cabinet work and in making other articles of luxury or superior quality, as yachts and fine furniture.
> 2. A particular variety of this wood; the variety meant is usually indicated by prefixing the name of its place of origin, as *African mahogany*, *Philippine mahogany*, *West Indian mahogany*.

What Malone objects to is the inclusion of any reference to the botanical classification *Swietenia mahagoni* as part of the ordinary meaning of the word. He writes:

> Only in botanical treatises and in dictionaries have I found this sense marked by the use of Swietenia mahagoni as a qualifier. In other words, current popular speech uses geographical, not botanical qualifiers. The reason for this is obvious: the general public knows little and cares less about the botanical classification of the various kinds of mahogany wood, but it IS interested in the place of origin of the wood, and associates specific kinds of mahogany with specific places of origin. (Malone 1940)

It is of interest to note that the first meaning of *mahogany* given in the *OED* begins 'The wood of *Swietenia Mahagoni*. . .'; so presumably this was one of the culpable dictionaries to which Malone was referring. Furthermore (although Malone does not mention this) the *OED* anachronistically dates this meaning back to the seventeenth century (i.e. before that botanical classification had been invented, and before the birth of van Swieten).

Is one dealing here with analytic or synthetic definitions? Robinson gives *mahogany* as an example of a word which falls between two stools. With Malone's criticisms of *Webster* evidently in mind, he writes:

> In so far as where a thing is found is neither clearly included in nor clearly excluded from the meaning of some word for the thing, it is not clear whether a definition of that word is analytic or synthetic. The word 'mahogany', for example, might be held by some to mean a certain type of wood wherever found, but by others to mean that type of wood only when found in certain species of trees; and then a definition which said that this wood was found in such and such species would be regarded as synthetic by one party but as analytic by the other. (Robinson 1954: 99)

But this is to miss Malone's point, which is that for the everyday meaning of the word *mahogany* the botanical species of the tree is not semantically relevant *at all*. Malone concedes that the word *can* be used in the way that the first meaning in *Webster* specifies; that is, by someone 'who has in mind the wood of Swietenia mahagoni'.

> But what of the man who speaks of mahogany wood without having in mind any particular botanical species or genus? Webster's ignores this use of the word *mahogany*, although it is by far the most common. (Malone 1940)

According to Malone, this use ignored by *Webster* occurred in about 70 per cent of his corpus of 1,500 (current American) examples. If this is right, a major American dictionary had failed both to identify and to record the most frequently occurring meaning of a frequently occurring word.

Although Malone is curiously reticent when it comes to spelling out what he takes the function of a definition to be, it is not difficult to infer his view from his own proposals for defining *mahogany*. In our view, Malone is making a very important point, although perhaps not quite seeing its full implications. Let us call this point 'Malone's principle' and try to state it more lucidly than he does:

> *Malone's principle*
> *What language-users neither know nor assume cannot be (any part of) the meaning of the words they use.*

In effect, this is to propose a 'communicational' concept of lexicographical definition, as distinct from assuming that all that is required of the lexicographer is a simple statement of correlation between word and thing. Just how big a step that is in lexicography must not be underestimated. To know the 'communicational' meaning of a word is to know how to use it for those communicational purposes for which it is most commonly used in the linguistic community in question; and to give a 'communicational' definition is to state how the word is thus used. This is, both in principle and in practice, quite different from knowing or stating what kind or class of thing the word is the name of. Malone – we think – is almost certainly right to contend that knowing how to use the word *mahogany* in English for communicational purposes very seldom requires either speaker or hearer to know or assume that it is the name of Swietenia mahagoni. That might be the case if the word were used exclusively by professors of botany talking to one another; but patently it is not.

Thus the first task of the lexicographer is to find out what the commonest uses of the word *mahogany* actually are. One of the commonest – we surmise – is in the buying and selling of items of furniture. Thus if John and Mary Smith buy a mahogany dining table from a High Street furniture store, it seems reasonable to assume that in the process the word *mahogany* will have been uttered a number of times, both by the Smiths ('We are looking for a mahogany dining table') and by the sales assistant ('As it happens, we have two very fine quality mahogany tables in our summer sale. Would you like to see them?'). By the time the purchase is eventually concluded, the word will in all likelihood have been used by all the parties concerned without occasioning any communicational problem. The Smiths will have used it (successfully) in communicating their requirements as customers, while the store employee(s) will have used it (no less successfully) in responding to these requirements.

From the communicational success of this episode, however, it does not follow that the Smiths and the sales assistant(s) in the store all have the same concept 'mahogany' in their minds. Nor does it follow that what the Smiths have purchased, or believe they have purchased, or what the sales staff in the store think the Smiths have purchased, is a table made of Swietenia mahagoni. Communicational success, in this instance, is based neither on familiarity with one specific concept nor, more generally, on being botanically knowledgeable about tropical trees. In fact, all that the *dramatis personae* in this particular episode have agreed on in public is the application of the word *mahogany* to a rather small number of pieces of furniture in the store. But that is sufficient for communicational success. All are delighted with the outcome. The store has sold a table and the Smiths have found one they are satisfied with. The 'definition' of *mahogany* was never an issue.

Communication often requires only a very slender basis in shared assumptions. That is not the only lesson to be learnt from the case, however. A harder lesson (at least, for lexicographers) is that *no one may know* – including the participants themselves – on exactly what assumptions about the word *mahogany* this successful episode of communication was based *other than*, as already stated, its applicability by certain customers and a sales assistant or assistants to a few tables in a certain furniture store.

Where does that leave the lexicographer in search of a definition of the word *mahogany*? Trapped between Malone's principle, on the one hand, and the laconic inscrutability of usage on the other. The way out that Malone offers – it seems to us – runs implicitly as follows. All the lexicographer can do when giving a definition of the main meaning of a word is to indicate what the majority of people most commonly 'have in mind' when using the word in ordinary (non-specialized) discourse. And this in turn comes down to what the average speaker knows or believes, and would expect to be known or believed, by their interlocutors or readers. In the case of 'words for things', this would be knowledge or belief about the thing designated: thus perhaps, for *mahogany*, what kind of wood it is ('hard', 'heavy'), its source ('derived from . . . tropical trees'), what it looks like (the grain, the colour), what it is used for ('fine cabinet work'), and so on. So the tacit criterion for inclusion in Malone's list of semantic features seems to be something approximating to the following: they are features such that, if you thought mahogany wood had *different* features from these, you would almost certainly be confusing it with, or be thought to be confusing it with, some other kind of wood.

If this 'communicational' concept of definition is to be taken seriously, however, empirical evidence is required that the majority of users *do* know or believe – and assume others to know or believe – these very things the lexicographer indicates. And unfortunately Malone produces no such evidence. Nor does he seem to have undertaken any research in the direction of producing such evidence. (He did not go around asking informants, for example, 'Do you think mahogany wood comes from tropical trees?' or 'What colour would you say mahogany wood is?') Like others before him, he appears just to have sat down with a corpus of written examples and guessed what they meant or were likely to have meant. And that will not do if what are needed are 'objective' criteria that eliminate reliance on the lexicographer's intuitions.

Nor do we think Malone had grasped the lexicographical problem of semantic differentiation. It is difficult to see why he counts his two meanings of *mahogany* as being different. The sole evidence, as far as we can see, is that his examples of the second meaning are regularly accompanied by an adjective indicating a geographical provenance, as in *African mahogany, Cuban mahogany,* and so on. But why the presence of the adjective should be taken to indicate a different meaning of the noun is far from clear. It is like supposing that *street* has a different meaning in the collocations *streets of Bristol, streets of Birmingham* and *streets of Liverpool.* The streets themselves are different streets, to be sure. But does the meaning of *street* therefore differ in these three cases? Maybe it does: but it would be helpful to have some supporting argument. Some supporting argument is likewise needed before one can happily accept that the meaning of *mahogany* differs systematically according to whether the word is preceded by *African* or *Cuban.* But Malone produces none, and the suspicion is that he has all along been confusing lexical definition with real definition.

* * *

Comparison of corresponding entries across dictionaries reveals at a glance the lack of consensus among lexicographers as to the content of definitions. For instance, someone who had never encountered the noun *shrimp* before and consulted a dictionary to discover what it meant might find any of the following definitions.

(*A*) '*shrimp*: a small crustacean.'

(*B*) '*shrimp*: 1. small edible sea crustacean caught in nets pushed along the sand. 2. diminutive person.'

(*C*) '*shrimp*: 1. any of many types of small sea creature with long legs and a fanlike tail. 2. *usu. derog.* a small person.'

(*D*) '*shrimp*: 1. any of various small (esp. marine) edible crustaceans, with ten legs, grey-green when alive and pink when boiled. 2. *colloq.* a very small slight person.'

(*E*) '*shrimp*: 1. any of numerous mostly small 10-legged invertebrate animals (suborder Natantia of the order Decapoda, class Crustacea) that have a semitransparent long slender flexible body, fanlike tail, long legs, and long whiplike antennae and that are commercially important as food; *also* a small invertebrate animal (e.g. an Amphipod or a Branchiopod) resembling the true shrimps. 2. *informal or humorous* a very small or puny person.'

(*F*) '*shrimp*: 1. any of various chiefly marine decapod crustaceans of the genus *Crangon* and related genera, having a slender flattened body with a long tail and a single pair of pincers. 2. any of various similar but unrelated crustaceans, such as the opposum shrimp and the mantis shrimp. 3. Also called: *freshwater shrimp.* any of various shrimplike amphipod crustaceans of the genus *Gammarus,* esp. *G. pulex.* 4. Also called: *sand shrimp.* any of various shrimplike amphipod crustaceans of the genus *Gammarus,* esp. *G. locusta.* 5. *Informal.* a diminutive person, esp. a child.'

All of the above examples were found in one-volume English dictionaries of various sizes. It comes as no surprise to find that the smaller dictionaries give the shorter definitions. But why the meaning of a word should apparently vary according to the space at the lexicographer's disposal is itself an interesting question.

There are large overlaps between these six entries, but the discrepancies are no less striking. Lexicographer *A* recognizes only one meaning for *shrimp*, but the definition given seems to cover prawns and many other crustaceans. Lexicographer *B* evidently thinks, for some reason, that knowing how shrimps are caught is part of knowing the meaning of the word *shrimp*, even though it must be obvious that shrimps are shrimps irrespective of whether or how they are caught by human beings. *Why* they are caught also features in three of the definitions: (*B*) 'edible', (*C*) 'edible', (*E*) 'commercially important as food'; but neither in the shortest (*A*) nor the longest (*F*) of the definitions. Apart from being eaten, what happens to them *after* they are caught is mentioned in (*D*), 'boiled', but nowhere else.

The range of physiological features listed varies from the single item 'crustacean' (*A*, *B*) to the lengthy and complex descriptions given in (*E*) and (*F*). The shape of the tail is mentioned in (*C*) and (*E*) but not in (*A*), (*B*) or (*D*). The length of the legs is mentioned in (*C*) and (*E*), but the number of legs only in (*D*) and (*E*). The antennae are mentioned only in (*E*), the body only in (*D*) and (*F*), the pincers only in (*F*), and the colour only in (*D*). The habitat is specified in (*B*) ('sea'), (*C*) ('sea'), (*D*) ('esp. marine'), and (*F*) ('chiefly marine'), but not in (*E*). (*E*) and (*F*) give the only definitions that explicitly mention other creatures than the 'true' shrimp that are also called *shrimp*. But whereas (*E*) puts them all together under a single meaning, (*F*) treats these as falling under separate meanings, presumably in order to indicate that in these uses – and these only – *shrimp* is synonymous with *freshwater shrimp* and *sand shrimp* respectively. This semantic subtlety is ignored in (*E*). Are definitions (*A*), (*B*), (*C*) and (*D*) intended to cover both the 'true' shrimps and the other invertebrates mentioned in (*E*) and (*F*)? Or have lexicographers (*A*), (*B*), (*C*) and (*D*) just failed to take these other creatures into account altogether? It is difficult to tell, because of the vagueness of the defining formulations given.

Five of the dictionaries list a separate meaning for *shrimp* when applied to human beings, but this is variously described as '*usu. derog*' (*C*), '*colloq.*' (*D*), '*informal or humorous*' (*E*) and '*informal*' (*F*). The divergence here is considerable: a usage may be colloquial without being derogatory, and informal without being either derogatory or humorous. All of which suggests that none of these lexicographers had done any serious research into the question. Lexicographer (*A*) does not reckon this as a separate meaning at all. Lexicographer (*B*) recognizes it, but evidently thinks there is no need to supply further semantic information about it. A learner who trusted in any of these dictionaries for this meaning of *shrimp* would – in our view – need to exercise considerable caution when applying the word to human beings.

How are definitions such as these constructed? What work has the lexicographer actually accomplished? A comparison between them strongly suggests that these definitions were based on three rather disparate sources of information: (1) information from marine biologists about the specialist classification of crustaceans, (2) information about food and food preparation from fishmongers and cooks, and (3) casual observation of the way the word *shrimp* is used in everyday discourse to refer to sea-food items and human beings. What the lexicographer has done in all six cases – it seems to us – is select and amalgamate various items from these sources in such a way as to provide a summary of what is deemed be most useful for the dictionary user to know. What is less clear – in fact, not clear at all – is how the lexicographer in each case has arrived at the relevant estimate of the user's needs. It is interesting, for instance, that none of these definitions provides details concerning the geographical distribution of shrimps, their reproduction and life cycle, their behaviour as aquatic creatures, what they live on in their natural environment, their nutritional value as a food for humans, whether they are esteemed as a delicacy, and many other facts about them. These facts were evidently not regarded by any of the six lexicographers as semantically relevant for their users' purposes. Thus the same question arises time and again. Why does knowing some of these things, but not others, count as part of knowing the meaning of *shrimp*?

Shrimp may not be a typical dictionary entry. We chose it at random. But we think it unlikely that there are no other words that lexicographers treat in much the same way. What it shows, in our view, in that some lexicographical definitions may in practice be no more than *ad hoc* collections of items of information, grouped together in virtue of having some connection with the usage of the word in question. In short, there are dictionary entries that are based on no coherent theory of definition at all.

* * *

To summarize: if we are right, modern lexicography has inherited from the nineteenth century extremely muddled concepts of meaning and definition. The origin of this muddle is not difficult to detect: it arises from confusions about denotation and connotation, which in turn reach back to the earlier conflation of real and lexical definition. These confusions are apparent in the lexicographical work of Murray, continued uncritically by his successors at Oxford. This is the only plausible explanation that can be offered for the fact that in so many cases the definitions offered by the *OED* do no more than present a brief statement of the denotation of the word, as established by nineteenth-century specialists, in their own terms, in whatever the relevant scientific discipline might be. Murray evidently thought that that sufficed as an account of the word's basic meaning, and that all connotations the word might have 'flowed from' the denotation, or had been acquired by analogical extension. The possibility that the connotation(s) might actually *determine* the denotation was clearly foreign to him.

We do not think that *general* lexicography can continue indefinitely on this unsatisfactory basis. Otherwise it will become more of a pretence than it already is. This is not to deny that such a basis may be adequate for specialized fields. If a dictionary designed for students of physics and chemistry defines *copper* as 'red-brown transition metal with the atomic number 29, relative atomic mass 63.546, relative density 8.93, melting point 1083.4 degrees Celsius and boiling point 2582 degrees Celsius' that denotational specification may be perfectly adequate for the purposes of the intended dictionary-users. But it tells them hardly anything about the meaning of the word *copper* as used for purposes of communication in daily life. To establish *that* would require as much time, money, effort, research and methodological rigour as went into establishing the atomic number, relative atomic mass and relative density of the metal copper. Perhaps more.

It goes without saying that, in the present state of lexicography, a systematic 'communicational' definition of words is nowhere to be found. But it would be pessimistic to assume that it will be beyond the reach of lexicography in the foreseeable future. (The current denotational definition of *copper* might well have seemed beyond the foreseeable reach of science in the days of Paracelsus.)

III. Definition and the Law

Chapter 8

The Definition of Law and Legal Definition

There exists a long and complex history of debate about the role of language within law. Concern with language frequently reflects anxiety about the potential capriciousness of authority, where claims to textual fidelity mask the arbitrariness of legal decision making, or the imposition by judges of a hidden political, social or ideological agenda. Legal decisions are generally of a 'yes-no' variety; language is frequently understood as inherently vague or uncertain, with linguistic categories having at best unclear boundaries, or subject to vicissitudes of context or individual interpretation. Legal decisions need to be justified with reference to the internal 'legal logic' of the case, but also must take their place within the wider coherence of law. They are also measured against prevalent commonsense standards of justice, morality and fair play. A constant source of uncertainty is whether the issues that arise in the definition of ordinary words and phrases are an external factor to be applied to the solution of legal problems as an independent variable, or whether all questions of language that arise in law are implicated in the legally contentious issues characterizing a particular case.

Underlying this concern with language are questions such as: the adequacy or inadequacy of language in the face of the various tasks that law sets for it; the need to balance legal certainty with flexibility and adaptability in the face of particular constellations of texts, intentions and factual events; the question of the transparency of law and the extent to which law can be known and understood on the basis of the 'plain meaning' of the texts that embody law; the issue of separation of powers, and the problem that in interpreting legal texts and ordinary terms judges may wittingly or unwittingly transgress into the realm of the legislature and 'make the law' rather than merely 'apply the law'. In setting a precedent by imposing a definition or an interpretation in a given context, judges may be legislating rather than adjudicating. As Bacon wrote in his essay 'Of judicature' ([1625] 1994: 141):

> Judges ought to remember, that their office is *jus dicere*, and not *jus dare*, to interpret law, and not to make law, or give law. Else will it be like the authority, claimed by the Church of Rome, which under pretext of exposition of Scripture, doth not stick to add and alter; and to pronounce that which they do not find; and by show of antiquity, to introduce novelty.

The question of interpretative authority is fundamental to any society that derives normative social rules from written texts. Posner speaks of two fundamental concerns: 'the autonomy of legal reasoning' and a preoccupation with objectivity 'used in the strong sense that persons with different political or ideological commitments can nevertheless be brought to agree on the answer to even the most testing, the most politically charged, legal question' (Posner 1990: 454).

Debates about construction, definition and meaning frequently take place against a tradition of lamenting that language is in principle an inadequate tool for the task which law sets for it. Within legal discourse, there is thus a strong 'complaint tradition' about the vagueness or intractability of ordinary language. This complaint tradition is expressed in scepticism about linguistic categories and the ability of language to give us a clear picture of reality: 'Metaphors in law are to be narrowly watched, for starting out as devices to liberate thought, they often end up enslaving it' (Cardozo J, in *Berkey v Third Ave Ry* 1926, at 94–5). This complaint tradition is often invoked by judges, and this comment below is much cited:

> The imperfection of human language renders it not only difficult, but absolutely impossible, to define the word 'building' with any approach to accuracy. One may say of this or that structure, this or that is not a building; but no general definition can be given; and our lexicographers do not attempt it. Without, therefore, presuming to do what others have failed to do, I may venture to suggest, that, by a 'building' is usually understood a structure of considerable size, and intended to be permanent, or at least to endure for a considerable time. A church, whether constructed of iron or wood, undoubtedly is a building. So, a 'cow house' or 'stable' has been held to be a building, the occupation of which as tenant entitles the party to be registered as a voter. On the other hand, it is equally clear that a bird cage is not a building, neither is a wig-box, or a dog-Kennel or a hen-coop – the very value of these things being their portability. (Byles J. in *Stevens v Gourley* 1859, at 112)

Many, however, would say that a 'general definition' is precisely what lexicographers do attempt. Complaints about the inadequacy of language, where they are expressed in an actual judgement, are not to be understood as a general commentary on the language of the law, but as a rhetorical device or strategy in the context of a particular case.

One focus of anxiety is the unstable or imprecise boundary between the 'inteior' of the text and its interpretative context. James Bradley Thayer was critical of attempts to draw a clear and objective line around the language of a text, since this gave a false impression of stable definitions and meanings:

> The Chief Justice [Holt] here retires into that lawyer's Paradise where all words have a fixed, precisely ascertained meaning; where men may express their purposes, not only with accuracy, but with fulness; and where, if the writer has been careful, a lawyer, having a document referred to him, may sit in his chair, inspect the texts, and answer all questions without raising his eyes. Men have dreamed of attaining for their solemn muniments of title such an

> absolute security; and some degree of security they have compassed by giving strict definitions and technical meanings to words and phrases, and by rigid rules of construction. But the fatal necessity of looking outside the text in order to identify persons or things, tends steadily to destroy such illusions and to reveal the essential imperfection of language, whether spoken or written.
> (Thayer 1898: 428–9, cited in Chafee 1941: 395)

One corollary of complaints about the imperfection or imprecision of language is the need for vigilance: 'Words are clumsy tools. And it is very easy to cut one's fingers with them, and they need the closest attention in handling; but they are the only tools we have, and imagination itself cannot work without them' (Frankfurter 1947: 546).

Against this evocation of the intrinsic uncertainty of language, we can find examples of the defence of common sense or robust plain meaning. Plain meaning can be presented as an antidote to judicial manipulation. One famous example of this is Lord Atkin's dissent in *Liversidge v Anderson* (1942) in a case which concerned the Home Secretary's right to order the detention of someone on grounds of national security. In effect, the court was asked to accept that the Home Secretary had reasonable grounds for detaining someone if he believed he had reasonable grounds:

> I know of only one authority which might justify the suggested method of construction; 'When I use a word,' Humpty Dumpty said in a rather scornful tone, 'it means just what I choose it to mean, neither more nor less.' 'The question is,' said Alice, 'whether you can make words mean different things.' 'The question is,' said Humpty Dumpty, 'which is to be master – that is all.' . . . After all this long discussion the question is whether the words, 'If a man has' can mean 'If a man thinks he has.' I am of the opinion that they cannot, and the case should be decided accordingly . . .'. (at 245)

For some, linguistic reform is required to ensure that the underlying conceptual structures are more faithfully reflected in the surface legal terminology and textual practices. Interpretative problems can be substantially remedied – or at least mitigated – by attention to clarity of definition and adjustment of the internal logic of legal terminology so as to reflect the underlying conceptual logic of law. Normative concern with legal terminology underlies Wesley Hohfeld's 'Some fundamental legal conceptions as applied in judicial reasoning' ([1913] 2001). Hohfeld sought to clarify the conceptual relationships underlying fundamental terms such as 'right' and 'duty' in terms of a set of opposites and correlatives: 'in any closely reasoned problem, whether legal or non-legal, chameleon-hued words are a peril both to clear thought and lucid expression'. Thus 'the term "right" tends to be used indiscriminately to cover what in any given case may be a privilege, a power, or an immunity, rather than a right in the strictest sense' (Hohfeld [1913] 2001: 53). Hohfeld employed what was essentially a structuralist technique *avant la lettre* to set out a systematic analysis of fundamental legal concepts, defining these in terms of 'jural opposites' (right vs no-right; privilege vs duty; power vs disability; immunity vs liability) and 'jural correlatives' (i.e. related aspects of the same legal relation): right-duty; privilege-power; power-liability; immunity-disability (Hohfeld [1913] 2001: 12). This approach treats law as an autonomous legal-linguistic system which needs to be constantly monitored to ensure that there exists a set of straightforward mappings between legal language and legal concepts.

Given the centrality of language, meaning and interpretation to all aspects of law, it is perhaps surprising that there is no strong tradition of looking at questions of definition. This may reflect the ambivalence with which legal practitioners and theorists regard their dependence on language and on definition in particular. Law is after all about normative social practice and coercion, grounded in practical reasoning authorized by explicit textual authorities and implicit reading and interpretative practice. Given that almost all substantive legal (as opposed to evidential) disputes can be framed as disputes about definition, it is nonetheless surprising that there is little or no theoretical discussion of how definitions are arrived at, how they should be interpreted, and what principles should govern their application in actual cases. Walton (Walton 2002: 70) observes that in the popular mind 'lawyers and philosophers have in common that they are both often criticized for arguing about definitions in a way that is seen as hair-splitting'. But disputes about definitions are far from trivial: 'billions of dollars can turn on how a term like "wetland" is to be defined'. The tendency to denigrate definitional debate is 'probably because of the great importance we place on empirical evidence, a heritage of the so-called Enlightenment ways of thinking in our culture' (Walton 2002: 70).

In recent debates about meaning and interpretation in legal theory, concern with definition has been submerged within wider issues of textual interpretation, notably the debate about indeterminacy associated with Stanley Fish, Jacques Derrida, and other theorists. That said, there does exist a longstanding concern with definitions in relation to statutory interpretation, but this appears as a rather autonomous strand of discussion not overlapping much with philosophical debates about interpretation in the law. The ubiquity of definitional questions in law complicates attempts to focus on this topic, as the boundary between definition and interpretation, and between so-called 'ordinary language' and legal language, and the strategic use of these boundaries, constantly shift within the analysis carried out by judges in particular cases, and in commentary on the cases. Any focus on definition potentially opens up a regress of explanation, since one can always ask that the language of the definition itself be defined further, or raises familiar problems of circularity. For example, in Hong Kong law, a triad member is someone who has been initiated into a triad society through a triad ritual, who carries triad writings, attends triad meetings, etc.: 'triad ritual means any ritual commonly used by triad societies, any ritual closely resembling any such ritual and any part of such ritual' (Bolton, Hutton and Ip 1996).

* * *

One way to approach a discussion of law and definition is by looking at attempts to define the word *law* itself and fundamental concepts within law:

> 'Law' is a word like 'religion', 'time', 'politics', 'democracy', and 'beauty' which can be used without creating serious problems of comprehension but cannot be defined unless the purpose of the definition is understood. . . . If you ask simply, What is law? you will touch off a jurisprudential debate. . . . But the general question seems to assume – what is most debatable – that 'law' is some kind of thing (or collection of things), like 'New York' or 'Dom Perignon' or 'salamanders', or perhaps a set of propositions, as in the expression 'the law of contracts'. (Posner 1990: 221)

On this view, *law* is an abstract noun which can only be defined if one understands the underlying purpose of the definitional question. But this would apply to any request for a definition. Posner seems to assume that in asking in an unqualified way for a general definition of a law, one is necessarily constructing a reification of law, but this is open to question. After all, asking for a definition is a routine preliminary for many kinds of discussion. Does it commit to a particular ontology, beyond implying that a definition should offer some useful insight or information of a general kind? Posner's strategy for dealing with the definitional problem is a familiar one. He points to three basic senses of the word: a 'distinctive social institution', 'a collection of sets of propositions' and 'a source of rights, duties, and powers', and then states that he will focus primarily on the third of these (Posner 1990: 221–2).

This raises a fundamental jurisprudential problem. If debate about the nature of law is carried on through stipulative definition, there is no reason to assume that any coherent discussion is taking place, unless an agreed definition has been set down at the outset. Much of jurisprudence can indeed be understood as a clash between narrow definitions of law (e.g. law as a set of explicit rules, independent of moral or social rules) and broader definitions which see law as normative moral, social and economic practice. Some definitions of law give language a central role: 'The law, then, is a language that lawyers and judges use when they try to prevent or resolve problems – human conflicts – using official rules made by the state as their starting point' (Carter and Burke 2002: 6). Glanville Williams suggests that law is a sub-category of language:

> For lawyers language has a special interest because it is the greatest instrument of social control. Lawyers are perhaps apt to regard law as the sole, or chief, means of social control, forgetting that law is only a special department of language and that, whereas the application of law is limited, language is all-pervasive. (Williams 1945: 71)

Following on from this, Williams argues (1945: 72) that jurisprudence is 'in much need of semantic analysis', in particular to avoid 'word fetishism' and the taking of 'verbal distinctions' for 'real distinctions', problems diagnosed by Ogden and Richards (1923). He evokes the metaphor of core meaning which legal theory shares with semantics:

> The upshot is that the words we use, though they have a central core of meaning that is relatively fixed, are of doubtful application to a considerable number of marginal cases. In general, we try in our language to sharpen our distinctions beyond what is warranted by the facts of the case. It is a necessary feature of language that we should have to make this effort, and thus it is inevitable that our linguistic distinctions should constantly break down.
> (Williams 1945: 191)

Williams' conclusion is that 'the theory here advanced destroys completely and for ever the illusion that the law can be completely certain. Since the law has to be expressed in words, and words have a penumbra of uncertainty, marginal cases are bound to occur'. As a consequence, 'the theory destroys the illusion that the function of the judge is simply to administer the law'. Williams denies the centrality of interpretative questions: 'less attention ought to be paid to dictionary meanings and more to legislative policy' (Williams 1945: 802–3). Here the determination that law is fundamentally linguistic in nature, and that language is fundamentally unreliable, leads paradoxically to the conclusion that we need to look to policy for an understanding of law.

The argument has been frequently made that it is either useless or impossible to define *law*. But what of *a law*? Jeremy Bentham offered this definition:

> an assemblage of signs declarative of a volition conceived or adopted by the *sovereign* in a state, concerning the conduct to be observed in a certain *case* by a certain person or class of persons, who in the case in question are or are supposed to be subject to his power: such volition trusting for its accomplishment to the expectation of certain events which it is intended such declaration should upon occasion be a means of bringing to pass, and the prospect of which it is intended should act as a motive upon those whose conduct is in question. (Bentham [1782] 1970: 1)

This definition gave rise to eight points of view from which a law could be considered: the source of law, the subjects to which it applies, its objects or acts, etc. Bentham did not however offer a definition of law itself in the abstract, no doubt because of his belief that the only things that can be defined are classes of objects:

> When a definition of a thing that is a definition of a class of objects (for classes of objects are the only things that can be defined) is given, the genus of which it is a species is narrowed down to the extent of that species by the application of certain circumstances which constitute the specific properties of that species. (Bentham [1782] 1970: 52)

Bentham was much concerned with the presence within law of terms designating fictitious entities. These were fundamental terms such as *duty, right, power, title.* Believing that ideas are derived from the senses, he disputed the utility of the Aristotelian method of *per genus et differentiam* or any other definitional methods which might apply to real entities (Bentham [1776] 1960: 106fn). Bentham's 'paraphrasis' method of definition, or his definitional test for names of fictitious entities, was basically a substitution test, the first stage of which ('phraseoplerosis') was to contextualize the word to be defined in a sentence. This could then be used 'to make a meaningful true or false statement on a particular occasion' (Hart 1982: 130). The second step, 'paraphrasis' proper, involved substituting the name of a real entity for that of a fictitious entity, in order to show that the fictitious entity was at least partly grounded in reality:

> A word may be said to be expounded by *paraphrasis,* when not that *word* alone is translated into other *words,* but some whole *sentence* of which it forms a part is translated into another *sentence*; the words of which latter are expressive of such ideas as are *simple,* or are more immediately resolvable into simple ones than those of the former. Such are those expressive of *substances* and *simple modes,* in respect of such *abstract* terms as are expressive of what LOCKE has called *mixed modes.* This, in short, is the only method in which any abstract terms can, at the long run, be expounded to any instructive purpose: that is in terms calculated to raise *images* either of *substances* perceived, or of *emotions*; – sources, one or other of which every idea must be drawn from, to be a clear one. (Bentham [1776] 1960: 106fn. Italics in the original.)

Thus the word *obligation* represents a fiction, but it can be contextualized in a sentence like 'X is under an obligation to pay Y £10'. This sentence must then be translated into one or more sentences 'where the word "obligation" does not appear' (Hart 1982: 130). According to Hart, Bentham in his 'Essay on Logic' added a third element to this, that of 'archetypation', which was the making explicit of the underlying imagery or metaphorical content of the expression. In the case of obligation, 'the emblematic or archetypal image is that of a man lying down with a heavy body pressing upon him, to wit in such sort as either to prevent him acting at all or so ordering matters that if he does act it cannot be in any other direction or manner than of the direction or manner requisite' (Bentham 1843: 247, quoted in Hart 1982: 131).

Bentham considered the notion of 'natural right' vacuous; however, other fictitious entities on which the law depended were not totally devoid of substance. Whilst natural rights were vacuous because they had no place in a legal system, terms like *right* which were contextualized within a legal system did have meaning, because the reality of law is rooted in 'pain and pleasure':

> The consequences of any Law, or of any act which is made the object of a Law, the only consequences that men are at all interested in, what are they but *pain* and *pleasure*? By some such words then as *pain* and *pleasure,* they may be

expressed: and *pain* and *pleasure* at least, are words which a man has no need, we may hope, to go to a Lawyer to know the meaning of.

(Bentham [1776] 1960: 26)

This mistrust of abstract definition forms the basis of a line of legal reasoning that seeks operational explications of legal concepts (rather than ontologically misleading definitions), or looks away from definitional issues to consider the contractual and cooperative basis of human communicative action.

It is not possible or desirable to review here the full history of debate about the definition of law. Debates about the scope and nature of law, or the scope and nature of theories of law, range between reductionist theories to sociological theories which define law as the totality of activities encompassed under that heading. On the reductionist side, there is Hans Kelsen's search for an autonomous theory of pure law or 'reine Rechtslehre' ([1934] 1997), and the American legal scholar Joseph Henry Beale's assertion, as summarized by Jerome Frank ([1930] 1970: 53), that law must be 'uniform, general, continuous, equal, certain, pure'. Just as for Saussure an utterance is not part of the *langue,* so a legal decision in a particular court is not for Beale 'Law'.

One discussion which is useful in this context is by Julius Stone (1964: 167). Stone disputes the view that law is an indefinable Kantian category, a 'limit-concept' or *summum genus*: 'an independent self-contained body of knowledge of which any definition would have to be "meta-juristic".' Though Stone does not accept that one cannot define law, he gives two prime reasons why a satisfactory definition of law is hard to achieve. Firstly, the wide range of uses of the word, even among lawyers; secondly, the 'meaning of *definition* is itself subject to debate' (Stone 1964: 167–8). Law lacks 'preordinated disciplines on which a sure foothold can be gained for the metajuridical steps towards definition'. In particular, logicians 'have recently destroyed any complacencies on the nature, scope, rules and kinds of definition'. To understand how to define law we must understand 'what logicians are now saying about definition' (Stone 1964: 168). Whilst commendable in its interdisciplinary spirit, this recommendation opens one of the many regresses that afflict the topic of definition. It requires that the definition of the word *law* be only available to someone who can master contemporary discussions in logic. Since what logicians think about language, meaning and definition is constantly changing, it must be the case that the definition of *law,* or our access to that definition, also undergoes constant change.

Stone points out that most definitions of *law* are hybrid, combining aspects of the conventional dictionary definition, whilst attempting to 'draw the conceptual boundaries of the law rather independently of what dictionaries say about "law"'. The task of defining *law* is not comparable to that of 'real definition' (i.e. definitions involving words which refer to objects), (Stone 1964: 172): 'For what is meant by the word "law" is not an entity with fixed boundaries of meaning, like the words "hydrogen", "man", or "tree". Its boundaries must be delineated before any explication can begin' (Stone 1964: 173). Attempts to define law aim to fix the boundaries of the concept by stipulative definition, but also subject the concept to rational analysis (Stone 1964: 173). Some definitions begin with the notion of a legal rule as a specific form of rule; others focus on social control. Questions as to the source of law and the scope of its rules can be solved if necessary by definitional fiat, 'for the conceptual boundaries of law in this regard seem not to be pre-established either by nature or by general convention' (Stone 1964: 174).

Stone further concedes that there are multiple viewpoints on the nature of law, so that a system of law 'looks different as viewed from the positions of (1) the lawmaker (2) the individual subject, (3) the judge, or (4) the legal adviser' (Stone 1964: 177). Nonetheless he lists what he terms seven *propria* of law, which include familiar features such as norms regulating behaviour, the social nature of legal norms, the existence of legal order, the coercive nature of that legal order, the institutional nature of coercion, and that coercion must operate with a degree of effectiveness. However the first property that Stone sets out is that law, by definitional fiat, must be recognized as 'a complex whole of many phenomena', i.e. he introduces an initial stipulation that there is unity to law.

In effect, following this logic, one can only define law by stipulating in advance a crucial feature of law, namely that it exists as an ordered, complex unity. There is a strong parallel here to linguistics, which in effect has stipulated a definition of language and/or languages, in order to make possible a science of language. This creates a clear dilemma, both for linguists and lawyers. Either it is denied that law or language itself can be defined, which is tantamount to denying the possibility of a coherent debate about the nature of either, or stipulative definitions of *law* and *language* are imposed as preconditions. The latter move implies that only those who accept the stipulations can be partners in the discussion. Integrational linguistics denies that there is any stipulative definition of *language* which is available as an external analytic tool in the search for insights into human communication. This would imply a single decontextualized definition of *language* which was of universal validity and applicability, whereas the properties and 'rules' of language and communication are the products of, and are at stake in, countless contextual acts of integration and interpretation.

An integrational view of law would regard the nature of law as being at stake in the legal conflicts and processes themselves, just as human communication reveals differing and contradictory understandings of what language is. Acts of textual analysis and interpretation rely on and realize particular theories of language (Love 1985). Another way of expressing this communality between language and law is by using the analogy from economics, where values do not exist prior to transactions: 'actual transactions are not subordinate to values: it is not the case that values come first, before transactions arise' (Toolan 2002: 160, Harris 1987: 230–1).

* * *

One of the few sustained theoretical discussions of definition in legal theory is H. L. A. Hart's inaugural lecture at Oxford University, 'Definition and theory in jurisprudence' (1954). This essay reflected the influence of Bentham and Hart's interest in debates in the philosophy of language, with its concerns about definition and the ability of abstract terms to mislead ontologically. Hart begins his lecture with a consideration of questions of the form 'What is a right?' He points out that people may pose questions in this form in order to 'demand a definition or the cause or the purpose or the justification of the origin of a legal or political institution'. What if we rephrase the question to: 'What is the meaning of the word "right"?' This may suggest a trivialization of the matter at hand: 'For what they want cannot be got out of a dictionary and this transformation of their question suggests it can' (Hart 1954: 37). Hart then discusses two anomalies of legal language when compared with ordinary language. The first is the diverse range of cases to which many legal terms apply, notably the word *law* itself:

> Whereas it would be patently absurd to ask for elucidation of the principle in accordance with which different men are called Tom, it is not felt absurd to ask why, within municipal law the immense variety of different types of rules are called law, nor why municipal law and international law, in spite of striking differences, are so called. (Hart 1954: 37)

This is an unpromising beginning to the discussion. In our view a better point of comparison with the word *law* be a noun like *happiness*; for it is hard to see any clear distinction of principle between abstract legal nouns and other so-called abstract everyday terms. Just as the word *law* may be used to refer to a highly diverse range of phenomena, so too can *happiness* arguably refer to an extremely wide range of states of mind and of circumstance. The second criterion applied by Hart is equally problematic, for he points out that efforts to define many legal terms such as *corporation, right, duty* 'reveal that these do not have the straightforward connection with counterparts in the world of fact which most ordinary words have and to which we appeal in our definition of ordinary words' (1954: 38). Hart appears here to take ostensive definition as the paradigm for definition in ordinary language. But this tells us nothing in particular about law, as some legal terms can be defined ostensively, at least in part (*court, judge*), and vast numbers of non-legal terms cannot.

Hart argues that this puzzle over definition has given rise to a vast and rarified edifice of legal theorizing about the ontological status of rights. From this he concludes that fundamental philosophical issues need to be separated from the question of definition: 'though theory is to be welcomed, the growth of theory on the back of definition is not' (1954: 41). Hart's basic point is that it is misleading to use the same technique to define legal terms as is used to define terms like *cat* and *table*. For behind the bare legal terms lie whole sets of procedures, inferences and sequences of actions with specified consequences. In making this distinction Hart arguably misleads as to the simplicity of definitions of terms like *cat*, and as to the boundary between 'ordinary usage' and legal language.

Hart points out that if one looks at legal terms like *right* in context, by which he means their use in sentences, one can see that this use 'silently assumes a special and very complicated setting, namely the existence of a legal system with all that this implies by way of general obedience, the operation of the sanctions of the system, and the general likelihood that this will continue' (1954: 42). Statements of the form '*A* has a right to be paid £10 by *B*' not only presuppose the existence of a legal system but 'the use of this statement has also a special connection with a particular rule of the system'. A further feature of legal language is that a statement of the form 'Smith has a right to be paid £10' has a different status if uttered by a judge than when it is uttered outside court, where it may involve stating a claim, or an admission, etc. The statement by the judge is final – subject to the hierarchy of the court system. Finally, Hart argues that rules. both legal and non-legal, often attach the same outcome to diverse sets of facts. The word *out* in cricket is used to reflect a range of possible states of affairs. Thus a diverse range of factual circumstances may lead to the same legal outcome, e.g. that someone is deemed to have possession of a property, and there may be or not be much 'similarity or analogy' among these states of affairs. This may be obvious in some cases but in others 'rules treat a *sequence* of different actions or states of affairs in a way which unifies them'. If one asks for a definition of the term *corporation*, looking for 'an underlying identical continuing thing or person or quality *in* the sequence', and finds a 'corporate spirit', this may be real in some sense, but it is not 'a criterion of identity' (Hart 1954: 45). Hart's polemical point is that treating definitional issues in relation to legal terms like *right* in the same way as terms like *cat* leads to futile ontological speculation.

In the second part of the lecture, Hart addresses the question of how legal terms should be defined. This basically involves 'a method of elucidation of quite general application which we can call definition, if we wish' (Hart 1954: 47). Following Bentham, legal definition does not involve a conventional definition (which involves a synonymous equivalent), but rather a process in which the term is put into a sentence in which it plays its characteristic role and explained 'first by specifying the conditions under which the whole sentence is true, and secondly by showing how it is used in drawing a conclusion from the rules in a particular case' (Hart 1954: 47). An explanation – or definition – of the legal concept of *right* thus takes this form:

> (1) A statement of the form 'X has a right' is true if the following conditions are satisfied: (a) There is in existence a legal system. (b) Under a rule or rules of the system some other person Y is, in the events which have happened. obliged to do or abstain from some action. (c) This obligation is made by law dependent on the choice either of X or some other person authorized to act on his behalf so that either Y is bound to do or abstain from some action only if X (or some authorized person) so choose or alternatively only until X (or some authorized person) chooses otherwise. (2) A statement of the form 'X has a right' is used to draw a conclusion of law in a particular case which falls under such rules. (Hart 1954: 53)

Hart is concerned to differentiate this approach to legal definition from the commonsense approach to terms like *corporation* which classifies statements about corporate bodies as 'disguised abbreviations for statements about the rights and duties of individuals' (Hart 1954: 54). While a sophisticated version of this theory, such as that presented by Hohfeld (who offers an analysis of the underlying conceptual logic of fundamental legal terms like *right* and *privilege*, see above), succeeds in giving the legal consequences upon the individuals of the original statement, 'it does not give us the force and meaning of that statement itself' (Hart 1954: 54).

These issues arise when judges 'who are supposed not to legislate' nonetheless extend to corporations liabilities which are associated with natural persons, e.g. for crimes involving knowledge or intent. In seeking to illuminate the question 'Can a limited company commit a crime involving knowledge and intention?', one should not start with a definition of a company, with a debate about its status as 'a mere abstraction, a fiction, a metaphysical entity' and seek to infer the answer logically. Hart objects in particular to the use of the word *fiction*, as in the ascription of a 'fictitious will' to a corporation: 'But if we talk of "fiction" we suggest that we are using words in their ordinary sense and are merely pretending that something exists to which they apply' (1954: 58). What is required is analogical thinking within the 'general structure of our law', in which an individual may be held liable for the actions of a servant, or, authority can be found for 'imputing to a company the actions and mental states of those who are substantially carrying on its work' (Hart 1954: 57).

One question raised by this discussion is whether traditional dictionary-style definitions nonetheless might have a role to play in the law. Hart sees in the definition a hypostatization of the entity, but a definition might have a useful role, even within Hart's terms, so long as it was not used as a starting-point for questions about the ontological status of *rights*, *corporations*, etc. This would mean that the casting of the definition in the form of truth conditions as suggested by Bentham would be unnecessary. The truth condition is required to make a link between a sentence (and the term embedded in it) and the world, without evoking misleading ideas of reference. Hart seems to correlate the form of a definition with a corresponding ontological claim. It might be that the standard definition could be more practical or fit more comfortably within the 'language games' of law than an explication in the style offered by Hart. In any case it is impossible to say *a priori* what kind of definitional style is most useful or practical within an individual case. There is no way to stand outside the case, identify the ideal outcome, and then work backwards to find the best style of definition or explication. Statements about what fits best in a case are always already implicated in a view of the best outcome of the case.

* * *

Mistrust of definition as ontologically misleading fits naturally with post-war philosophy of language's concern with the rules underlying human interaction.

There has been constant interaction with law and with questions of rule, norm and the contractual nature of communication. For example, Austin's speech act theory (Austin 1962), with its notion of felicity conditions for speech acts, reflects a jurisprudence of everyday interaction. The paradigm cases of speech acts include some with legal effect such as 'I name this ship', 'I now pronounce you man and wife', 'I sentence you to three years in prison'. The speech act of promising is understood in quasi-contractual terms and set against a set of felicity conditions. If felicity conditions are not fulfilled, the speech act 'misfires' or is 'insincere'. Austin's speech act theory thus offers a rewriting of tacit social rules in quasi-legalistic terms.

Ordinary language philosophy was presented by Austin as drawing on time-tested linguistic distinctions:

> Our common stock of words embodies all the distinctions men have found worth drawing, and the connexions they have found worth marking, in the lifetimes of many generations; these surely are likely to be more numerous, more sound, since they have stood up to the long test of the survival of the fittest, and more subtle, at least in all ordinary and reasonably practical matters, than any that you or I are likely to think up in our arm-chairs of an afternoon. (Austin 1956: 8)

This concern with ordinary language leads to a particular focus on distinctions, on the boundaries between concepts, as reflecting 'the inherited experience and acumen of many generations of men' (Austin 1956: 11). The importance of the legal framework for the understanding of ordinary language becomes clear when Austin argues that we should pay attention to distinctions which work well 'for practical purposes in ordinary life'. That these distinctions work is 'no mean feat, for even ordinary life is full of *hard cases*' (Austin 1956: 11, emphasis added). Language usage is understood as an exercise in correct characterization of situations, and guidance to correct characterization is found by paying careful attention to established usage. A corollary of this model of language is an emphasis on relative uniformity of usage – differences in usage are held by Austin to be generally traceable to an underlying difference in how a situation has been imagined (Austin 1956: 9–10), rather than to what a linguist might call differences in the linguistic system itself.

The law itself however does not or cannot respect the niceties and nuanced distinctions of ordinary language:

> In the law a constant stream of actual cases, more novel and more tortuous than the mere imagination could contrive, are brought up *for decision* – that is, formulae for docketing them must somehow be found. Hence it is necessary first to be careful with, but also to be brutal with, to torture, to fake and to override, ordinary language: we cannot here evade or forget the whole affair. (Austin 1956: 12. Italics in the original.)

The implicit contrast is between the non-contentious, harmonious, communal nature of ordinary usage, which is normally adequate even for the hard cases that confront it, and the tortured language of the law, as a basically consensual system is twisted and stretched to meet the extraordinary demands of the contentious legal process.

We reject this contrast between ordinary usage and legal language, and would diagnose here a recurring problem in the academic study of human language and communication, namely the almost obsessive emphasis that is placed on consensus, order and shared knowledge. One can find as much order in law as in ordinary life, and as much conflict and contentiousness.

This contractualism is even clearer in Paul Grice's model of human communication (1975). Parties are enjoined under a consensus model of conversation to calculate the degree of relevance which the addressee of a remark is expecting and to which therefore he or she is entitled. Underlying human interaction is a contract, a shared agreement as to how conversation should be conducted. On this model, breaches of contract are sanctionable, or – to use the ethnomethodological term – 'accountable'.

A case where this contractual view of language was at stake is *Bronston v United States* 1973 (Solan 2004). Bronston, whose film production company was in bankruptcy, was asked about his own personal assets: 'Q. Do you have any bank accounts in Swiss banks, Mr Bronston? A. No, Sir. Q. Have you ever? A. The company had an account there for about six months in Zurich' (Solan 2004: 184). It turned out that Bronston had had an account earlier in Zurich but that he no longer had a bank account there. Bronston was prosecuted for lying under oath when giving evidence, i.e. for perjury, even though everything he said was true. He was convicted but his appeal was upheld by the Supreme Court of the United States, where it was held unanimously that Bronston had not lied under oath.

Definitional anxieties play little role in the works of J. L. Austin and Grice. What dominates is not anxiety about the inability of linguistic categories to obtain precision, but rather attention to the preconditions which allow the contract of language to function. This reflects a belief that attention to definition in the abstract creates uncertainty, since it seeks to reify meaning in an unnatural way, but that when it is focused on the 'use' of words, many of the puzzles about meaning disappear. However, in our view the problem with this form of contractualism is that law itself, and social life in general, are not built upon an unproblematic consensus. Law as a form of social life can be understood as a dynamic form of decision-making, in which there is strong pressure for coherence, and for the alignment of practical reasoning with the demands of social justice and moral order. But, while *Bronston v United States* can be used to illustrate the operation of relevance within human communicational order, it also illustrates the disputatious nature of that 'order'. An integrational view of law would suggest that law can never coalesce into an organic whole, just as to regard human language or languages as an organic structure is deeply misleading when set against the often scrappy and contentious nature of human interaction.

Developing Bentham's ideas, and in step with the 'linguistic turn' in the philosophy of language, Hart represents a tradition of seeing the definitional problems relating to abstract nouns as solved by the application of a general theory of meaning as use. The result of the general neglect of definition is a gap between theoretical debates about the status of legal language and the vast sea of cases and articles in which questions of definition are raised in respect of particular terms. There is no way of knowing what relation if any theorists' formulation of definitional issues connects with problems perceived by legal practitioners involved in deciding or analysing actual cases.

Hart himself pointed to a divide 'between jurisprudence and the study of law at work', which had led to the impression that 'there are certain fundamental concepts that the lawyer cannot hope to elucidate without entering a forbidding jungle of philosophical argument' (Hart 1954: 37). Hart's own success in bridging this divide is open to question. The concern about definitions misleading us as to the ontological nature of legal entities and scruples about 'fictions' cannot be translated directly into the concerns of actual cases. It is hard to see in practice what difference there is between Hart's explication of *right* and a conventional dictionary definition, since practitioners can bring their understanding of law as an operational system to their reading of conventional definitions. Just like the lay users of a conventional dictionary, lawyers have the ability to make a bridge between decontextualized abstract or general statements and actual contextualized instances.

Criticisms of statutory definitions within English legal discourse have an extensive history: 'In English Acts of Parliament a somewhat reckless use is made of the "interpretation clauses", by which, instead of a word or a sentence being simply guarded against misapprehensions or abuse, the word or sentence is made to cover a number of artificial meanings which in the absence of the clause, no interpreter would ever think of attaching to them' (Amos 1874: 66). Amos, an American jurist, looked to 'wise' definition 'to secure that words or sentences, having been used in one sense by the legislator, be strictly confined to that sense, and be rescued, as it were, from the perils of vacillation and uncertainty to which all language is naturally exposed' (Amos 1874: 65). On the borderline between definition and interpretation is the modification of written rules as they are applied in practice. The legislator cannot have foreseen all possible circumstances to which the language would have to be applied, so the language of the rule 'is either made to cover a larger meaning or a narrower meaning than that impressed upon it by the legislator'. This is termed by Amos 'extensive' versus 'restrictive' interpretation (Amos 1874: 67).

The entry on *definition* in the *Oxford Companion to Law* stresses the fundamental role of definition within law, noting that a legal system which formulates its rules and principles 'in verbal terms' has to offer definitions of many of its terms and concepts 'to enable courts and lawyers to know with some approach to certainty whether a particular set of facts amount to a particular category for the purposes of legal consequences' (Walker 1980: 346). But the remainder of the entry does not reflect the full range of issues that one could treat under this topic. It offers a critique of some statutory definitions as unhelpful, in 'merely saying that X includes or does not include Y, but giving no assistance on the meaning of X', and notes that definitions given in decided cases can give guidance 'but decided cases always discuss terms and concepts in the light of the facts and circumstances then before the court, and these interpretations may be unhelpful if the term or concept arises again in a very different context' (Walker 1980: 346).

Extensive discussion of definition can however be found in guides to statutory interpretation (see Bennion 2002: 479ff.). Statutory interpretation as an academic discipline wavers between the descriptive analysis of actual decisions and the search for prescriptive rules or norms to determine how decisions ideally should be arrived at. For Bennion, the *definition* of a word or phrase 'which must then be understood in the stipulated sense' should be understood as a limited rule of construction applicable within a statute or set of statutes. Bennion offers a detailed taxonomy of types of definition, e.g. 'clarifying definition', 'labelling definition', 'referential definition' (where reference is to an established legal concept), 'exclusionary definition', 'enlarging definition' and 'comprehensive definition'. Parliament also has passed *Interpretation Acts* (1889, replaced by 1978), which clarify the general legal import of various terms, such as *person*, but which are not intended to affect the substantive legal content of other Acts (Bennion 2002: 491–7). One general property of stipulative definition is, following Robinson (1954: 77), its relative weakness in the face of the established meaning:

> Whatever meaning may be expressly attached to a term, it is important to realize that its dictionary meaning is likely to exercise influence over the way the definition will be understood by the court. It is impossible to cancel the ingrained emotion of a word merely by an announcement.
>
> (Bennion 2002: 480)

One example cited by Bennion is *British Amusement Catering Trades Association v Westminster City Council* 1988, in which the House of Lords decided that a 'cinematograph exhibition' as defined in the relevant act should not be construed as including video games, 'although they were within the literal meaning of the definition'. The judge stated that the use of the term 'immediately brings to mind a film show' (Lord Griffiths, at 491, cited in Bennion 2002: 481). The Court of Appeal had held that the operation of a video game was an 'exhibition of moving pictures', the language used in the Cinematograph Act 1909 (amended 1952, 1982). The 1952 (9) (1)Act defined *cinematograph exhibition* as 'an exhibition of moving pictures produced on a screen by means which include the projection of light'; this was amended in 1982 to include 'all exhibitions of moving pictures which are produced otherwise than by the simultaneous reception and exhibition of television programmes broadcast by the British Broadcasting Corporation or the Independent Broadcasting Authority or distributed by a system licensed by the Secretary of State under section 89 of the Post Office Act 1969' (at 149).

Below are cited extracts from the case to illustrate how reasoning about definition is presented in a fairly routine case. The plaintiffs (who sought to exempt video games from the control of the statute) pointed to the language of the original 1909 statute:

> To construe the true meaning of the definition it would be helpful to examine section 1 of the Act of 1909 in its original unamended form. The references there to 'inflammable films' and 'regulations . . . for securing safety' are strong indications that the primary legislative purpose of the Act was to provide for the safety of persons attending cinematograph exhibitions, even though the licensing authority had power to impose conditions unrelated to safety considerations[.] (at 149)

They also suggested that a video game was not an 'exhibition':

> The moving pictures which are seen on the screen of a video game do not amount to an exhibition of moving pictures. The word 'exhibition' in its ordinary and natural meaning imports two characteristics, neither of which is possessed by the images that a video game produces. The first characteristic of an exhibition is that the thing exhibited takes a predetermined form. The expression 'to give an exhibition' implies the existence firstly of a giver, who determines the form that the exhibition will take, and secondly of a recipient whose role is a passive one. That is not characteristic of a video game because the person who sees the pictures on the screen is also the person who determines which pictures appear, in what sequence and for how long. Those pictures are computer-generated graphics produced by a circuit board inside the video game in response to the manipulation of the controls by the player. This means that a video game is quite different in kind from a video film, where a predetermined recording in tape form produces the video film on a screen. (at 150)

The second characteristic of an exhibition was that 'the thing exhibited is seen for its own sake', unlike a video game 'where the pictures that appear on the screen are seen by the player only as a means to an end, namely the playing of the game' (at 151). Further, the *Shorter Oxford English Dictionary* defined *cinematograph* as meaning: 'A device by which a series of instantaneous photographs of moving objects is projected on a screen so as to produce the effect of a single motion scene.' The respondents answered these points as follows:

> The literal interpretation used in the Act of 1909 is clear and unambiguous. Section 1(3) states that a 'cinematograph exhibition means any exhibition of moving pictures.' It is not appropriate when examining the legislation to think in terms of a cinematograph exhibition. The proper approach is to think of it in terms of 'any exhibition of moving pictures.' The words are clear and unambiguous and must be taken to express the intention of Parliament.

> The Shorter Oxford English Dictionary defines 'exhibit' inter alia as 'expose to view; to show; especially to show publicly for the purpose of amusement or instruction, or in a competition' and 'exhibition' inter alia as 'The action of exhibiting, submitting for inspection, displaying, or holding up to view.' The dictionary definition describes exactly what occurs in the moving pictures in a video game. Since a video game machine exhibits moving pictures, it is irrelevant that it does so for the purpose of the viewer playing a game or that the viewer has some control over some of the content of the exhibition by effecting choices. (at 151–2)

The respondents also contested the relevance of the player's perspective:

> It is necessary to consider what the machine is doing, namely exhibiting moving pictures, rather than [look] at the activity of the viewer or player. It is irrelevant that the exhibition of moving pictures is only part of the overall activity involved in the playing of a video game. The Acts apply to 'all' exhibitions of and to 'any' exhibition of moving pictures: see section 1 of the Act of 1982 and section 1(3) of the Act of 1909 (as amended by the Act of 1982). (at 152)

There was also debate about the mischief addressed, and the reconstruction of the original purpose of the statute.

One feature of common law argumentation that this case illustrates is the common technique of bombarding the court with as many points as possible. Thus the appellants' opening gambit was as follows:

> The above propositions [against including video games under the act] are supported by (1) the plain and ordinary meaning of the words used in the definition contained in section 1(3) of the Act of 1909 as amended, in particular 'In this Act "cinematograph exhibition" means any exhibition of . . .'; (2) the context in which the word 'exhibition' is used in the legislation; (3) the regulations made under the legislation which are consistent with that interpretation; (4) the legislative controls which already exist over video games of the kind under consideration; (5) the absurdities which would result from an application of the legislation to the extent contended by the respondents and (6) the requirement that it is for Parliament alone to legislate. (at 148)

It is then left to the judges to sort out the argument and prioritize the points made, but often judgements use the same technique. They engage in criticism of the reasoning of lower courts, and cite definitions and various interpretative principles, rather than giving a clear *ratio* for the decision,

Lord Griffiths, in the only written judgement, asserted that 'an exhibition of moving pictures is a film show'. He then looked at the background to the enactment of the statute, which was concerned with the flammable nature of cinema films. This led him to a firm conclusion:

> I am left in no doubt that in the phrase 'an exhibition of pictures . . . by means of a cinematograph' the word 'exhibition' is being used in its primary sense as a show to an audience and the entire phrase means a film show. The principal object of the Act of 1909 and of the regulations made thereunder which were published contemporaneously with the Act was to provide for the safety of the audience at such an exhibition and in particular to eliminate the fire risks. The word 'exhibition' used in this sense appears throughout the Act of which a good example appears in section 7(2) in which an exception is provided to the requirement of a licence if: 'the occupier thereof has given to the county council and to the chief officer of police of the police area, not less than seven days before the exhibition, notice in writing of his intention so to use the premises . . .' (at 154–5)

This analysis by the judge could be said to combine a straightforward decontextualized, literal reading, with an evocation of the context in which that literal reading makes sense. In the associative style of common law judgements, Lord Griffiths then takes on the lower court, citing this paragraph of the judgement by Balcombe L. J.:

> I know of no warrant for the proposition that the use of the word 'exhibition', whether or not used in conjunction with the word 'given', requires the assumption of a passive recipient of that which is exhibited. That does not accord with my understanding of the meaning of 'exhibition', nor is it supported by the definition in the Shorter Oxford English Dictionary to which we were referred. There 'exhibit' is defined as including: 'To expose to view; to show; [especially] to show publicly for the purpose of amusement or instruction, or in a competition'; while 'exhibition' is defined as including: 'The action of exhibiting, submitting for inspection, displaying, or holding up to view.' That exactly fits what happens to the moving pictures in a video game: they are exhibited to, or held up to the view of, the player in particular, although possibly to others as well; the fact that the pictures are not displayed as an end in themselves, and that by his choice and actions the player may alter the pictures is *nihil ad rem*. The use of the word 'given' in relation to the 'exhibition' of moving pictures in no way affects the position.
> (1987, at 981)

In response to this, the judge offers a different reading of the dictionary definition:

> This approach fails in my opinion to take into account the different shades of meaning attached in the English language to the use of the word 'exhibition' according to the context in which it is used and, in particular, fails to give sufficient weight to the primary dictionary meaning of 'exhibit "especially to show publicly for the purpose of amusement or instruction."' It is true that the Act of 1982 now covers exhibitions for private gain (in order to catch the

> pornographic cinema clubs) but reading the Act as a whole and the Regulations made thereunder, I have no doubt that 'exhibition' is used in the sense of a show to an audience and not in the sense of a display of moving objects on the screen of a video game. (at 156)

The judge then returns to the intuitive or common sense point: 'In arriving at this conclusion I have given weight to the title of the Acts. The use of the word "cinematograph" immediately brings to mind a film show but hardly alerts one to the possibility that it is to deal with the totally different activity involved in a video game' (at 157).

This looks on the surface like a good example of the free-standing use of judicial intuitions about meaning, the kind which have drawn criticism in particular from linguists. But it is hard to make the reasoning absolutely explicit. Reading through the case, one is met with a continual stream of criteria either applied or dismissed, and one is left unsure whether the House of Lords made the decision primarily on plain commonsense intuitive grounds, but backed it up with lots of supplementary reasoning, or whether some more complex process of decision making was at work. If we accept that the literal wording of the statute would have included video games, but the ordinary meaning of 'cinematograph exhibition' does not, we are faced with the intractable problem of finding some external interpretative principle by which to decide which meaning is relevant. But the court did not make that precise determination, and discussion moved continually between the dictionary definition of the two key terms and the legislative context and its policy background.

A contrasting type of case is one where the legal technical meaning of a term is applied where the everyday commonsense meaning might logically have been intended. In *Fisher v Bell* (1961), a shopkeeper had placed a flick-knife in the window of his store, and was subsequently charged under the Restriction of Offensive Weapons Act 1959. Section (1(1)) stated that any person 'who manufactures, sells or offers for sale or hire' knives that were dangerous weapons commits an offence. However, in contract law, it is not the shopkeeper but the customer who makes the first offer, and thus technically the shopkeeper was not 'offering' the knife 'for sale' but merely extending an invitation for offers ('Display of an article with a price on it is merely an invitation to treat. It is in no sense an offer for sale the acceptance of which constitutes a contract'). Thus the court took the term in a technical legal sense, rather than an everyday sense in which items displayed in windows are 'offered for sale'.

Bennion defends this decision against criticism that it gave 'insufficient weight to the mischief', on the grounds that 'part of the context is always legal' (Bennion 2002: 1034). But this raises the question: how does one know how much of the context is 'legal' in advance of addressing the specific question raised by the case, i.e. the status and definition of 'offering for sale'? Once one addresses the specific definitional problem raised by a case, one is already inevitably caught up in its 'hecceity', the particular constellation of facts, terms and circumstances. One cannot then step back to make an objective judgement about such matters as whether the term is being used only or primarily in its legal sense or in its everyday sense. This reflects the wider integrational principle that in communication and interpretation people are always *in medias res.* This does not prevent them from using certain tools such as reference works in the search for a resolution of an interpretative difficulty, but it is difficult to make sense of Bennion's underlying confidence that issues that are ideally or theoretically distinct in principle can also be separated rigorously in practice. As Harris (1981: 204) puts it, 'the search for some fixed point of linguistic reference outside the continuum of creative activity which itself is language', is bound to be in vain. The same would apply to the continuum of creative activity which is law.

* * *

One relatively elaborate general discussion of definition in law which also looks at lexicographic definition is given in Tiersma (2000). Tiersma grounds his discussion of definition in the law in a distinction between the general dictionary, which is – or should be – descriptive, in that 'it describes actual usage by the speech community', and legal definition, which 'resembles the prescriptive practice of bygone eras, because it dictates how the word ought to be used in that statute or contract' (Tiersma 2000: 116). The difference between general linguistic prescriptivism and legal prescriptivism is that 'statutory definitions *are* authoritative' (Tiersma 2000: 116; emphasis in original). For example, the California Consumer Legal Remedies Act defines *person* as 'an individual, partnership, corporation, limited liability association, or other group, however organized'. Whilst for Tiersma this is from a descriptive standpoint 'nonsense', that is what the word means in the statute: 'Although the legislature cannot change the ordinary meaning of *person,* it does have the power to define the term for the purposes of its legislation' (Tiersma 2000: 116–17). This form of definition Tiersma terms 'declaratory definition'. Whilst a speaker or academic writer may in some circumstances 'assert a degree of authority over her own language use' by asserting that a particular word is being used with a specific, well-defined meaning, 'few fields use declaratory definitions anyway nearly as much as the law'. Declaratory definitions enhance precision by 'making explicit which of various possible meanings a word has in a particular legal document' (Tiersma 2000: 117). If done properly, in general they 'minimize problems caused by overly vague and flexible terms'. However Tiersma cites a 150-word definition of *buttocks* from a local Florida ordinance (in the context of restrictions on the level of nudity allowed for professional dancers in clubs and entertainment establishment) which is comic in its attempt at a very high level of precision:

> the area at the rear of the body (sometimes referred to as the gluteus maximus) which lies between two imaginary lines running parallel to the ground when a person is standing, the first or top of such lines being one-half inch below the top of the vertical cleavage of the nates (i.e., the prominence

> formed by the muscles running from the back of the hip to the back of the leg) and the second or bottom line being one-half inch above the lowest point of the curvature of the fleshy protuberance (sometimes referred to as the gluteal fold), and between two imaginary lines, one on each side of the body (the outside lines), which outside lines are perpendicular to the ground and to the horizontal lines described above and which perpendicular outside lines pass through the outermost point(s) at which each nate meets the outer side of each leg[.] (Tiersma 2000: 118)

Tiersma discusses a common type of statutory definition which he terms the 'incorporating definition'. This is where an ordinary word is used in the body of the statute, but a separate section then defines the term, often by listing items that fall under the term. For example, the meaning of the term *document* may be defined to include a wide variety of means of recording or registering information (Tiersma 2000: 119). One potential problem Tiersma recognizes with this is that the text of the statute may be very straightforward (e.g. giving the right to seize 'documents'), but the incorporating definition may be highly technical. Thus a substantive point of law may be buried in the definitions.

The discussion also covers that class of problematic cases which arise at the intersection of so-called ordinary usage and legal usage. For example, Tiersma cites a Canadian case in which the court decided that the testator had used the word *wife* to refer to his 'legally married spouse' (from whom he was alienated) rather than 'the person he factually treated as his wife', even though from the context the more likely beneficiary was the latter (Tiersma 2000: 191). Here the point at issue is whether the term should be construed in its strict legal meaning, or in the meaning implied by knowledge of the lifestyle and (possibly idiosyncratic) linguistic habits of the testator. The interesting meta-issue concerns how the judge is to go about choosing between these competing approaches to the problem. What meta-principle of construction allows the judge to choose between the (alleged) plain meaning of the text (*wife* as 'legally married spouse') and the apparent intent of the testator?

One arguable omission in Tiersma's account is any close analysis of what exactly is meant by *definition*, and a discussion of the general principles by which definitions are, or should be, applied or 'operationalized' in actual hard cases. It is relatively clear what the declaratory definition aims to achieve and why it is so prevalent in law, but beyond pointing to the familiar conflict between precision and flexibility, he offers little discussion of the underlying theoretical issues. Further, the distinction drawn by Tiersma between the descriptive general dictionary and the prescriptive use of definition in law is open to question at a fundamental level. The idea of a dictionary which is devoid of prescriptive intent, or which regardless of editorial intent has no prescriptive effect, is in our view implausible. Dictionaries are contextualized by users in multiple ways as authoritative, even when the dictionary claims only to offer an accurate description of usage. A simple example of this is the use by Scrabble players of *The Official Scrabble Players Dictionary* to determine for them whether a particular string of letters counts as a word in the English language or not. Further, the fact that there is a published work of fiction with the title *Down with Skool* has not led to the inclusion of *skool* in general dictionaries of English. Debates about the inclusion or exclusion of certain words (e.g. *herstory*) reflect an investment in the authority of the dictionary.

It might be argued that there is nonetheless a distinction to be drawn between the prescriptive authority of the general dictionary and the declaratory definition in a statute, since the declaratory definition has the force of law, is in fact literally law, whereas submission to the authority of the dictionary (e.g. in a Scrabble game) is a matter of choice or contextual authority (teacher, examination, etc.). But this reduces the distinction to the truism that legal definitions embedded in statutes have the force of law and general definitions do not. This is not at all the same as saying that legal definitions are prescriptive and general definitions are descriptive.

* * *

Another source of legal definitions is the legal dictionary. This is a work of reference which offers definitions of words and phrases which are either primarily legal terms of art, or which appear in legal texts with specialized meanings. An example of the first kind would be *estoppel*, of the second *negligence*. These two categories do not exhaustively cover all the entries in a legal dictionary, nor are they absolutely distinct. A third category of entries might be words which raise special problems of interpretation or scope when used in a legal context. For example *and* has an entry in Curzon's *Dictionary of Law*. The legal dictionary is sometimes sub-categorized into two basic types, the law dictionary and the judicial dictionary: 'A judicial dictionary is both broader and narrower than a law dictionary because it collects whatever words and phrases judges have had occasion to define' (Garner 2003: 38). It is broader because it includes judges' definitions of ordinary words or phrases which have arisen in particular cases (e.g. *Boston cream pie*), and narrower because judges have not had to interpret all legal terms. For example, *Black's Seventh* contains legal terms such as *legal realism, legal research, legal secretary*, but these are not found in *Words and Phrases*, the leading judicial dictionary (Garner 2003: 38).

As with general dictionaries, there is an unclear (and uneasy) boundary between the dictionary – often understood as defining words and phrases – and the encyclopedia sometimes thought of as defining the things or concepts (the referents) themselves. The boundaries between a general dictionary, an encyclopedia, a law dictionary and a legal encyclopedia are inevitably unclear, both in theory and as a matter of practice. For example, general dictionaries also often define common legal terms such as *estoppel*. Legal dictionaries do not exclusively define legal terms. According to Mellinkoff (1963: 37), the many ways in which the law is concerned with whisky 'have been recognized by its inclusion in American law dictionaries'. The *Dictionary of Law* has entries for a diverse range of expressions, such as *ecstasy, EEC, ISA* (*Individual Savings Account*).

Bryan Garner, the editor of *Black's Seventh*, applied this following tenet among others: 'Distinguish between definitions and encyclopedic information (that is, textbook descriptions)' (Garner 2003: 38). In the history of legal lexicography one can find widely varying practices, from glossaries with short explanations to quasi-encyclopedic attempts to 'expound the law according to an alphabetical arrangement' (Garner 2003: 33). One early example was Giles Jacob's *New Law Dictionary* (1729), described by Mersky (2004: 25) as 'more like an encyclopedia than a dictionary in that it combined definitions with an abridgement of the law and a vocabulary of Anglo-Saxon and Law-French words'.

In *Black's Seventh*, Garner initiated a policy of separating the definition proper from 'discursive information' by use of a bullet-point. The encyclopedic information includes quotations from major legal authorities, i.e. distinguished law treatises, rather than from 'some appellate judge in Louisiana'. Garner preferred law treatises to cases because of the greater depth of reading behind a law treatise, the relatively ease now of electronic access to cases, and 'the chance that a reader of Black's law Dictionary is actually looking for a Louisiana precedent seems remote' (Garner 2003: 37).

To this one might respond that one does not always know what one is looking for when one opens a dictionary. A definition cited from a case is simply a different theoretical entity from a general definition offered by the author of a textbook or treatise. Garner notes disapprovingly that *Black's Sixth* included the following definition of *hotel* from the Utah Supreme Court:

> A building held out to the public as a place where all transient persons who come will be received and entertained as guests for compensation and it opens its facilities to the public as a whole rather than limited accessibility to a well-defined private group. (Garner 2003: 40)

This is 'ill-phrased' and 'inaccurate, even if a state supreme court said it'. An impatience with diverse citations can perhaps be traced to a desire to maintain consistency between the definition and the attached encyclopedic information. Garner comments that this definition is 'inaccurate', rather begging the question of the underlying normative stance of the dictionary. If one wished to find examples of how different courts have tried to define particular words in the context of particular cases, then a reference work which included definitions from sources such as the Utah Supreme Court would be of great interest. If one is looking for coherence between definition and encyclopedic information summarizing the received wisdom of the great minds of legal theory, then Garner's more normative approach has its own rationale.

Chapter 9

Strategies of Construction

While there have been clear shifts in theoretical debates about interpretation in law, it is much harder to discern clear long-term trends in the world of common law adjudication. In judicial practice, a number of definitional and interpretative strategies have commended themselves, at least within common law systems. One is for judges simply to muddle through on a case by case basis. A second is for particular judges to evince leanings towards particular forms of construction, either preferring some variant of literal or strict construction or supporting a so-called purposive approach. A striking example of a judge with a theory of interpretation is Antonin Scalia, a judge on the present United States Supreme Court, who has elaborated a theory now called 'new textualism' (Scalia 1997). In Britain, Lord Denning (1899–1999) was the most famous modern exponent of the gap-filling, purposive or creative construction. It is often difficult to classify judges strictly according to interpretative type, and the so-called 'literal' approach is itself not easily defined. Scalia does include contextual factors (in the sense of relevant aspects of the linguistic context, including other parts of the statute) in his textualist construction, while rejecting attempts to reconstruct the legislative intention.

In *Magor and St Mellons v Newport Borough Council* 1952, remarks by Lord Denning, made as part of his dissent in the Court of Appeal, were cited in the House of Lords judgement:

> We do not sit here to pull the language of Parliament to pieces and make nonsense of it. We sit here to find out the intention of Parliament and carry it out and we do this better by filling in the gaps and making sense of the enactment than by opening it up to destructive analysis. (at 189)

This method of interpretation was condemned in strong language by Lord Simonds:

> The court, having discovered the intention of Parliament and of Ministers too, must proceed to fill in the gaps. What the legislature has not written, the court must write. This proposition, which restates in a new form the view expressed by the Lord Justice [Denning] in the earlier case of Seaford Court Estates Ld. v. Asher (to which the Lord Justice himself refers), cannot be supported. It appears to me to be a naked usurpation of the legislative function

> under the thin disguise of interpretation, and it is the less justifiable when it is guesswork with what material the legislature would, if it had discovered the gap, have filled it in. If a gap is disclosed, the remedy lies in an amending Act. (at 190)

In the context of English law over the past two centuries, claims have been made that the 'literal rule' was dominant for the past hundred or one hundred and fifty years, but that judges have been increasingly 'moving away from [such] literal mindedness' (Zander 1999: 111, 127). Zander cites *Whitely v Chappell* 1868–9 as a foolish example of this literal mindedness. In this case a statute which made it an offence 'to impersonate any person entitled to vote' was held not to apply to a case where the defendant was impersonating someone who was dead. A dead person was not entitled to vote, so no offence had been committed. Zander is also highly critical of *Re Rowland* 1963, in which the question arose of interpreting a will left by a couple with distinct provisions depending on whether their death was coincident or one party predeceased the other. Husband and wife disappeared together along with a small vessel in the South Pacific, but the exact circumstances of their death were unknown. The court ruled that the plain meaning of the word 'coinciding' was not covered by these facts (Zander 1999: 126, 115–20). Lord Denning dissented, criticizing what he characterized as nineteenth-century literalism which asked for the 'ordinary and grammatical meaning'. Denning preferred an alternative approach, one which involved an attempt to reconstruct the intention of the testator:

> In order to discover the meaning which he [the testator] intended, you will not get much help from a dictionary. It is very unlikely that he used a dictionary, and even less likely that he used the same one as you. What you should do is place yourself as far as possible in his position, taking note of the facts and circumstances known to him at the time and then say what he meant by his words. I decline, therefore, to ask myself: what do the words mean to a grammarian? (at 9)

Lord Denning also remarked (*Re Rowland* 1963, at 9–10): 'I have myself known a judge to say: "I believe this to be contrary to the true intention of the testator but nevertheless it is the result of the words he has used"'. However in 1962 the Master of the Rolls Lord Evershed noted that 'the length and detail of modern legislation has undoubtedly reinforced the claim of literal construction as the only safe rule' (preface to Wilson and Galpin 1962: vi).

Denning has been accused of adopting the interpretative method most suited to the result which he had identified in advance on subjective, moral grounds. In *Royal College of Nursing v Department of Health and Social Security* 1981, the question arose as to whether the phrase 'terminated by a registered medical practitioner' could be understood to cover those cases where a doctor set up and initiated the procedure and was available for consultation during it, but was not present during the actual carrying out of the abortion. Denning took this view of the interpretative politics of the case: 'Emotions run so high on both sides that I feel that we as judges must go by the very words of the statute – without stretching it one way or the other – and writing nothing in which is not there' (at 804). Denning's conclusion was that the strict constriction of the statute was the correct one and the 'treatment' had to be carried out from beginning to end by a doctor:

> I think the word 'treatment' in those sections means 'the actual act of terminating the pregnancy.' When the medical induction method is used, this means the continuous act of administering prostaglandin from the moment it is started until the unborn child is expelled from the mother's body. This continuous act must be done by the doctor personally. It is not sufficient that it is done by a nurse when he is not present. (at 805)

But the rhetoric of Denning's judgement makes clear his hostility to legalized abortion, and his adoption of a literalist reading rings rather hollow in the context of his wider career as a judge.

Judges occasionally talk in the language of change, as if it were possible to leave behind one style of interpretation and develop another. The House of Lords' decision in *Investors Compensation Scheme Ltd v West Bromwich Building Society* 1998 affirmed that the result of a fundamental change in the construction of contracts had been 'to assimilate the way in which such documents are interpreted by judges to the commonsense principles by which any serious utterance would be interpreted in ordinary life'. It was asserted that 'almost all the old intellectual baggage of "legal" interpretation has been discarded.' Interpretation was defined as 'the ascertainment of the meaning which the document would convey to a reasonable person having all the background knowledge which would reasonably have been available to the parties in the situation in which they were at the time of the contract', i.e. against the 'matrix of fact'. In only exceptional cases did the law distinguish between 'legal interpretation' and 'the way we would interpret utterances in ordinary life' (judgement of Lord Hoffmann, at 912).

Whether this case and the authority it cites really offers such a radical departure is difficult to say. The difficulty of imagining a history – as opposed to a chronological narrative – remains. Discussing US patent law, Barney (2003: 104–5) argues that there has been a shift since 1999 from scepticism about the possibility of construing 'ordinary meaning' to 'a claim construction system that is primarily focused on the "ordinary meaning" of claim terms', i.e. one that begins with the presumption in favour of their 'ordinary and accustomed meaning'. In the past two decades the United States Supreme Court has become increasingly textualist and consequently highly critical of a search for explicit legislative intent (i.e. of the practice of solving hard cases by looking for statements of intent from discussions preceding the enactment). However the House of Lords in *Pepper v Hart* 1993 approved for the first time research into the background to the enactment as an interpretative strategy in certain circumstances. Toolan suggests that this ruling 'is only one of many indications that, in the last couple of decades, English law has qualified its preference for statutory interpretation to be literalist and its treatment of the text of a statute as freestanding' (Toolan 2002: 171).

* * *

To aid them in the interpretation of legal texts ('construction'), judges have available a set of 'canons'. Principles of interpretation are often described as rules: the 'literal rule' (that the court should give effect to the plain meaning of the statute as this best reflects the intentions of the legislature), 'the 'golden rule' (that the court should not construe a statute literally if an absurd result will follow), the 'mischief rule' (where the court will focus on the problem the statute is intending to address rather than follow the strict wording). For example, one much quoted statement of the thinking behind the literal rule is as follows:

> the only rule for the construction of Acts of Parliament is, that they should be construed according to the intent of the Parliament which passed the Act. If the words of the statute are in themselves precise and unambiguous, then no more can be necessary than to expound those words in their natural and ordinary sense. The words themselves alone do, in such case, best declare the intention of the lawgiver. (Tindal C. J., *Sussex Peerage Case* 1844, at 85)

Lord Esher in *R v Judge of the City of London Court* 1892 said (at 290): 'If the words of an Act are clear then you must follow them even though they lead to a manifest absurdity. The court has nothing to do with the question whether the legislature has committed an absurdity.'

These canons are perhaps best characterized as 'tendencies or approaches' (Zander 1999: 109). Often known by Latin tags, so-called intrinsic textual rules include *ejusdem generis* ('when general words follow particular words, the general words are understood as being limited to the class of things indicated by the particular words'); *expressio unius est exclusio alterius* ('mention of one thing means exclusion of another'). So-called 'substantive canons' are principles of policy guiding construction, such as the 'rule of lenity' which states that statutes imposing criminal liability should be narrowly construed in favour of the defendant.

In a famous article, the American legal theorist Karl Llewellyn argued that the canons of statutory interpretation were mutually contradictory, i.e. that they were not capable of guiding how statutes should be interpreted (Llewellyn 1950). Llewellyn juxtaposed a series of 'thrusts' with contradictory 'parries', thereby reducing to nonsense the received body of interpretative maxims and guidelines: 'A statute cannot go beyond its text', but 'To effect its purpose a statute may be implemented beyond its text'; 'If language is plain and unambiguous it must be given effect', but 'Not when literal interpretation would lead to absurd or mischievous consequences or thwart manifest purpose'. Whether

Llewellyn is a straightforward indeterminacy theorist is open to question. Winter (2001: 217) shows how for Llewellyn legal certainty must be achieved by semantic change in the interpretation of the rule, since within an evolving socio-political scene lack of change or too radical change creates the appearance of uncertainty, whereas changes in judicial decision-making that are in step with social change offer a (somewhat paradoxical) certainty: 'if the change on the judge's part is keeping up perfectly [with semantic change], neither judge nor layman realizes that any change has occurred . . . and legal certainty prevails. It *can* only prevail through change.'

The last pair of maxims cited above is often seen as a contrast between 'plain meaning' and 'purposive' techniques of interpretation, or as a related – albeit theoretically distinguishable – opposition between 'strict construction' and 'liberal construction' (Mullins 2000). Purposive construction involves a metaphorical 'going beyond' the plain or literal meaning:

> Of course it is true that words, even in their literal sense, are the primary, and ordinarily the most reliable, source of interpreting the meaning of any writing: be it statute, a contract, or anything else. But it is one of the surest indexes of a mature and developed jurisprudence not to make a fortress out of the dictionary; but to remember that statutes have some purpose or object to accomplish, whose sympathetic and imaginative discovery is the surest guide to their meaning. (Judge Learned Hand in *Cabell v Markham* 1945, at 739).

A separate theoretical problem concerns how 'purpose' is to be ascertained, and whether the court can look behind the statute to consider the political debate and the drafting of the law.

Critics of legal decision making and of maxims of interpretation taught to first-year law students point to the lack of a meta-rule of interpretation that can be applied to decide which of these two approaches should be followed. Judges in effect offer a form of *post hoc* reasoning. A decision is presented as following logically from a particular rule of interpretation, but there is no explanation as to why that particular rule was selected. If the judge does not wish to apply the literal rule, then there remains ample room for manoeuvre:

> For words, which are no other than the Verberation of the Air, do not constitute the Statute, but are only the Image of it, and the Life of the Statute rests in the Minds of the Expositors of the Words, that is the Makers of the Statutes. (*Partridge v Strange and Croker* 1553, at 130)

Bennion's guide to statutory interpretation dismisses the idea that 'the court selects which "rule" it prefers, and then applies it in order to reach a result' as 'perhaps the biggest mistake made about statutory interpretation' (Bennion 2002: 468). Bennion argues that it is in any case an oversimplification to reduce statutory interpretation to these three rules: 'What the court does (or should do) is take an overall view, weigh all the relevant interpretative factors, and arrive at a balanced conclusion' (Bennion 2002: 469). The basic rule of statutory interpretation 'is that it is taken to be the legislator's intention that the enactment shall be construed in accordance with the general guides to legislative intention laid down by law; and that where these conflict the problem shall be resolved by weighing and balancing the interpretative factors concerned' (Bennion 2002: 468). This is presented as a *rule* because the court is obliged to follow it in every case (Bennion 2002: 469). This approach Bennion terms 'the global method' of statutory interpretation ('pertaining to or embracing the totality of a number of items, categories, etc.; comprehensive, all-inclusive, unified, total'); alternatively it can be called 'pluralistic' (Bennion 2002: 7).

It would be wrong to present Bennion as a naive advocate of statutory interpretation ('to aspire to so direct, for years into future, the endlessly varied actions of millions of people by a brief verbal formula, necessarily bearing the cramping impress of its own day, is remarkably ambitious', Bennion 2002: 3), though he does shift much of the blame for the overall difficulties to the fact that 'Acts of Parliament are prepared unscientifically and in haste' (Bennion 2002: 4). The reference to 'science' suggests a lost discipline of precise drafting. Bennion subscribes to a belief in the underlying importance of 'literal meaning', and adopts a 'telementional' view of communication (see discussion above, and Harris 1998: 32):

> The whole idea of governing by fixed words inscribed on tablets is fascinating and strange. The words, because of the inadequacy of language and the infinite variety of circumstances can from the beginning never be better than approximate, are frozen in their imperfect state unless and until amended. Parliamentary amendment is difficult, and subject to the same constraints. Meanwhile, the inadequate words grow less and less apt. The temptation the court feels is to depart from the literal meaning in order to do justice or make sense. Yet this natural urge marks a failure in communication. Words are designed for no other purpose than to transmit a message. If what the words say is rejected in favour of a meaning reached by other means, the message has not got through. Those who trustingly read it, and in good faith acted accordingly, are confounded. (Bennion 2002: 5)

This suggests a correlation between belief in the inadequacy of language and the idea that communication should ideally involve the intact transmission of an idea from producer to recipient. However, from an integrational perspective, it makes no sense to speak of language as inadequate when measured against an ideal which no human system of communication could ever attain.

It is doubtful whether Bennion's discussions would be persuasive for those who believe that the apparently authoritative language of the law in reality represents a set of indeterminate surface forms underlying which are political, ideological or economic deep structures. For these theorists, claims for actual or potential certainty and consistency in legal language represent a mystification of the essentially socio-political nature of law. After all, terms such as 'relevant' and 'balanced' are all subject to potentially contentious interpretation in the context of a particular case.

In *Church of the Holy Trinity v United States* 1892, an underlying set of socio-political assumptions were brought to bear on a dilemma created by appeal to the strict wording of a statute. The Church of Holy Trinity in New York concluded an employment agreement with an English minister who was to serve as its new pastor. A federal statute made it unlawful for any person to 'in any way assist or encourage the importation or migration of any alien [. .] into the United States [. .] under contract or agreement [. .] made previous to the importation or migration of such alien [. . .] to perform labor or service of any kind in the United States'. A decision of the Circuit Court for the Southern District of New York found that the church was liable for breaching the statute and imposed a fine; the Supreme Court reversed the decision. Its reasoning was as follows:

> It must be conceded that the act of the corporation is within the letter of this section, for the relation of rector to his church is one of service, and implies labor on the one side with compensation on the other. Not only are the general words 'labor' and 'service' both used, but also, as it were to guard against any narrow interpretation and emphasize a breadth of meaning, to them is added 'of any kind;' and, further, as noticed by the circuit judge in his opinion, the fifth section, which makes specific exceptions, among them professional actors, artists, lecturers, singers, and domestic servants, strengthens the idea that every other kind of labor and service was intended to be reached by the first section. While there is great force to this reasoning, we cannot think congress intended to denounce with penalties a transaction like that in the present case. It is a familiar rule that a thing may be within the letter of the statute and yet not within the statute, because not within its spirit nor within the intention of its makers. This has been often asserted, and the Reports are full of cases illustrating its application. This is not the substitution of the will of the judge for that of the legislator; for frequently words of general meaning are used in a statute, words broad enough to include an act in question, and yet a consideration of the whole legislation, or of the circumstances surrounding its enactment, or of the absurd results which follow from giving such broad meaning to the words, makes it unreasonable to believe that the legislator intended to include the particular act.
>
> (at 458–9)

The court appealed to a general common law principle that a statute should not be construed literally if this would lead to an absurd result, citing *Stradling v Morgan* 1560, and Lord Coke: 'Acts of parliament are to be so construed as no man that is innocent or free from injury or wrong be, by a literal construction, punished or endangered' (cited by Abbott C. J. in *Margate Pier Co. v Hannam* 1819, at 270).

The court's confidence that the literal construction was not what congress had intended was based on a reading of intent of the statute, as that of preventing undesirable, uneducated foreign unskilled labour from entering the United States. The statute was therefore not directed at 'brainworkers', as the legislative history also showed. In particular, the United States was a fundamentally religious, indeed Christian, nation, and it was impossible to believe 'that a congress of the United States intended to make it a misdemeanor for a church of this country to contract for the services of a Christian minister residing in another nation':

> The construction invoked cannot be accepted as correct. It is a case where there was presented a definite evil, in view of which the legislature used general terms with the purpose of reaching all phases of that evil; and thereafter, unexpectedly, it is developed that the general language thus employed is broad enough to reach cases and acts which the whole history and life of the country affirm could not have been intentionally legislated against. It is the duty of the courts, under these circumstances, to say that, however broad the language of the statute may be, the act, although within the letter, is not within the intention of the legislature, and therefore cannot be within the statute. (at 471–2)

For legal realists, and critical legal theorists, cases such as this represent clear evidence for the ease with which rules or canons of interpretation can be applied in a creative manner, given that what counts as an 'absurd' result is so manifestly manipulable if the court wishes to achieve a particular result. This decision is also criticized by Scalia as 'the prototypical case involving the triumph of so-called "legislative intent"' (Scalia 1997: 24).

A contrasting case is *John Angus Smith v United States* 1993, where in effect two potential literal readings were in competition, so none of the rules or canons could apply, even in theory. Smith offered to trade an automatic weapon (MAC-10) for cocaine and was arrested by an undercover police officer. The relevant statute required specific penalties if the defendant 'during and in relation to [a] drug trafficking crime uses . . . a firearm'. The Court of Appeals affirmed Smith's conviction and sentence as the

> plain language imposes no requirement that a firearm be used as a weapon – trading the firearm was a way of using a firearm as understood by the statute. The statute mandated that a defendant who uses a firearm must be sentenced to five years in prison; and if the firearm is a machinegun or is fitted with a silencer – as in this case – the sentence is thirty years. Case law conflicted on the interpretation of this statute, with the Court of Appeals for the Ninth Circuit holding for example that trading a gun was not 'use of a firearm' (*United States v Phelps* 877 F.2d 28 (1989)).
>
> (*United States v John Angus Smith* 1992, at 3)

The Supreme Court confirmed the decision, on the grounds that any non-technical word or a word not specifically defined in the statute should be construed 'in accord with its ordinary or natural meaning'. The majority quoted definitions from *Webster* (2nd edition, 1939) and *Black's Law Dictionary* (6th edition, 1990) in support of its claim that 'to use' had a range of meanings including 'to employ', 'to utilize', 'to derive service from'. The words 'as a weapon' did not appear on the statute: 'Had congress intended the narrow construction . . . it could so have indicated' (at 229). The majority recognized that the ordinary meaning of 'uses a firearm' included the use of a firearm as a weapon, but argued that this did not exclude other uses.

The dissenting opinion was led by Scalia (in a court which divided 6–3). He used the analogy between using a cane as an adornment in the hallway, i.e. to show that some 'uses' lay outside the normal scope of the verb (at 242): 'When someone asks, "Do you use a cane?" he is not inquiring whether you have your grandfather's silverhandled walking stick on display in the hall; he wants to know whether you *walk* with a cane'. The principle of 'lenity' required that where a criminal statute is ambiguous the court should use narrow construction in favour of the defendant. However the majority argued that '[t]he mere possibility of articulating a narrower construction, however, does not by itself make the rule of lenity applicable', since not only did the petitioner's use of a MAC-10 fall 'squarely within the common usage and dictionary definitions of the terms 'uses a firearm', 'but Congress affirmatively demonstrated that it meant to include transactions like petitioner's as "using a firearm" by so employing those terms in §924(d)', where both belligerent and non-belligerent 'uses' for firearms are criminalized, including items of 'barter or commerce'.

The dissent argued that the majority had failed to 'grasp the distinction between how a word *can be* used and how it is *ordinarily is* used, so that to speak of using a weapon is to speak of using it for 'its distinctive purpose', as opposed to scratching one's head (at 242): 'The ordinary meaning of "uses a firearm" does *not* include using it as an article of commerce. I think it perfectly obvious, for example, that the objective falsity requirement would not be satisfied if a witness answered "no" to a prosecutor's inquiry whether he had ever "used a firearm", even though he had once sold his grandfather's Enfield rifle to a collector' (at 242, fn. 1). Disputing the majority's reading of §924(d), the dissent argues that '[s]tretching language in order to write a more effective statute than Congress devised is not an exercise we should indulge in. But in any case, the ready ability to use a gun that is at hand as a weapon is perhaps one of the reasons the statute sanctions not only *using* a firearm, but *carrying* one. Here, however, the Government chose not to indict under that provision' (at 247, fn. 4). For Scalia, this decision was literal-minded nonsense, since the ordinary contextually available meaning of the word 'uses', combined with the principle of 'lenity', gave a clear right answer in this case.

Scalia (1997: 23) cited *Smith v United States* to illustrate the distinction between 'textualism' and 'strict contructionism': '[a] text should not be construed strictly, it should not be construed leniently; it should be construed reasonably'. In this case, a 'proper textualist' would have voted to acquit. Textualism is viewed by Scalia as a check on the misuse of implied legislative intent as a cover for unelected judges to usurp the legislative branch. Indeterminacy theories are dismissed as 'nihilistic' (Scalia 1997: 24): 'But while the good textualist is not a literalist, neither is he a nihilist. Words do have a limited range of meanings, and no interpretation that goes beyond that range is permissible.'

* * *

This new textualism is at the head of a trend for the United States Supreme Court to make greater and greater use of dictionaries. This has involved assigning to the dictionary a significantly enhanced theoretical role. Traditionally the dictionary was used as a means of refreshing the judge's memory about the meaning of a word 'or to provide potential meanings from which the Court would select based on statutory purpose, legislative intent, common sense, or some other contextual argument' (Werbach 1994: 1439–40). The Court first took judicial notice of the use of a dictionary for establishing 'the meanings of words in the vernacular language' more than fifty years after it began consulting dictionaries (Thumma and Kirchmeier 1999: 246). The question of when it was appropriate to rely on the dictionary was raised in relation to uncertainty about whether the language in question (*mineral, ore, mine*) was 'technical' or 'words of common speech, and as such, their interpretation is within the judicial knowledge and therefore a matter of law' such that *Webster's* dictionary could be employed (*Marvel v Merritt* 1885, cited in Thumma and Kirchmeier 1999: 246). Historically, judges vary greatly in the frequency of their use of the dictionary, but Scalia is the most prolific in a Supreme Court where the justices are all using the dictionary (both general and legal) more than their predecessors (Thumma and Kirchmeier 1999: 262).

Werbach argues that in recent decades the US Supreme Court has been using dictionaries 'as the focal point of the interpretative inquiry' and has 'relegated arguments about policy, history or structure to a secondary role' (Werbach 1994: 1440). Dictionaries however are 'neither as neutral nor as reductive as the Court supposes them to be, and they do not provide the kind of meaning the Court seeks to determine' (Werbach 1994: 1445). The problem with dictionaries is two-fold. Firstly, they are sources external to the legal process and not 'perfect repositories of the ordinary meaning of statutory terms' (Werbach 1994: 1445). This does not disqualify them altogether but it does undermine them in this primary role: '[o]ne of the most significant flaws of dictionaries as interpretative tools is the imperfect relationship of dictionaries to statutory context' (Werbach 1994: 1449). A contextualist position is put forward: '[t]he essence of words can never be described fully in the absence of contextual cues; in fact, some theorists have argued that meaning, as we understand it, does not exist without context. Consequently, no dictionary can completely capture the particular historical and textual framework of a statutory term' (Werbach 1994: 1449).

The second objection raised is the 'fundamental indeterminacy' of dictionaries, in that dictionaries often provide more than one meaning for a term, and in any case do not agree among themselves. Use of the dictionary is therefore subjective, and does not subtract from the overall subjectivity of the legal process (Werbach 1994: 1446). The Court has failed to use the dictionary in a consistent or principled manner, using a wide range of general dictionaries in addition to *Black*'s law dictionary. There is also inconsistency which reflects an ambiguity in textualism's understanding of the status of the text both as historical artifact (embedded in a particular historical context) and authoritative text directed at a contemporary readership. This calls into question the extent to which judges are actually employing dictionaries 'for ascertaining ordinary meaning'; many of the textualists are on the political right and 'can use dictionaries subjectively either to concretize or to blur statutory or constitutional terms, without abandoning the veneer of textual objectivity' (Werbach 1994: 1448).

Citing the case of *Nix v Hedden* 1893, Werbach further points out that dictionary definitions may run directly counter to popular understandings of statutory language. In that case the issue at stake was whether a tomato was a fruit or a vegetable. The court preferred the ordinary understanding of tomatoes as vegetables rather than the technical botanical classification reflected in the dictionary. The note sees this as exemplifying the correct methodology, namely seeking 'to determine the appropriateness of a definition for the particular statutory context'. In *Nixon v United States* 1993 the Chief Justice defined the word *sole* 'only by reference to Webster's Third New International Dictionary and ignored arguments that looked at the term's usage in relation to the structure of the Constitution'; in *Chapman v United States* 1991, the Chief Justice used 'an abstract technical definition to reach the awkward conclusion that blotter paper soaked with LSD is a "mixture"' (Werbach 1994: 1450–1).

Much the same argument is made by Thumma and Kirchmeier (1999: 264–75), who state that there are 'few articulated principles to provide guidance to the Court's use of dictionaries', i.e. selecting which word is in need of definition, the appropriate type of dictionary and specific dictionary and edition within that type; e.g. should the dictionary be contemporaneous with the enactment of the statute? (Thumma and Kirchmeier 1999: 299). They argue that the dictionary should be used at the outset of the analysis rather than as a tool for resolving legal questions as these involve questions of 'context, conduct, purpose, history and other similar factors' (Thumma and Kirchmeier 1999: 301).

Historically, the use of dictionaries has been rather limited in cases where the interpretation of the United States Constitution has been at issue. Justice Holmes wrote in *Gompers v United States* 1914 that the provisions of the constitution 'were not mathematical formulas having their essence in their form; they are organic, living institutions transplanted from English soil' whose significance was 'vital not formal' and 'not to be gathered by taking the words and a dictionary, but by considering their origin and the line of their growth' (cited in Thumma and Kirchmeier 1999: 277).

One underlying issue is whether a case hinges on the 'ordinary' meaning of a word or not, and how this determination is made. One can look at an English case like *Adler v George* 1964, which is taught to beginning law students studying problems of statutory interpretation. The Official Secrets Act 1920 (UK) s. 3 stated: 'No person in the vicinity of any prohibited place shall obstruct, knowingly mislead or otherwise interfere with or impede, the chief officer or a superintendent or other officer of police, or any member of His Majesty's forces engaged on guard, sentry, patrol, or other similar duty in relation to the prohibited place. . . .' A protester was arrested *inside* a military facility and charged under the act. The question for the court was whether 'in the vicinity' also included the meaning 'inside'. The court found the defendant guilty, even though it is hard to make this case in the abstract: if one considers a cat inside a box, it would be odd to say of such a cat that it was 'in the vicinity of the box'. But this raises a further question about the distinction between something being 'literally false' or merely a potentially misleading or usual characterization (see discussion of *Bronston v United States*, above). Are we dealing in such a case with the ordinary definition of the word *vicinity*, or are we looking at a specifically legal usage within a statute? Does recognizing the legal context mean that we are required to take the overall purpose of the statute into account, and thus make the definitional-interpretative determination from the point of view of what the statute would regard as the right answer, i.e. that national security should be protected?

Whether such cases can in fact be taken as involving purely ordinary language is unclear, not least because there is no way to operationalize the concept of 'ordinary language', except by using a non-specialist dictionary to provide definitions. Judges may get into arguments about whether they are using terms in their ordinary everyday meaning alone or with a special legal significance. In *R v Caldwell*, Lord Edmund-Davies (dissenting) rejected an attempt to ground a legal term (*recklessness*) in everyday usage:

> I have to say that I am in respectful, but profound, disagreement. The law in action compiles its own dictionary. In time, what was originally the common coinage of speech acquires a different value in the pocket of the lawyer than when in the layman's purse. Professor Kenny [in *Outlines of Criminal Law*] used lawyers' words in a lawyer's sense to express his distillation of an important part of the established law relating to *mens rea*, and he did so in a manner accurate not only in respect of the law as it stood in 1902 but also as it has been applied in countless cases ever since, both in the United Kingdom and in other countries where the common law prevails. (at 23)

Once a word is used in a statute, its interpretation is in some sense dependent on a reading of that statute as a whole, and the case law that surrounds it. Further, case law will offer in effect an evolving definition of terms like *recklessness*. Judges will make yes–no judgements about whether a particular set of actions falls under the category or not, and that accumulation of 'fact patterns' and judgements is then considered for relevance and for underlying principles when the court is faced with a new scenario. In this sense, even statutory language which is defined or the interpretation of which is constrained within the statute yields to the case law which has interpreted a particular section, phrase or term. It is therefore in principle not possible to understand a section of a statute from a plain reading of its language, if there is an accumulation of case law which has interpreted it. But it is open to a court to reinvigorate the plain or 'ordinary' language of the statute if the court feels that this throws light on a particular case.

* * *

The question of definition is at the centre of Hart's most celebrated contribution to legal theory, namely his discussion of the 'penumbra of uncertainty' which he perceives as surrounding a core of certainty in word meaning (Hart 1994). In a social order constructed in part from a set of prescriptive rules or norms laid down in writing, where there is a requirement that the decision of the arbitrator must cohere with or at least not contradict decisions taken in the past (unless they are being explicitly overruled) as well as principles derived from those decisions, there will arise situations where the application of the rule to a particular set of facts is problematic. These are known as 'hard cases' and the attempt to solve these problems gives rise to issues of interpretative methodology and definition.

A municipal ordinance prohibiting 'taking vehicles into the city park' yields a set of core or clear cases (car, motorcycle) and a set of marginal cases (baby carriages, roller skates, skateboards, etc.). For Hart, the 'open texture' of law means that in hard cases judges have to use their discretion and balance various policy considerations, whereas in 'clear cases' they can simply apply the language and linguistic categories of the relevant legal textual authority:

> In all fields of experience, not only that of rules, there is a limit, inherent in the nature of language, to the guidance which general language can provide. There will indeed be plain cases constantly recurring in similar contexts to which general expressions are clearly applicable ('If anything is a vehicle a motor-car is one') but there will also be cases where it is not clear whether they apply or not. ('Does "vehicle" used here include bicycles, airplanes, roller skates?') The latter are fact-situations, continually thrown up by nature or human invention, which possess only some of the features of the plain cases but others which they lack. Canons of 'interpretation' cannot eliminate, through they can diminish, these uncertainties; for these canons are themselves general rules for the use of language, and make use of general terms which themselves require interpretation. They cannot, any more than other rules, provide for their own interpretation. The plain case, where the general terms seem to need no interpretation and where the recognition of instances seems unproblematic or 'automatic', are only the familiar ones, constantly recurring in similar contexts, where there is a general agreement in judgments as to the applicability of the classifying terms. (Hart 1994: 126)

Fundamental to debate about legal interpretation is the question of 'hard cases'. An influential model for understanding the distinction between 'clear' and 'hard' cases was laid out by Hart. Hart's general position was that there is a core of certainty surrounded by a 'penumbra of uncertainty' attaching to any rule:

> All rules involve recognizing or classifying particular cases as instances of general terms, and in the case of everything which we are prepared to call a rule it is possible to distinguish clear central cases, where it certainly applies and others where there are reasons for both asserting and denying that it applies. Nothing can eliminate this duality of a core of certainty and a penumbra of doubt when we are engaged in bringing particular situations under general rules. (Hart 1994: 123)

The metaphor of the 'penumbra' has a substantial lineage in legal writing (Henly 1987). Hart is generally viewed as deriving his ideas on language and 'open texture' in part from Friedrich Waismann's *Principles of Linguistic Philosophy*, itself an attempt to formalize and develop Wittgenstein's philosophy of language. Bix quotes this comment by way of illustration:

> The idea of a closed system of laws lasting for all time, and able to solve any imaginable conflict, is a Utopian fantasy which has no foundation to stand upon. In actual fact every system of law has gaps which are, as a rule, noticed and filled out only when they are brought to light by particular events. Similarly we must admit that grammar is incomplete, and that should the circumstances arise we would make it more complete by introducing new rules to provide for such situations. No language is prepared for all possibilities. To deplore the insufficiency of language would be merely misguided. (Bix 1993: 12, quoting Waismann 1965: 76)

Waismann (1965: 222) makes what Bix describes as the same point, this time in relation to definition, i.e. whether there is any possibility of providing 'anything like an exhaustive definition – a definition that limits the concept in all possible directions':

> Try as we may, no concept is outlined in such a way that there is no room for any doubt. We introduce a concept and limit in *some* directions; we say, for example, 'This is gold' in contrast to silver, platinum, etc. This suffices for most practical purposes, and we do not probe any further. We *forget* that there are other directions in which we have not limited our concept. And if we did, we could imagine hundreds of situations which would necessitate new limitations. Are our concepts therefore incomplete, inexact? But what would then be an exact concept? . . . A concept is good if it fulfills the purpose for which it has been devised. (Waismann 1965: 223)

Bix distinguishes between Waismann's and Hart's conceptions of 'open texture', on the grounds that Waismann's examples are more extreme ('cats growing to gigantic sizes and people disappearing'), whereas Hart's exceptional or difficult cases are well within the compass of ordinary human experience (Bix 1993: 17). One criticism of Hart's concept of a stable core of meaning came from Fuller (1958), arguing that a rule such as 'no vehicles in the park' if applied strictly would exclude a war monument made up of a working truck. There was no core of certainty which could be isolated. However, Bix argues that this does not disturb the notion of core meaning (the truck is still a core example of 'vehicle') but this example proves that 'the strict application of rules sometimes produces absurd results (or, at the least, results inconsistent with the rules' purposes)' (Bix 1993: 30).

Bix denies that Wittgenstein takes an indeterminate view of language, pointing to his concept of the 'grammar' of an expression: 'For Wittgenstein, the clarity of clear cases derives from certain background facts regarding agreement in judgments, agreement in social context, and stability of the world'. However Bix does not follow Langville in arguing that Wittgenstein's evocation of clear language games (where the only puzzle is that created by asking questions that stretch the grammar of ordinary expressions) provides an answer to the sceptical critic of law (Bix 1993: 46). For Bix, the difference between a rule such as 'add 2' and legal rules is that 'law is a reflective activity: the participants consider, discuss, and argue over how they should go on. . . . Legal practice, locally and generally, *is* subject to criticism and *is* in need of further justification' (Bix 1993: 48).

From an integrationist perspective, Hart's conception of a linguistic 'core of certainty' surrounded by a 'penumbra of uncertainty' is an all-too-familiar but unhappy compromise between trying simultaneously to adopt and reject a fixed-code model for languages. It is unhappy, in the first place, because Hart's discussion lacks the theoretical sophistication to make it clear which of various possible positions he is adopting. He does not say, for example, as many linguists do, that certainty belongs to *la langue* and uncertainty to the vicissitudes of *la parole.* Nor is it clear that, if he were familiar with that Saussurean distinction, he would want to make that claim. So where exactly does he stand? His problem is that if he holds, as integrationist do, that *any* feature of context may affect what the meaning of a word is taken to be, there is actually no 'core of certainty' for the 'penumbra of uncertainty' to surround. But if he clings to the notion of a 'core of certainty', then he has to spell out where certainty stops and uncertainty begins. And this he fails to do. So in the end his contention is no more coherent than that of a monarch who claims that the frontiers of the kingdom are established beyond doubt, but cannot, when asked, say exactly where they lie.

* * *

How easily any everyday word may unexpectedly become legally contentious is illustrated by the term *vehicle.* One celebrated case is *McBoyle v US* 1931. McBoyle was convicted of transporting across a state line a stolen airplane, and the judgement was upheld by the Circuit Court of Appeals for the Tenth Circuit. The Supreme Court then considered an appeal in relation to whether the National

Motor Vehicle Theft Act (1919) applied to aircraft. The relevant statute stated (s. 2) that '(a) The term "motor vehicle" shall include an automobile, automobile truck, automobile wagon, motor cycle, or any other self-propelled vehicle not designed for running on rails'.

Justice Holmes conceded that the term *vehicle* could be and had been used to include aircraft in some legislation (at 26): 'No doubt etymologically it is possible to use the word to signify a conveyance working on land, water or air, and sometimes legislation extends the use in that direction . . . But in everyday speech "vehicle" calls up the picture of a thing moving on land.' Legislative intent gave no guidance: 'Airplanes were well known in 1919, when this statute was passed; but it is admitted that they were not mentioned in the reports or in the debates in Congress.' On balance, Justice Holmes held that the line should be drawn clearly, on grounds that (at 27) 'it is reasonable that a fair warning should be given to the world in language that the common world will understand, of what the law intends to do if a certain line is passed'. Holmes argued that the rule laid down 'in words that evoke in the common mind only the picture of vehicles moving on land'. The court should not extend this to aircraft, 'simply because it may seem to us that a similar policy applies, or upon the speculation that, if the legislature had thought of it, very likely broader words would have been used' (at 27).

A more recent *vehicle* case, *Garner v Burr* 1951, is discussed by Endicott (Endicott 2002). In that case, the offence in question was using a vehicle on the road without pneumatic tyres. Burr had equipped a chicken coop with iron wheels and pulled it behind his tractor. He was acquitted by the magistrates on the apparent grounds that the chicken coop was not a vehicle. The appeal court reversed this decision, criticizing the magistrates for their overly narrow interpretation of the word *vehicle*:

> It is true that, according to the dictionary definition, a 'vehicle' is primarily to be regarded as a means of conveyance provided with wheels or runners and used for the carriage of persons or goods.

While nothing was actually being carried in the chicken coop, 'I think that the Act is clearly aimed at anything which will run on wheels which is being drawn by a tractor or other motor-vehicle' (at 33).

While one can read these contrasting decisions as drawing a different balance between a lenient reading (where criminal liability is only created if the language of the statute is unequivocal) and a reading of parliament's intent (namely to protect the surface of the roads), as Endicott points out the Chief Justice actually stated that the magistrates should have concluded that the chicken coop was a vehicle within the meaning of the Road Traffic Act (Endicott 2002: 6). Endicott identifies a paradox here: 'competent speakers of the English language presumably share a knowledge of the meaning of the word "vehicle", yet they disagree – apparently sincerely – over how to use the word' (Endicott 2002: 6).

This paradox only arises however on the presumption that speakers of a language have shared knowledge of meanings of the words of that language. It is this that generates a 'puzzle' as to how people who know the meaning of a word can nevertheless disagree about how to use it. Endicott seeks to resolve the paradox by defining that shared knowledge in a more abstract way: 'what speakers of the English language share is an ability to use words like "vehicle" in a way that depends on the context' (Endicott 2002: 6). The judge was correct that the dictionary definition could not answer the question posed in the case 'because the purpose of a dictionary definition is to point the reader to features of the use of the word that can be important in a variety of more-or-less analogical ways in various contexts', so the shared meaning (which Endicott seems to identify with the dictionary meaning) 'does not tell the reader whether a more-or-less analogical extension of the word to chicken-coop on wheels is warranted or unwarranted by the meaning of the word' (Endicott 2002: 6). Endicott offers this further formulation:

> Another way of stating this resolution of the apparent paradox is to distinguish between the meaning of a word (which the magistrates and the appeal judges all knew) and a decision about how to interpret a communicative act using the word (over which they disagreed). What the courts in *Garner v Burr* shared was a knowledge of the meaning of the word 'vehicle', and what they disagreed over was the effect of the statute. (Endicott 2002: 6)

It is important for Endicott in this discussion that an underlying consensus model of linguistic knowledge be preserved. Quite why this should be so important is unclear, since in the face of these facts one could adopt a much simpler explanation, namely that there is no particular underlying consensus about the meanings of words, because the routines of everyday interaction do not require it. Once a consensus is required, i.e. where there is a dispute or a contentious 'hard case', it becomes clear that there is no easy way to arrive at one. It would be a strange kind of shared knowledge that was always unavailable at the very moment it was required.

One possible conclusion to be drawn from these cases is that hard cases are decided on what are at best arbitrary grounds, or on grounds that have nothing to do with the language of the relevant authoritative text. But it is important to be clear that there is frequently no consensus as to whether a particular case is hard or not, and no meta-rule or even procedure which can answer this question independent of the issues that arise in the particular case. The integrational position is that each case has in effect its own interpretative politics, and the distinctions that are drawn between ordinary language and legal language, or between literal and purposive interpretation, 'clear' and 'hard' cases, cannot be mapped neatly from one case to another. Even within the terms of a model of an autonomous linguistic-legal system, the boundary between clear and hard cases can be shown to be contentious. Once we accept that 'there is no clear dividing line between clear cases and hard cases' (MacCormick 1994: 197), we can imagine a number of marginal situations. It might for example be that in a given case there is general assent that the case falls into a grey area between hard and clear. Perhaps the case looked at first sight to be clear, but on a second inspection an element of doubt creeps in. Or it might describe a situation where there is fundamental disagreement (e.g. among a panel of judges) as to whether the case is actually hard or clear, but with all agreed however that the case is one or the other. Another way of looking at this question is through the simple observation that judges who decide that a case is 'clear' or routine 'also make a judgment' (Fletcher 1996: 58).

* * *

Lawyers are fond of pointing to the gap between commonsense understandings of everyday terms and their legal meaning and import. One good example of this is the term *land*, which for the land lawyer represents fundamentally a bundle of abstract relations (rights, privileges, duties, etc.) rather than a physical entity which can be owned absolutely. As a matter of legal principle, the Crown owns all land in England and Wales, so all other forms of 'ownership' are inherently relative to that underlying legal reality. *The New Oxford Dictionary of English* (2001) defines *land* simply as 'the part of the earth's surface that is not covered by water, as opposed to the sea or the air', though it also gives a subsidiary (and partially circular) definition: 'an expanse of land; an area of ground, especially in terms of its ownership or use'. The Law of Property Act 1925, s. 205 (1)(ix) states:

> Land includes land of any tenure, and mines and minerals, whether or not held apart from the surface, buildings or parts of buildings (whether the division is horizontal, vertical or made in any other way) and other corporeal hereditaments; also a manor, advowson, and a rent and other incorporeal hereditaments, and an easement, right, privilege, or benefit in, over, or derived from land; but not an undivided share in land; and 'mines and minerals' include any strata or seam of minerals or substances in or under any land, and powers of working and getting the same but not an undivided share thereof; and 'manor' includes a lordship, and reputed manor or lordship; and 'hereditament' means any real property which on any intestacy occurring before the commencement of this Act might have devolved upon an heir.

This falls short of an attempt at definition, but it does contain within it subsidiary clarifications and definitions of some of the key terms. Even given the fundamentally abstract nature of land, there is a key distinction made between the physical or corporeal and the non-physical or incorporeal. Blackstone's *Commentary* stated that 'corporeal hereditaments' were comprised of 'substantial and permanent objects' which 'affect the senses' (cited in Gray and Gray 2005: 15). These would include not only the physical soil, rocks, etc. but buildings, trees and other permanent or immovable features. They do not include flowing water. Gray and Gray (2005: 13fn.) quote Ward L. J. in *Thames Heliports Plc v LB of Tower Hamlets* 1997, at 177) as follows: 'No ordinary users of the language will be surprised by the conclusion that water is not land'.

But this appeal to the ordinary language user is disingenuous, since there are large parts of the language and theory of land law which might well surprise the ordinary language user, starting with the proposition that the holder of the freehold title does not actually own the land in question absolutely. The idea that a building or other 'fixture' is itself land (*superficies solo cedit*), as opposed to a 'chattel' is unfamiliar to the ordinary language user. The boundary between fixtures and chattels is determined by tests and distinctions grounded in case law which are foreign to the ordinary language user, such as the extent to which the object is fastened to 'annexed' to the land, whether the object was intended primarily to benefit the use of land, or is an object 'of intrinsic enjoyment', etc. (see Gray and Gray 2005: 35ff.).

In addition to this and other statutory definitions of *land*, there are free-standing maxims, most famously: *Cuius est solum eius est usque ad coelum et ad inferos* ('whoever owns the land owns everything reaching up to the very heavens and down to the depths of the earth'). As a definition of what it means to own land, this is seriously deficient. It has been declared to be 'worthless as a statement of contemporary law', but able to serve 'as a crude approximation of the extent of the rights pertaining to owners of land and of the extent of ownership which is transferred by conveyance' (Gray and Gray 2005: 15). One question that this raises is why one would teach, cite and discuss a maxim which offers only a 'crude approximation' of what is generally recognized as the contemporary legal situation.

If the meaning or definition of the term *land* is embedded in case law, and that case law is neither 'uniform nor consistent' (Gray and Gray 2005: 43), then there can be no static or decontextualized definition of *land* which is simply operationalized in order to determine the result of a particular case. The purpose of definitions and maxims then is not to be applied strictly to the facts of each case, but to counter the centrifugal forces which pull the definition of key terms in different directions, as lines of cases provide their own specialized definitions. Law, in particular common law, can thus be understood as undergoing a continual process of fragmentation as different areas develop autonomously, and within those areas, particular lines of cases follow a certain line of reasoning. At the same time, judges may look across from one area or from one line of cases to another, and are also continually aware of the overall coherence of law as a set of definitions, as interpretative practice, practical reasoning and as moral discourse. In this process, 'ordinary language' or extra-legal meanings are inevitably involved, as a force for greater coherence, at the same time as technical discussion and case law may lead to increased fragmentation.

* * *

A particular line of cases may develop a set of definitions of everyday English words, as well as a specific metalanguage. Trust law is centrally concerned with particular forms of certainty, and one of the so-called 'three certainties' is the question of whether the settler of a trust has identified with sufficient accuracy the property involved and the beneficiaries who are to receive it. Some particular words that have come under close scrutiny in this regard are *friend, relative, customer.* If one leaves one's estate to one's 'old friends', is this sufficiently clear and unambiguous to allow the trustee to carry out one's instructions? In dealing with such terms, the courts do not work from single, overall definitions, but rather require different levels of certainty dependent on the type of trust being created.

Trusts vary in the amount of discretion which they allow the trustee in distributing the benefits of the trust. In the case of a fixed trust, where there the trustee has no discretion, the so-called 'class ascertainably' or 'fixed list' applies to the determination of the beneficiaries, since the trustee is under an absolute obligation to distribute the gift and therefore must know in advance how many individuals qualify for a share. This test was previously also applied to discretionary trusts, i.e. to trusts where the trustees have substantial discretion in the distribution of the benefits (*IRC v Broadway Cottages* 1955). In the case of a so-called 'mere power', where the trustee can decide whether to exercise a power without being legally obliged to do so (though the trustee is required in a reasonable manner to consider from time to time whether to use the power), the test was determined in *Re Gestetner Settlement* 1953 to be an 'individual ascertainability' test, otherwise known as an 'is or is not test'. The House of Lords ruled in *Re Gulbenkian* 1968 that it was not required that in the case of a power that the trustee be able to draw up a complete list of beneficiaries under the trust, but rather that it was necessary to be able to say of any individual that they did or did not fall under the trust. The problem with this approach is that, if it is strictly applied, a single problematic case will invalidate the trust.

In *MacPhail v Doulton* 1971 the House of Lords considered a deed providing for trustees to make grants at their absolute discretion 'to or for the benefit of any of the officers and employees or ex-officers or ex-employees of the company or to any relatives or dependents or relatives of any such persons'. The court held that this deed created a discretionary trust and not a power, but decided that the test for certainty should be the same as for a power, i.e. the 'is or is not' test of *Re Gulbenkian.* In *Re Baden's Deed Trust (No 2)* 1973 which was a further stage in the *MacPhail v Doulton* case (also known as *Re Baden No 1*), the Court of Appeal considered the 'is or is not' test in detail, applying a distinction set out by Lord Wilberforce in *MacPhail v Doulton* between the 'conceptual' or 'linguistic' uncertainty that may attach to a general term like *relative* or *employee* and the evidential uncertainty that may arise in trying to identify members of the category, even where the category itself is deemed conceptually clear. It was argued for the settlor's personal representatives that following the test laid down in *Re Gulbenkian* the trust was invalid for uncertainty:

> The appellants contend that there is conceptual uncertainty as regards 'dependants' and 'relatives' and therefore the Gulbenkian test is not satisfied; alternatively, the test applied by Brightman J. is not satisfied. Conceptual uncertainty arises (a) where the trustees are required to make an evaluative judgment, e.g., as in In re Leek, decd. [1969] 1 Ch. 563 where power was given to benefit persons to whom the deceased was under a moral obligation, or e.g., to benefit 'handsome barristers'; (b) where the concept itself is inherently vague, e.g., 'old friends'; or (c) where the concept itself is clear but there is no way in which the trustees can say whether it applies or not because the evidence is missing, e.g., a power to benefit 'persons with whom the donor had ever travelled in a railway coach.' Linguistic or semantic uncertainty does not invalidate a trust provided that the court is able to give some interpretation to it. The word 'dependants' is conceptually uncertain under category (b) above and that invalidates the trust. (at 13)

Counsel quoted Lord Wilberforce from *MacPhail v Doulton* (*Re Baden No 1*) to the effect that (at 13) 'I do not think that a discretionary trust for "relatives" even of a living person falls within "the category" where the meaning of the words used is clear but the definition of beneficiaries is so hopelessly wide as not to form "anything like a class" so that the trust is administratively unworkable.' He cited cases where *dependant* had been ruled too vague, or a clear definition had been supplied in the deed. As for the word *relative*:

> even if the concept is clear there is uncertainty whether any given individual is a member of the class. There is no certain stopping point as to how far 'relative' goes and therefore it is not possible to say whether any given individual is or is not a 'relative.' The use of the word 'relatives' is fatal if the Gulbenkian [1970] A. C. 508 test is to be applied. . . . The word 'relatives' can go back ad infinitum; unless it is stated how far back in cases of relationship the class is not defined. (at 14)

Against this, it was argued:

> The trust deed was for the benefit of the company's officers and employees. It would be surprising if the inclusion of 'dependants' and 'relatives' should result in the deed being void. The term 'relatives' is certain as a concept. Any uncertainty as to who is a relative is a pure question of fact. If the concept is certain the factual or evidential difficulties do not matter. Alternatively, if 'relatives' is not sufficiently certain in itself, the courts have always given it a workable meaning in order to validate a trust, and the proper course would be to so construe it as to make it workable in such sense. The term 'dependants' is similarly certain as a concept. (at 14)

The meaning 'all persons claiming descent through a common ancestor' was conceptually certain. Since this was a discretionary trust, there was no need to allow possible uncertainties at the margin of the concept to invalidate the trust:

> In a trust such as the present there is no reason to give any artificial narrow construction to the word 'relatives' because the court is not obliged to distribute equally between all objects if the trustees fail to distribute. . . . Numerative certainty of the beneficiaries is not required. There is no reason why 'relatives' should not be given its ordinary and proper meaning. Where there is a discretionary power to distribute the test is: 'can the beneficiary be shown to be a relative?' (at 15)

One suggestion was that the *relative* be understood as 'next of kin', i.e. that a legally better defined term be used to define the more general, ordinary term.

Sachs L. J. commented (at 16) that 'two constructions of "relatives", one wide and the other restricted to next-of-kin' had been suggested and asked: 'Do we have to decide which one should be applied? If the court finds that the widest meaning is conceptually certain it is not necessary to decide the other; but if the court comes to the conclusion that the widest meaning is too wide for certainty then the court may say whether the restricted meaning is acceptable.' He concluded that the term was conceptually certain, and noted that the courts were generally unwilling 'to hold that a settlement which has been deliberately made is and was from the start invalid for uncertainty'. If conceptual certainty could be established, then the bequest could not be defeated just because there were difficult questions of fact: 'The suggestion that such trusts could be invalid because it was impossible to prove of a given individual that he was *not* in the relevant class is almost unarguable'. In reply, counsel for the appellants argued that:

> The term 'relatives' is not within this definite class and the court cannot direct an inquiry as to whether a person is a relative or not. That term does not define a class and is a conceptual uncertainty. The test is whether the person is 'in' or 'out'. If the trust is invalid because of the conceptual uncertainty of 'relatives' in its widest meaning the court cannot escape declaring it invalid by giving it a narrower meaning such as 'presumptive next-of-kin.' It would not be right to do so because it would thereby cut out intended beneficiaries and also bring in the Crown as a beneficiary if there is no next-of-kin. (at 17)

On the word *dependant*, there was 'a wide area of doubt':

> Is the class one which includes only dependants of a living person? Does the word conjure up a clear conception in all cases? If there is a fuzzy line there is uncertainty and the deed is void. It may be tempting to say that the trustees can make the trust work despite its imperfections or that the uncertain bits can be cut out. If the trustees were always honest and competent persons this might be so, but trustees are not always reasonable and not always honest and

> therefore the trust must be clearly defined so that the beneficiaries can intervene if not properly administered. If it were permitted to cut out the uncertain parts this would change the substance of the settlement and the court has no power to do so. There is no half-way house. If it is not certain whether any given individual is 'in' or 'out' the trust is invalid. (at 17)

Sachs L. J. was however unsympathetic to attempts to use definitional difficulties in relation to *dependant* to undermine the trust, arguing (at 19) that the deed should be looked at from the point of view of a businessman 'seeking to advance the welfare of the employees of his firm' and those connected with them: 'He would not necessarily be looking at the words he uses with the same eyes as those of a man making a will. Accordingly, whether a court is considering the concept implicit in relevant words, or whether it is exercising the function of a court of construction, it should adopt that same practical and common-sense approach which . . . would be used by an employer setting up such a fund.' The court was not sitting primarily 'as a court of construction' required to give exhaustive definitions of the words 'dependant' and 'relative'. That is to say, even if the court decided that the term was conceptually or semantically clear, and the widest meaning attributable to those words did not produce uncertainty, it was not required to provide a complete definition of the term.

As regards the word *relative*, Sachs cited one definition which required the tracing of 'legal descent from a common ancestor' (at 22). Dismissing the argument that this was evidentially unworkable, the requirement of proof soon narrowed down the field: 'Further, a settlor using the word "relatives" in the context of this deed (which is not the same context as that of a will) would assume that the trustees would, in the exercise of their discretion, make their selection in a sensible way from the field, however wide' (at 22).

The court was anxious to ground the definitional problem in a practical approach which would select those whom a 'reasonable and honest employee' who would introduce as 'relative', rather than as a 'kinsman' or as a 'distant relative'. However a definition was not required in this case (at 22): 'Indeed, on a construction summons some such definition might emerge for the word "relative" – but that is not relevant to the present appeal, as the widest meaning that has been suggested for that word does not, in my judgment, produce uncertainty.' There was no decided case where a trust had been declared invalid because of uncertainty about the meaning of the word *relative*.

Megaw L. J. argued that there was no particular uncertainty attached to the word *dependant*:

> I do not find any greater uncertainty in it than is inherent in, or can by ingenuity be conjured up in relation to, any ordinary, well understood word. It would be odd indeed, and wholly regrettable, if a word which was regarded as sufficiently certain to be used, without further explanation or definition, for the purposes of an Act of Parliament (see, for example, section 46 (1) (vi) of the Administration of Estates Act 1925) had nevertheless to be

condemned by the courts as being so uncertain as to involve the validity of a trust deed. (at 22)

Megaw then considered the strict application of the 'is or is not test' from *Re Gulbenkian*, which could be taken to imply that if one could not say with certainty that someone was *not* a relative, then the trust must fail, rejecting this as an unreasonable obstacle to the trust. The third judgement by Stamp L. J. adopted a strict view of the 'is or is not test', concurred in finding that the term *relative* was conceptually clear, but defined it as 'next of kin' rather than in terms of 'descent from a common ancestor' (at 29).

In effect, the definitional problems with the terms *dependant* and *relative* were resolved by the court's insistence on the importance of the distinction between conceptual or semantic clarity on the one hand, and evidential issues on the other. This led the courts to insist that there is nothing particularly problematic about such terms. Looking at these cases from the outside, the distinction between conceptual and evidential certainty looks somewhat *ad hoc*, but it works to devolve away from the judges the need to define exactly what these terms mean and allows them to assert that everyday English words have ordinary, clear meanings.

However, one cannot conclude that there is an overall determination or meta-principle at work here: there is 'no evenly applied test' (Hudson 2003: 99). In *Brown v Gould* 1972, a trust to benefit 'old friends' was declared void: 'It was held that if the court cannot determine who an "old friend" is then the trustees will not be able to' (Hudson 2003: 99). In *Sparfax v Dommett* 1972, a trust in favour of 'customers' failed for uncertainty, given among other uncertainties the fact that it was unclear whether someone would have need to have made a purchase, as opposed to just visiting the shop, in order to qualify.

This raises the general issue that any ordinary English word which establishes a social category (*friend, old friend, relative, customer, employee*) might from one point of view be considered conceptually or semantically clear. This is especially true if the court feels it can delegate the evidential or practical stage to a competent, qualified person (see *Re Tuck's Settlement Trust* 1978, where the court or the trustee could be asked who might qualify as having 'married into the Jewish faith'). Equally plausibly, one can argue that these terms are hopelessly vague, when set against a strict 'is or is not test'.

In the case of *Re Barlow's Will Trusts* 1979 the testatrix left a collection of valuable paintings with a direction to the executor 'to allow any member of my family and any friends of mine who may wish to do so to purchase any of such pictures'. The court considered whether this direction was void for uncertainty because the meaning of *friend* was too vague, and the determination of family members too uncertain. It was presented with two possible tests, that of *Re Gulbenkian* and that applied in *Re Allen* 1953, where a gift was valid if it was possible to identify one or more persons who were qualified to receive it, even if there were other uncertain cases. Lord Browne-Wilkinson commented as follows:

> The distinction between the *Gulbenkian* test and the *Re Allen* test is, in my judgment, well exemplified by the word 'friends'. The word has a great range of meanings; indeed, its exact meaning probably varies from person to person. Some would include only those with whom they had been on intimate terms over a long period; others would include acquaintances whom they liked. Indeed, many people, if asked to draw up a complete list of their friends, would probably have some difficulty in deciding whether certain of the people they knew were really 'friends' as opposed to 'acquaintances'. Therefore, if the nature of the gift was such that it was legally necessary to draw up a complete list of 'friends' of the testatrix, or to be able to say of any person that 'he is not a friend', the whole gift would probably fail even as to those who, by any conceivable test, were friends. (at 281)

But since this case could be construed as involving a gift, rather than a bequest in which all members of the class were to be established, the court could give effect to the will. This was not a case of 'linguistic or semantic uncertainty':

> I therefore hold that the disposition does not fail for uncertainty, but that anyone who can prove that by reasonable test he or she must have been a friend of the testatrix is entitled to exercise the option. Without seeking to lay down an exhaustive definition of such test, it may be helpful if I indicate certain minimum requirements: (a) the relationship must have been a long-standing one. (b) The relationship must have been a social relationship as opposed to a business or professional relationship. (c) Although there may have been long periods when circumstances prevented the testatrix and the applicant from meeting, when circumstances did permit they must have met frequently. (at 282)

This point (c) was perhaps an appropriate moment to stop, as the criterion of meeting frequently where possible starts to get the learned judge into difficult definitional terrain: 'If in any case the executors entertain any real doubt as to whether an applicant qualifies, they can apply to the court to decide the issue.'

Browne-Wilkinson also mentions two other cases in which the meaning of the term *friend* was discussed (at 282). In the first, *Re Gibbard's Will Trust* 1967, it was held that the term 'any of my old friends' could be given effect to, since the *Re Allen* test was the appropriate one, whereas *in Re Lloyd's Trust Instruments* (June 24, 1970, unreported, but quoted in *Brown v. Gould* 1972, at 56–7) a trust for 'my old friends' was declared void, on the grounds that friendship 'is a concept with almost infinite shades of meaning'. However this was a trust intended for a whole class, so the more stringent test was appropriate.

What do these and similar cases tell us about the role of definition in law? What is striking here is that judges have held both that the term *friend* can be reasonably clearly defined (and indeed, as we have seen, one judge embarked on a sketch of such a definition) and that the word has 'infinite shades of meaning', and could not be defined accurately enough within the context of the case. There is however no overall contradiction here, since the legal context is different in each case and a different level of precision is required. It makes no sense to talk thus of a general attempt to define *friend* within the law, or within trust law, or even within the law of certainty of object within trust law: we are dealing with localized questions couched in general terms.

There is also a potential distinction in approach between those cases where the intended meaning of a particular phrase is at issue and a case which can be understood as involving definition proper. In *Sprange v Barnard* 1789, a wife left a legacy to her husband 'for his sole use' but 'at his death the remaining part of what is left that he does not want for his own wants and use' was to go a third party. The court held that there was no trust and that the husband took free of the legacy. Such cases are typically understood primarily as involving the court's attempt to understand or clarify the intentions of the testator, rather than general questions of definition (though these may also arise). One would not perhaps understand this case as turning on the definition of *sole use*, in the same way that the judges in the case discussed above felt it necessary to make general comments about the definition of terms like *relative* or *friend*. But arguably those cases also did not ultimately turn on finding a satisfactory decontextualized definition of a term and applying it into the law, even though they were couched in more lexicographic terms. One could say also of *sole use* that it has a great range of meanings. In other words, the courts are constantly moving between (1) analysing language as expressing the particular intentions of an individual on a particular occasion and (2) considering what terms like *friend* mean as a decontextualized question of definition.

Chapter 10

Linguistics, Science and Meaning

One fundamental question in the modern era has been whether law could be a science, and if so, in what sense. As in the history of linguistics, there is a tension here between the idea that the enterprise can be a science on the lines of the natural sciences, or a science but in a distinct form with its own subject matter and methodology. John Austin (1790–1859), appointed the first professor of jurisprudence at University College London in 1827, limited the scope of jurisprudential discussion by reference to a 'command theory of law' (J. W. Harris 1980: 26). He rejected the parallel between judicial law and natural laws, the latter not involving the application of concepts of reason, duty and the will: 'Yet through the misapplication of a *name*, flagrant as the metaphor is, has the field of jurisprudence and morals has been deluged with muddy speculations' (Austin 1879: 90). Austin's view was supported by Karl Pearson in his *Grammar of Science*.

> The civil law involves a command and a duty; the scientific law is a description, not a prescription. The civil law is valid only for a *special* community at a *special* time; the scientific law is valid for *all* normal human beings, and is unchangeable so long as their perceptive faculties remain at their present state of development. (Pearson 1892: 104)

However, commenting on this in the 1930s, Robson (1935: 295) argued that 'eminent contemporary scientists, working in what are regarded as the most severely disciplined and objective departments of study, have seen fit to apply the Command and Obedience concept to the very processes of nature themselves'. For Robson, this possibility was grounded in the fundamental nature of human beings, as there was 'ground for believing that the law is not a chance product but the result of a reasonable impulse innate in human beings, a sociological process arising from the material and spiritual needs of mankind'. Law, like 'other evolutionary processes', was governed by 'its own principles and laws' (Robson 1935: 291).

The figure in American jurisprudence most associated with the promotion of law as science is Christopher Langdell (1826–1906), the first dean of Harvard Law School. For Langdell, case method was a logical enterprise involving both induction and deduction; it was intended to attain generalizability and predictability. Like other sciences, law should thus be able to be in a position to predict events, i.e. the decisions of the courts (Dimock 2001: 204–6).

Frank ([1930] 1970: 284), summarizing Dickinson (1929), gave a sketch of the history of attempts in legal theory to find 'the law behind the law'. Following the eighteenth-century search for a mediating principle in 'natural reason' or 'the reason of the law', the early nineteenth-century theory was that 'popular custom, that social and economic institutions and mores dictate specific legal rules or that the "sense of justice of the people" specifically points to the rule to be applied in any given situation'. The late nineteenth century developed the theory that 'law is an inductive science which can discover, in the precedents, authoritative jural principles capable of demonstrating the objective correctness of the rule to be applied to any new situation which may arise'. This was displaced in the 1920s and 1930s by the conception that there was 'a science of human nature and society in such a sense as to dictate in advance with objective precision and authority the specific legal rule', and the related notion that a coherent body of theories, principles or premises could be discovered behind the operations of the law. Legal realism rejected the idea that 'the law itself supplies a basic scale of values to serve as a standard for all situations', or that the judgements of policy involved in the work of judges can be 'generalized into a coherent system of policy which can be said to underlie the whole law, and dictate all its specific rules' (Frank [1930] 1970: 284).

Realism in legal theory was generally framed as an attack on formalism, sometimes pejoratively termed 'mechanical jurisprudence'. On the formalist model, the judge's function was that of applying 'to an ascertained set of facts a rigidly defined legal formula definitely prescribed as such or exactly deduced from authoritatively prescribed premises'. A definition would thus provide a template for distinguishing entities or states of affairs that fell under it from those that did not. Frank characterized this as 'a slot machine theory of judicial administration' (Frank [1930] 1970: 221): 'the facts being inserted in one end of the machine and the decision, through the use of mechanical logic, coming out at the other end' ([1930] 1970: 223). Other 'realists' saw a sociological or socio-economic policy logic behind decisions, rather than no logic at all. It was possible to seek coherence on a different level, e.g. in the application of sociological method, or in a critique which embedded law within politics, such as those offered by Marxists and feminists, where the coherence or systematicity of law is viewed as a negative or politically oppressive coherence. One can speak of a three-way division within legal theory: pure realism, in which legal decisions may be seen as undetermined, or radically underdetermined; sociological realism in which it is asserted that there is a coherence to legal decision making, but that it cannot be found by looking purely at legal rules and principles; formalism, in which it is asserted that the legal rules and principles do generate or substantially determine legal decision making.

More recent theoretical debates within legal theory continue this disagreement about the basis and nature of adjudication. The realist challenge within law was an attack on notions of law's internal coherence, and involved a denial that there was a well-defined domain of law with its own coherent set of rules. The realists' successors in jurisprudence were interpretative sceptics, influenced by indeterminacy theories found in philosophy and literary deconstruction. Critical Legal Studies was marked by a tension between a radical political agenda and deconstructionist theory of the text and reading praxis, between the postmodern denial of coherence on any level of legal decision making as against an analysis that identifies the priority of ideological and political factors in judicial decision-making.

This is not to say that there are no coherence theorists within contemporary jurisprudence. For example, Ronald Dworkin has argued that law does provide a set of right answers for hard cases, when one looks at judges' decisions within the total context of their commitment to the ideals of law, including principles which are not formally part of positive law (Dworkin 1996). Further, a critique of legal interpretative practice which relies on the indeterminacy of legal language to support an underlying and coherent socio-political critique asserts the coherence of law on one level, even while denying it on another. Between the defence of 'plain meaning' as constraining legal interpretation and indeterminacy can be found diverse attempts to define a partial sphere of legal-linguistic certainty, or to distinguish indeterminacy from 'underdeterminacy' where the outcome in a given legal case is 'constrained by the law, but not determined by it' (Solum 1996: 489). A related distinction is one between cases that have no complete answer versus cases that have no required answer (Bix 1993: 25).

Linguistics would seem to have a good *prima facie* case to mediate in, or at least be relevant to, the definitional and interpretative questions that confront law, given the analogies and links between the disciplines. There is a somewhat patchy history of links between the two disciplines, in spite of an array of conceptual, metaphorical and methodological parallels. M. Jori, for example, makes the following comparison between a legal system and a linguistic system:

> In fact, both are double-faced notions, designating a set of rules and a part of social reality; both notions are under attack for being part of too abstract an approach to the facts that they purport to describe (a language, the law, respectively). The discussion of the concept of a linguistic system has been of direct inspiration to legal theorists; however, the discussion of the concept of a legal system, wholly unknown to linguists, could be of some utility to them, due to some interesting peculiarities of legal rules and systems.
>
> (Jori 1994: 2122)

Debates about the domain and coherence of the object of study feature in both linguistics and legal studies. As in linguistics, some legal theorists separate systematic from non-systematic parts of the object of inquiry. The legal realist Roscoe Pound recognized areas of judicial discretion, the need for flexibility based on unique circumstances, in particular where matters of human conduct were concerned, but nonetheless argued that in matters pertaining to property and commercial or business transactions and contracts, commercial law and the 'creation, incidence and transfer of obligations' then the judge should employ rules 'authoritatively prescribed in advance and mechanically applied' (quoted in Frank

[1930] 1970: 222). Frank argues that both Pound and Dickinson depart from the realist position by drawing a distinction between legal rules and discretion: he sees Dickinson as reasserting a foundationalist theory of law in holding that law is made up entirely of rules developed by the courts, these rules being authoritative and thus distinct from judicial discretion (Frank [1930] 1970: 285–6).

Within linguistics, the defence of partial certainty in questions of legal meaning has in general echoed Hart's model, since the notion of invariant core meanings underlying contextual variants is fundamental to orthodox theories of the linguistic sign within the discipline. Hart's theory implies a large domain of consensus where the linguistic-legal system operates relatively unproblematically, and a smaller domain where marginal cases present problems that require an adjudicator to reach outside the linguistic-legal system proper for their solution, so-called 'second-order justification' (MacCormick 1994: 197).

A recent example of the application of a theory from linguistics to legal questions is Winter (2001), who applies the cognitive theory of conceptual metaphor associated with George Lakoff to law to defend a 'relative indeterminacy' thesis according to which:

> Legal decisionmaking does reproduce in predictable patterns that are no more or less regular, no more or less susceptible to study and categorization than any other human phenomenon. On the other hand, there is nothing about this process that is 'objective' or 'determinate' in the way promised by the analytic logic that dominates the surface of the discipline.
>
> (Winter 2001: 3–4)

For Winter, the extent to which law is predictable and determinate is the extent to which it reflects the reality of human cognitive processes rather than objective rational models of human reasoning: 'An imaginative rationality is indeterminate in more or less predictable ways' (Winter 2001: 7).

Winter attempts to tread a middle path between the indeterminacy theorist and the idea of legal professionals applying objective and rational tools. He does this by grounding an understanding of legal reasoning in what he perceives as the true, underlying nature of human cognition:

> A cognitive account denies neither that there is indeterminacy in legal reasoning nor that social, political, and policy considerations play an important role in legal decisionmaking. What a cognitive account does claim is that it is possible to explicate the kinds, degrees, and reasons for the relative indeterminacy that one experiences in working with legal materials.
>
> (Winter 2001: 163)

For Winter, one source of indeterminacy is the 'rationalist model' of legal reasoning itself, i.e. the mismatch between the surface language of rational reasoning and the underlying actual processes of human cognition and the human imagination.

Lakoff's linguistics is a decontextualized, consensus model which presents cognitive structures as shared by speakers of a given language, frequently reflecting substantive universal or near-universal structures. In general, linguistics, with its emphasis on like-mindedness as a product of a shared linguistic code operating within the speech community, has severe difficulty dealing with the contentious nature of legal discourse. Solan quotes Benjamin Cardozo on the ideal system of law, one Cardozo sees as unattainable:

> No doubt the ideal system, if it were attainable, would be a code at once so flexible and so minute, as to supply in advance for every conceivable situation the just and fitting rule. But life is too complex to bring the attainment of this ideal within the compass of human powers.
>
> (Cardozo 1921: 143, cited in Solan 1993: 13)

This reflects a sense of the law's deficiencies when set against its ideal, one where we would have 'a system of law so certain and rigid that it could be applied to any conceivable situation with mathematical precision and accuracy' (Goble 1933: 229). For Solan, this is not a chimera but an actual ideal realized in the operation of the linguistic system. Thus, Chomsky's understanding of generative grammar can offer the judge a solution:

> The core of our linguistic knowledge, the part that linguists call a 'generative grammar', is, however, indeed the type of 'code' for which Cardozo yearns. Therefore, to the extent that a judge can decide a case by resort to this special human power, he can avoid the difficulties of having to rely, for example, on one set of precedents when he and the parties know full well that a different body of precedents could have been invoked to justify the opposite result.
>
> (Solan 1993: 15)

But even if one accepts this view of the nature of language, it is evident that a technique of 'letting the language decide' must rely on each unique constellation of circumstances having only one characterization in terms of the linguistic code. Otherwise the contentious nature of legal characterization is simply replaced by the multiple and no doubt in part equally contentious characterizations that could be produced in ordinary language.

This consensus model of language and speech community lies behind the idea that linguists can represent the ordinary meaning of a word to the courts when these face difficulties in determining the meaning of ordinary English words. Judges have generally either relied on their own intuitions, or consulted dictionaries for guidance as to ordinary meaning and usage. In their intervention in *NOW v Schneider* 1994, the authors put the case for the superiority of linguistic analysis of meaning over traditional lexicography:

> Unfortunately, compared to the analysis of a particular textual problem by a trained linguist, dictionaries are a crude and frequently unreliable aid to

> word meaning and usage. In fact, for one of the three cases [concerning the definition of the word *enterprise*], the leading dictionaries have definitions that differ exactly as the parties differ over the meaning of the statutory term, and thus provide no objective way of resolving that dispute over ordinary language meaning. (Cunningham *et al.* 1994: 1563)

The linguist can produce an analysis which 'articulates linguistic distinctions that all members of the relevant speech community can recognize once they are brought to conscious attention' (Cunningham *et al.* 1994: 1563). In other words, the linguist can, like Solan's code, answer the question for the court of what the word really means; it can bring to conscious awareness a latent or underlying shared understanding to be found in the speech community. Although the authors do not fully embrace Solan's view of a language as an ideal code, they do make the claim that 'linguistics has made considerable progress in finding and analyzing the predictable order in the seeming infinite variety of speech'; further the methods used by linguists can assist judges in 'finding and analyzing predictable order in the complex textual issues which so frequently make cases hard' (Cunningham *et al.* 1994: 1568). There are again two *non sequiturs* here: firstly, there is no clear relation between the idea of a language as an ideal code able to characterize any possible situation, and predictability; secondly, the Chomskian model that is being borrowed here even its own terms makes no special claim about offering insights into issues of textual interpretation, which clearly fall into the realm of 'performance' rather than 'competence'.

In practice, we are not always able to say whether a case concerns an everyday word in its ordinary meaning, or a legal term in its specialized meaning. This complicates considerably attempts to apply linguistic analysis to legal problems. In *NOW v Scheidler* 1994 the issue was whether the Pro-Life Action Network (PLAN), a network of anti-abortion activists whose aim was to shut down abortion clinics, was an 'enterprise' as that word was used in the Racketeer Influenced and Corrupt Organizations Act (RICO, 1988). This was one of three cases selected by a research group of lawyers and linguists. The court would be presented with a review article in proof while the case was pending, with the hope that the court would take into account expertise in relation to language and the meanings of ordinary terms or expressions. The specific provision of RICO invoked by the plaintiffs provides:

> It shall be unlawful for any person employed by or associated with any enterprise engaged in, or the activities of which affect, interstate or foreign commerce, to conduct or participate, directly or indirectly, in the conduct of such enterprise's affairs through a pattern of racketeering activity or through collection of an unlawful debt.

The National Organization of Women (NOW) sought damages and an injunction to prevent PLAN from disrupting their business. The argument hinged on whether PLAN would only fall under the statute if it were primarily defined in terms of economic activity:

> In other words, according to the defendants, *enterprise* was a synonym or near-synonym of *business*. The plaintiffs argued that the word *enterprise* as used in the statute had a wider denotation, containing both economically-focused and non-economically focused entities. The case law in the lower courts conflicted. (Kaplan *et al.* 1995: 90)

Court decisions varied between the narrow, economically focused definition, where an enterprise was held to 'exist for the purpose of maintaining operations directed towards an economic goal', and wider definitions: 'an ongoing organization, either formal or informal in nature in which the various associates functioned as a continuing unit. The enterprise must have an existence separate and apart from the pattern of activity in which it engages'; 'a group of persons associated together for a common purpose of engaging in a course of conduct' (Kaplan *et al.* 1995: 91).

The definitions section of the statute did not define the word but stated that '"Enterprise" includes any individual, partnership, corporation, association, or other legal entity, and any union or group of individuals associated in fact, although not a legal entity.' Kaplan et al argue that this falls short of being a definition, since it provides no additional criteria for something to be an enterprise. These criteria were necessary since 'if the statutory word *includes* were interpreted as 'means', any individual would be an enterprise – surely an unacceptable result'. Dictionary definitions were also found to be deficient, since '[d]epending on the dictionary consulted, support could be found for either interpretation of the word' (Kaplan *et al.* 1995: 91).

The team approached the question of the meaning of *enterprise* by using the NEXIS database, and in the relevant count noun usage found that uses 'included not only many referring to organized profit-seeking entities, but also a significant minority unambiguously referring to non-business entities'. Terms such as *business enterprise, commercial enterprise, economic enterprise* were judged to be non-redundant (Kaplan *et al.* 1995: 91). The conclusion was therefore that '(1) *enterprise* was most commonly used to refer to businesses but (2) many uses of *enterprise* were found which referred to entities that did not have an economic goal.' The conclusion was therefore that *enterprise* was not synonymous with *business*, but rather was a broader category 'which included but was not limited to business'.

The next stage involved a questionnaire survey designed to ascertain 'what criteria speakers would use in deciding whether a candidate organization was an enterprise'. This was grounded in 'the standard assumption within linguistics that identifying the meaning of an expression which is used in a speech community is not a matter of mere intuition and may require empirical research' (Kaplan *et al.* 1995: 92). It was not being suggested that judges could delegate to others 'the task of ascertaining just how statutory terms should be applied to particular cases', rather it was an exercise in consciousness raising for the judge. However judges were seen as being required to take seriously such survey data: 'It is very hard to maintain that a particular utterance is capable of only one interpretation if large numbers of speakers can be shown to disagree about its interpretation'. The results of the survey followed the database, with informants dividing into two groups, one which took as the primary criterion 'whether an entity had a clear goal', the second which saw the pursuit of profit as primary. This followed the split in the lower courts (Kaplan *et al.* 1995: 94). However the court appeared to rely on its own linguistic intuition, issuing a unanimous verdict that PLAN was an enterprise, the court apparently not regarding this as a hard case, stating that the 'the statutory language is unambiguous' (Kaplan *et al.* 1995: 95).

This decision is read by the authors as involving the use of free-standing judicial intuition about meaning, and was thus an evident disappointment. But their discussion contains a series of *non sequiturs.* Firstly, the dictionaries were divided in the same way as the courts and the general public, and thus the dismissal of dictionary definitions is somewhat ironic, since it seems predicated on the idea that all dictionaries should agree in order for any dictionary to be authoritative in a forensic context. Further, the results of the corpus investigation cannot be summarized by saying that *enterprise* is not a *synonym* of business, since in many contexts it clearly is. The statute in question just might be one of those. Asking what evidence is needed to in order to know whether the statute is one such context simply leads back to the original problem. There is a further methodological issue raised here with respect of the concept of speech community. The necessary implication is that a speech community is homogenous in all other respects apart from its language use, or rather that any additional variation in the speech community is necessarily independent of views about the primary definition of *enterprise.* Further, since, according to the authors, it is not intended that judges delegate the task of definition to linguists (though the linguist claims to offer a superior product to dictionaries and to the intuition of judges), it remains unclear how a judge can determine the degree of relevance of the linguists' findings.

To argue that judges should not assert that an utterance has only one interpretation, if the community view suggests that the term has more than one meaning, is to confuse definition with interpretation. A judge may conclude that an utterance or a contextualized statement is unambiguous, whilst recognizing that the terms within it have various potential meanings. It does not follow from the findings of the survey that the court was bound to find that the statute was ambiguous, since the judge is interpreting a statute rather than applying a definition directly into the context. The court was necessarily aware of alternative possible readings of the term *enterprise* in the context of the statute, as these had been at the heart of the conflicting decisions that led to the appeal. It is of course open to judges to use definitions in that way, but that again is a matter of contextual judgement. There is no meta-rule.

The grounds on which linguistics is held to be relevant to law are often contradictory. One argument is that the new textualist reliance on plain meaning and dictionaries would give room for a more systematic account of meaning as offered by linguists. On the other, linguistics is seen as supporting an essentially purposive, contextual approach. Sullivan credits linguistics with this insight:

> The plain meaning rule is based on the fundamental proposition that once a text is written, it 'contains' a meaning that does not change, but remains stable regardless of the context in which the text is read and regardless of the different knowledge and expectations readers bring to the text. Recent work in linguistics has discredited this view. Texts do not 'contain' meanings; rather they invite readers to infer meanings from the words chosen, the arrangement of the words, the circumstance of utterance and other aspects of context. The text of legislation may be fixed once and for all, but the context cannot be. (Sullivan n.d.: [11])

But it is far from clear that lawyers have hitherto believed that texts are stable objects in which fixed meanings inhere.

Discussing recent proposals that linguists be brought into legal cases that hinge on meaning (Cunningham *et al.* 1994), Golanski concludes that linguistics may only be able to contribute to those cases where the question comes down to the clear ordinary meaning of the words, and this meaning is not in conflict with a specialized legal meaning:

> In general, Cunningham/Levi's influential recommendation that linguists be brought into legal cases complements the increasing concern among legal scholars that law lags behind, and fails adequately to comprehend, science and social science. Courts should be wary, however, about assigning non-legal experts an enhanced role in adjudication. These experts will likely overlook many of the policy and interpretative factors that inform law's public outcomes, and that subtle legal training and experience have sought jurists to synthesize. (Golanski 2002: 120)

In other words, legal language is not a subordinate variety of ordinary language, but a specialized language with its own rules and traditions: 'It helps very little to know what the man on the street makes of "word" or "consideration"; it does not even appear that these terms can be translated into ordinary, educated English' (Schroth 1998: 22). Schroth reluctantly concludes that 'scientific linguistics has very little assistance to offer to statutory construction'. The further question this raises is whether linguists have any expertise of forensic relevance when the law is confronted with problems of the definition and meaning of ordinary words which have become contentious in a legal context. It is also evident that whether a case hinges on the so-called 'clear ordinary meaning' of a word or phrase is extremely hard to determine, and is frequently itself in dispute. It is not something that can be determined as an independent question, outside the other interpretative and legal issues raised by the case.

The trust cases concerning words like *friend, relative* are perhaps most revealing of why linguists have little to contribute to the definitional complexities of law. For what emerges is the paradox that appeals to decontextualized definition are contextually motivated, and the courts are equally able to justify denying the definability of an ordinary English term, or asserting its conceptual clarity. There is no obvious point in those cases at which one could confidently assert that the court was in need of an 'objective' definition of *friend*, etc. The court or one of the parties might of course assert such a need at a certain point, but that determination will arise out of one view of the interpretative politics of the case. Here Bennion's point, made almost as an aside, that 'part of the context is always legal', becomes crucial, because the determination of how much of the context is legal cannot be made in advance of an analysis of the situation itself in which the question arises.

* * *

Discussion of issues of definition within legal theory is highly fragmented. One problem is that arguably every single legal issue, case or controversy can be cast in terms of a problem, to which definitional clarity might give an answer ('It all depends on how we define X'). There is no consensus as to the issues that are raised by considering definition, and a divided set of opinions about how fundamental linguistic issues are to law and whether those issues can be dealt with systematically through the extant discipline of statutory interpretation, or by the importation of external expertise such as that found in linguistics. One could distinguish three theoretically distinct questions of meaning in law. The first involves a question of the meanings of legal terms of art, for example whether something can be counted as *land* or not. This would be a question primarily of the legal meanings(s) of the term *land*, though courts do sometimes make reference to ordinary or commonsense understandings. While such a case might be couched in definitional terms ('Is X land or not?'), it will ultimately involve the application or prioritizing of various legal principles to a factual situation, including perhaps various statutory definitions, other textual authorities (decided cases), but also principles of justice, equity, etc. The second would be questions of the intent attached to the language of a document, such as a will, or a statute. For example, the court will look for a firm and explicit intention to make a trust and discount what are termed 'precatory words' ('in the hope that X will act justly in relation to our children') which express general wishes or expectations but fall short of a creating a legally enforceable trust. Thirdly, there are cases which come to hinge centrally on the meaning of an ordinary term in its so-called ordinary meaning. In practice however there is often a doubt as to which of these three issues are at stake, and that doubt arises within the interpretative politics of the case and cannot be resolved 'neutrally' from the outside.

Judges may make statements of interpretative principle within the context of a case but these are not automatically elevated to general principles of common law interpretation. There can be no such principles. The way the common law evolves gives to a particular judge or court the task of situating a particular case within the wider patterns of law. That decision is subject to review by higher courts, and ultimately by Parliament if it dislikes the decision. The way the common law operates means that judges have available an extensive set of tools of construction, canons, terminology ('literal meaning', 'plain meaning'), reference works, maxims; they can appeal to 'reasonableness' or 'absurdity'; they can quote from statements of interpretative principle made by judges and others; they can decide which cases are relevant, and which statements made in which cases will throw light on the point at issue; they can appeal to wider notions of 'policy' or even justice, morality, and they can use equitable principles to give themselves room for manoeuvre. Distinctions such as that between 'conceptual clarity' and 'evidential clarity', or between a meaning that 'can be found' as opposed to 'being ordinarily found' may become important within an individual case or a line of cases, but their relevance is localized and specific. Even the superficially general distinction between 'legal language' and 'ordinary language' actually operates in this same way.

It makes little sense to see law as a separate linguistic domain with its own autonomous linguistic culture; nor does it make sense however to assert that ordinary language simply includes legal language. For the question of whether a term or a text involves ordinary language or legal language is itself contentious in many contexts where this distinction is raised. 'Ordinary language' exists only as a reification when a particular context directs attention to a special variety or context of use against which ordinary language is to be contrasted; there is no decontextualized sense one can make of the concept, as it is inherently relative. What is often meant by the determination that a word belongs to 'ordinary language' is that it is justifiable to use a non-specialist dictionary to define it.

* * *

A more productive way to think about the relationship of linguistics to law is to focus on the insights the legal situation offers into general questions of meaning, definition and interpretation. Following a discussion of two cases where the meanings of ordinary words came into question (i.e. *souvenir*, in *Hudson v Marshall* 1976, and *carriage*, *Corkery v Carpenter* 1951), Harris comments as follows:

> The kind of descriptive diagnostic which operates in the case of the law is merely one very clear example of a principle which applies to communicational interactions generally. It is not a 'special case'. Except that it probes and lays bare to an unusual degree the procedures and the rationale which underlie a determination of 'what is meant'. It comes to terms with the fact that there is no way in which language can provide explicitly and specifically for all conceivable eventualities. (Harris 1981: 192)

What this suggests is not that linguists have much to teach lawyers about meaning, but rather linguists have much to learn about meaning from looking at how the law operates. For the law makes manifest the lack of consensus that exists at the level of definition, at the level of attempts to make precise the meanings of individual word and phrase, but also the lack of a meta-consensus about how those difficulties should be tackled. There is no agreement as to the weighting that should be given to particular factors or considerations (e.g. in choosing between a 'narrow' or a 'broad' definition, or the everyday or the legal meaning, of a term at issue), and, on a further level of abstraction, no agreement about how we should theorize this difficulty. The discipline (craft, art, science, . . .) of statutory interpretation is largely a taxonomy of, and a commentary on, difficulties that have arisen in construing statutes and offers an attempt to lay down principles which should be followed in hard cases. But those principles are inevitably couched in terms of reasonableness, coherence, and a search for as much 'order' (Bennion 2002: 1) as possible.

Indeterminacy theorists reject an understanding of the distinction between clear and hard cases, since it suggests that the law and judges normally operate apolitically in applying the categories of law automatically and only look to policy concerns (which are inevitably political) when the language of the law as it were 'runs out' in a particular constellation of circumstances. This points to the fundamental weakness of both Hart and Winter's approaches, i.e. the inability of these models to deal with the contentious nature of law. The strength of the indeterminacy model is that it focuses precisely on the contentious and non-autonomous nature of the legal-linguistic construct of law; its weakness is that some versions either offer indeterminacy as the substance of an entire political critique, or translate the indeterminacy and contingency of law into fixed underlying race, class and gender positions, or into categories of economic relationships. The argument for the indeterminate, non-autonomous nature of legal decision-making is frequently sustained by a determinate political or economic reading of law itself. The integrational view is that indeterminacy is not to be equated with disorder, or with simplistic political attacks on the use of linguistic reifications in law, but rather is the background against which participants construct, impose, contest and debate meaning and seek to impose or deny order, coherence and narrative.

Bix concludes his discussion in *Law, Language and Legal Determinacy* with the blunt statement that 'language has, for the most part, been a false focus for legal theory'. This is because language and theories of language 'have been used as an excuse for decisions that are more properly attributable to political – or at least policy – decisions about how we want the various institutions in our legal system to interact' (Bix 1993: 178). One ground for this assertion is that by contrast with a general theory of language and communication 'different factors' need to be stressed in the special context of drafting, interpreting, and enforcing legal rules' (Bix 1993: 179). But this suggests that if we focus on language, we are somehow excluding the political and policy dimensions of legal decision making. For the integrationist, this distinction between a linguistic domain and a political domain makes no sense. The assumption behind Bix's comments seems to be that ordinary language itself, or at least theories of ordinary non-legal language, exist in a kind of free zone independent of social pressures, questions of purpose, policy in its widest sense, and social conflict.

Law like language can be understood as existing in tension between attempts at reification and generalization on the one hand (e.g. appeals to 'context-free' definition), and the invocation by participants of contextually appropriate interpretative strategies (appeals to the intention of parliament, the testator, etc.). Participants work against the threat of fragmentation towards goals of coherence and consensus on various levels, but fragmentation may also be a necessary or a conscious strategy, where perhaps coherence on one level (in law, for example the application of a precedent to a particular set of facts) creates incoherence on another (e.g. where the decided outcome would be incoherent when set against the court's understanding of underlying norms of justice and equity). Comments on the definitions of individual words, on intentions that may be attached to particular words, and discussion of matters of interpretative strategy that arise within the context of legal cases must be seen within this overall dynamic of coherence versus fragmentation. In this sense, each case has its own interpretative politics, and creates its own strategic alignment within the wider context of law. The interpretative politics of the case cannot be separated from the legal (moral, social) issues that are at stake, as participants look forward towards potential outcomes, look back to previous cases and decisions, while reaching for 'decontextualized' interpretative tools such as definitions, canons and maxims.

IV. Conclusion

Chapter 11

Definition, Indeterminacy and Reference

In *The Search for the Perfect Language*, Umberto Eco discusses various idealistic projects for artificial languages, in which the authors seem to have assumed that it would be possible to give every word an exact definition (Eco 1995). The notion of a perfect language goes hand-in-hand with that of a perfect definition, since it is obvious that if definitions are imperfect, for whatever reason, the language itself must de deficient too. More down-to-earth theorists, however, often seem to be engaged in a search for the perfect definition, even when they acknowledge that the languages they are dealing with are, unfortunately, far from perfect. They appear to be seeking, and hoping to find, ways of building an intellectual structure with materials intrinsically inadequate to the task. Thus arises a paradox which haunts the subject: does it make sense to look for determinacy in the midst of indeterminacy? Before surrendering to this paradox, we propose to scrutinize the notion of indeterminacy more closely.

Most modern theorists who proclaim the semantic indeterminacy of words as used in 'ordinary language' seem to have in mind nothing more profound than the fact that different users manifestly apply certain terms in different ways, coupled with the fact that the same user may apply a given term differently on different occasions. In short, there is both inter-user and intra-user inconsistency in usage; i.e. both as between user *A* and user *B*, and also as between user *A* on one occasion and user *A* on another, even though both *A* and *B*, as with *A* on different occasions, seem in such cases to be using 'the same language' and not two different languages.

This rather obvious level of indeterminacy might be called, for purposes of discussion, 'applicational indeterminacy'. It does not seriously threaten the theoretical assumption that languages can be treated, for purposes of linguistic analysis, as fixed codes; for the evidence on which this kind of indeterminacy rests is evidence from *parole*, and the orthodox theorist of *langue* can easily shrug this off as the kind of discrepancy that will inevitably arise when individual cases of *parole* are examined. In the rough and tumble of everyday speech speakers are given to speaking casually, without paying particular attention to matters of consistency, and listeners are accustomed to making due allowance for this. All that is demanded by interlocutors is that the words used serve the purposes of the moment, and do not cause manifest misunderstandings. In brief, 'applicational indeterminacy' can be dismissed by the orthodox theorist as no more than the kind of variation that would emerge if one were to investigate the measurement of certain distances as measured by a random set of individuals. Some figures given will doubtless be greater than others given for the same distance, depending on how great the distances are, the thoroughness of the person carrying out the measurement, or the purpose for which the measurement is deemed to be required (property boundaries, road signs, pipe lines, cycle races, ordnance survey, etc.). But these observable variations, it will be argued, do not in any way undermine the supposition that exactly the same system of measurement is being applied in all cases. It certainly does not oblige one to suppose that every measurer has his or her own system of measurement, or that there is something wrong with the measuring instruments, or that in some mysterious way the distances themselves are affected by the process of measurement.

Analogously, it may be claimed, the fact that different English dictionaries do not all give identical definitions for certain English words is no reason for supposing that they are not describing 'the same language', viz. 'English'. The variations are simply due to the fact that different lexicographers choose to emphasize certain semantic features of a word rather than others, or give fuller or briefer accounts depending on their assessment of the likely needs of the user. So whereas it may seem perfectly clear from one dictionary that word *W* is not applicable to items of category *z*, this may not be at all clear from another dictionary. These 'inconsistencies' do not warrant any suspicion that different English dictionaries are describing different languages, or that some lexicographers are incompetent, or that – *horribile dictu* – the meanings of words are not invariant under lexicographical scrutiny.

So appeal to the mere facts of everyday 'applicational indeterminacy' and its lexicographical counterpart do not in the end make much of a dent in the orthodox conception of a language as a fixed code shared by all its (competent) users. There is nothing that compels the orthodox theorist to revise his basic assumption that every word has its own meaning or meanings, and that these meanings can, in principle, be ascertained and stated.

A stronger version of indeterminacy is espoused by those philosophers who argue that all 'empirical' concepts are necessarily indeterminate. This is sometimes called the 'open texture' thesis. It has nothing to do with inconsistency or lack of consensus within the linguistic community: it is a thesis about the human mind. Nevertheless, the two theses are often confused. In particular, some who think they are arguing for open texture are doing no more than producing evidence of applicational indeterminacy. To avoid possible misunderstanding, let us call this stronger philosophical version 'intrinsic indeterminacy'. (Variants of it were developed by Waismann and by Quine.)

The thinking behind intrinsic indeterminacy is this. However clearly one may suppose one has grasped some conceptual distinction (e.g. between 'cats' and 'dogs'), it is always possible to imagine a case which straddles that distinction in such a way that there would be no non-arbitrary means of deciding on which side it fell. It does not matter whether such cases ever occur in the 'real world'. Being able to imagine a creature with a dog's head and bark but a cat's body is sufficient to cast doubt on the determinacy of the difference between the concept 'cat' and the concept 'dog'. The claim is that all conceptual systems, however apparently comprehensive, have holes in them, i.e. do not exhaust all conceivable possibilities, because that is beyond the power of the human mind.

From an integrational perspective, intrinsic indeterminacy is a thesis that is not so much philosophically contentious as linguistically uninteresting. That is to say, it would not occur to an integrationist to doubt that one can imagine all kinds of hypothetical borderline cases that would test *any* apparently clear conceptual distinction. But the integrationist would argue that in practice human beings are sufficiently resourceful to deal with such problems. The conceptual quandary appears to be a quandary only because it is presented in a communicational vacuum. In practice, given a communicational context, it would not be impossible to decide (1) whether to call the problematic creature a 'cat' or a 'dog', or (2) whether to declare it was neither. A reason could be found, and doubtless different reasons in different cases. The reason chosen would doubtless depend on why it mattered to resolve that particular question at that particular time, i.e. on what chain of integrated activities waited upon that decision and hence conferred meaning upon the use of one term rather than another.

* * *

The integrationist position rests neither on applicational indeterminacy nor on intrinsic indeterminacy. It is more far-reaching than either and appeals to different considerations altogether. We will call this 'radical indeterminacy'.

Neither applicational indeterminacy nor intrinsic indeterminacy are quite as revolutionary positions as they sound (and are often taken to be). Both in fact allow for a large measure of semantic determinacy. In this respect both are compromises with the orthodox doctrine of the fixed code. Thus it is perfectly possible for someone who upholds the thesis of applicational indeterminacy to concede that there will always be some terms with meanings on which all speakers of a given language agree, even while disagreeing about others. This is a very old form of compromise: it is first articulated clearly by Socrates in Plato's *Phaedrus*. In other words, some terms are regarded as having determinate meanings, while other have variable or controversial meanings. (For Socrates, the Greek words for *iron* and *silver* have meanings on which everyone agrees, whereas *just* and *good* have meanings on which opinions are divided.)

Similarly, apologists for intrinsic indeterminacy usually allow that it is only at the margins that concepts are indeterminate. So there are many uncontroversial applications of such concepts as 'cat' and 'dog', and these, as it were, form the normal background against which hypothetical creatures which have both cat-type and dog-type characteristics appear in a problematic light.

Both theses, in fact, need the notion that there *is* determinacy in the system up to a point, in order to be able make the case that *beyond* that point indeterminacy takes over. What neither explains is how it comes about that the allegedly determinate meanings are fixed, or the supposedly agreed usages come to be agreed. Neither can afford to dispense with the premise that, in principle, semantic determinacy is possible, but both remain silent about how it is achieved and – no less important – about it can be shown to have been achieved. In the history of Western thought, no attempt to locate the putative source of semantic determinacy (from Plato's sempiternal forms to Skinner's behaviourist universals) has ever commanded general acceptance.

The 'radical indeterminacy' recognized by integrationists goes far beyond either applicational or intrinsic indeterminacy. It questions the notion of semantic determinacy altogether. In integrational semiology, the sign does not 'have' its own meaning: it is 'made to mean' whatever the circumstances require. And may be made to mean different things by different individuals on the same occasion. More exactly, the contextualization that makes a sign mean something is simultaneously what establishes its identity as a sign. So *even if* by some miracle human beings woke up tomorrow equipped with those concepts with 'sharp boundaries' that Frege longed for, (or, equivalently, even if intrinsic indeterminacy were abolished overnight) radical indeterminacy would still be the order of the day. For there would still be no guarantee that *A*'s system of determinate concepts matched *B*'s. In other words, once integrationist premises are adopted, the notion of semantic determinacy is theoretically superfluous to requirements. Occam's razor demands that it be discarded.

This does not make it impossible for members of the community ever to agree. But it does imply that no agreement automatically carries over from one occasion to the next, any more than the price you paid for a pint of beer in one pub last week somehow fixes in advance the price you will be charged in another pub next week. All verbal continuities are subject to recontextualization. There is no standing guarantee that an author who uses a word twice on the same page, or even twice in the same sentence, is using it in the same way on both occasions.

This is why, from an integrationist perspective, all cases of what are usually given as examples of communicational consensus are actually contextualized products of communicational independence. This is far less paradoxical than it sounds. When *A* and *B* both call Fido a dog and Tibbles a cat, this is not evidence of the existence of determinate meanings of the words *dog* and *cat* that *A* and *B* share, or of a determinate conceptual distinction between 'dog' and 'cat' that their minds grasp in common, any more than *A* and *B* crossing the road together would be evidence of their sharing a determinate reason for wanting to get to the other side. The postulated semantic consensus underlying everyday talk about cats and dogs is a theoretical illusion conjured up by generalizing across separate, individual decisions to call Fido a dog and Tibbles a cat for the communicational purposes to hand. But it is an idle cog in the explanatory wheel. For *even if* it were true that all members of a linguistic community had reached an agreement in advance on what to call Fido and Tibbles, their implementation of that agreement would still require an individual decision by each of them on each occasion.

One is dealing here with the same kind of philosophical mistake that would be involved in forgetting that a 'unanimous decision' taken at a meeting does not warrant supposing that all were of one mind: those present might have voted as they did for all kinds of disparate and incompatible motives. That possibility, to be sure, does not somehow invalidate the decision or make it less than unanimous. But it does make it quite unnecessary to postulate a common view of the issue in order to explain the result of the vote.

Adopting the semantic terminology popularized by J. S. Mill, as far as words like *cat* and *dog* are concerned the crucial point might perhaps be put as follows. It is a mistake to imagine that denotation is determined by connotation. The denotation of a term is not *determined* at all. Rather, it is the contextualized reference of a term that (in part) establishes the function of that term as a sign (on a particular occasion). It is only the misguided attempt to generalize from one referential use to another that results in the curious metaphysical belief that a term somehow carries its denotation around with it. Once that fallacy is recognized for what it is, and the full implications are realized, the vacuity of supposing that *any* signs are semantically determinate should be apparent.

How does the illusion of semantic determinacy arise? Its psychological source is shrewdly suggested by Locke, when he observes in his *Essay Concerning Human Understanding* that men 'suppose their words to be marks of the ideas in the minds also of other men, with whom they communicate'. Since no one can observe what is going on in the mind of another, this is a supposition of which people have no direct assurance, but which they nevertheless take to be indirectly confirmed by their own communicational experience. Thus while speaker *A* egocentrically projects his own understanding of words on to hearer *B*, and continues to do so in the absence of any contra-indication from *B*, at the same time *B* egocentrically projects his own understanding of *A*'s words back on to *A*, and assumes that *A* intended him to understand what *B* in fact understands. In this way a conspiracy of false assumptions on both sides reinforces the impression of mutual comprehension. This in turn seems to be corroborated by further episodes of communication between *A*, *B* and other interlocutors. Since interlocutors vary from one episode to the next, it then becomes tempting to believe that success in communication is due not to the efforts of any individual participants but to the fact that the words they use already have invariant meanings that exist, and continue to exist, irrespective of variations in interlocutors or situations. Finally, in literate communities, the assumption that word meanings are independent of users provides a powerful inducement to believe that written texts offer reliable access to the minds of individuals no longer alive, as well as a reliable instrument for preserving messages for generations not yet born. In this way, a cumulative picture is built up of a homogeneous linguistic community continuing over time, united by the shared use of a fixed code that determines in advance for all members, without requiring any initiative on their part, what shall be meant by the words used.

Thus the postulate of semantic determinacy makes it possible to transfer the responsibility for making meaning from the individual to the collectivity, and from the circumstantial to the macrosocial level. At the same time, this transference ensures that the role of nonverbal context in the communicational process is marginalized or ignored altogether. Words come to be construed as autonomous signs that can and do function semantically without support from any other semiological source, providing the essential self-sustaining mechanisms for the facilitation and regulation not only of human interactions but of human thought itself.

* * *

We have argued in earlier chapters that a confusion between lexical definition and real definition underlies many of the problems that arise in connexion with definition in the Western tradition. But that does not explain how the confusion arises or why it is so common. In order to pursue that question it becomes necessary to move from the theory of definition to the theory of reference, and to introduce the integrationist concept of 'referential focus'.

Reference, as far as integrationists are concerned, encompasses all those communicational devices enlisted to make it possible for *A* and *B* to make it clear to each other *who* or *what* it is that is being talked or written about in a given context. (Whether successfully or not is another matter.) No one disputes that some of these devices are non-verbal: they include touching, pointing, nodding and looking in the direction of the referent. But it is also recognized that people can identify who or what is being referred to because their language supplies the words and expressions necessary to do this. Prominent among them are proper names (*Napoleon, London, Switzerland, Asia,* etc.). Particular events can be identified by description (*the invention of the internal combustion engine*), times and dates can be specified (*the first of January 2001*), and so on. But giving examples simply postpones the theoretical question, which concerns *how* these various types of verbal device manage to fulfil their referential function.

Perhaps it is as well to make clear at the outset that reference – at least for purposes of the present discussion – is not a type of mental act or process. However hard a person concentrates his or her thoughts on, say, the current president of the United States, this does not constitute *referring to* the president of the United States. In order to do that, it would be necessary to employ some overt communicational device by means of which an *act of reference* to that individual could be made. Just thinking about someone does not count as referring to that person. The point is worth emphasizing because reference is commonly held to involve making someone *think of* the referent. The communicational success or otherwise of *A*'s attempt to refer to a particular individual is often thought to depend on getting *B* to think of that individual. This is the standard telementational view of reference: the thought of the individual in question is 'transferred from' *A*'s mind to *B*'s. This is a disguised causal explanation: the tacit assumption being that, by employing the right words or other communicational devices, *A* causes *B* to think of the right person. Since integrationists reject all telementational accounts of communication, they reject by the same token telementational accounts of reference. This does not mean, however, that they deny the possibility of any such mental event as thinking of a particular individual, or, for that matter, deny that thinking of a particular individual may be triggered by hearing someone refer to that individual.

How does the theory of definition connect with the theory of reference? If you do not know what carbon tetrachloride is, it seems reasonable to claim that you are in no position to define the expression *carbon tetrachloride*. That task, regardless of how it is to be accomplished, is best left to someone who *does* know what it is. If this is right, then it seems that the first step in trying to offer a definition would be finding out what people who talk about carbon tetrachloride are referring to by their use of this term. If we call carbon tetrachloride the 'referent' of the expression *carbon tetrachloride*, it would follow that giving a definition requires as one of its pre-conditions identification of the referent. If that is not possible, no definition is possible either.

Do people *have to know* what carbon tetrachloride is in order to be able to refer to it? Evidently not. There is nothing to prevent *A* from giving the instruction 'Bring me some carbon tetrachloride' in order to see what they will bring him, thus hoping to find out (or at least get a better idea of) what carbon tetrachloride is. It hardly needs pointing out that *A* will be in no position to judge whether what they bring him is carbon tetrachloride or not. Nor does it need pointing out that if *A*'s strategy is to work (i.e. if his instruction is to be carried out), *someone* has to know what carbon tetrachloride is, even though *A* himself does not.

Can one be sure that there always is someone who can identify the referent in question? If not, then the enterprise of defining the corresponding expression seems doomed in advance to failure. That is why theorists of definition become alarmed when it is argued that reference itself is subject to 'indeterminacy' or 'inscrutablity'. 'Indeterminacy of reference' or 'inscrutablity of reference' is a doctrine primarily associated with Quine, whose view of language we commented on in Chapter 4. We return to the question here because the integrationist tenet of radical indeterminacy might appear automatically to support – or even be just another version of – Quinean indeterminacy of reference. This is not the case, however.

The imaginary scenario which provides the setting for Quine's argument introduces a (rather naive) linguist trying to compile, on the basis of observational evidence alone, a dictionary of a previously unknown native language. The kind of indeterminacy that Quine is concerned with is – to take one of his own examples – whether a referring expression that seems to be regularly used by the natives whenever rabbits appear actually has as its referent the whole animal, or just a time-slice of the animal, or the quality of rabbithood, some characteristic feature of rabbit behaviour, or any one of a number of other logically possible referents connected with rabbits. The contention is that there is no overt evidence in the observable application of the term when rabbits are present that could, even in principle, lead an impartial observer to decide which of these various possibilities was correct. So the referent remains 'indeterminate': its ultimate identity is 'inscrutable'. The linguist cannot be sure how to translate the word.

Quine's somewhat far-fetched example may most charitably be regarded as a *reductio ad absurdum* of some long-standing and widespread assumptions about reference, of which integrationists are also critical. But Quine's forced dilemma of the translator confronted with many problematic rabbit-reference possibilities makes little impression on integrationists as an argument for 'indeterminacy'. Quine sounds rather like a cantankerous Frenchman insisting that the English word *chair* is hopelessly vague because it does not distinguish a *chaise* from a *fauteuil*. Indeterminacy, for integrationists, has nothing to do with being unable to decide between hypothetically distinguishable but communicationally irrelevant options.

Quine is right, however, to be sceptical of the traditional explanation of reference offered by Western philosophers and grammarians, which construes reference as a *relation*. The relation allegedly holds between a particular word or combination of words and a particular item or items in the world. The classic example is the proper name: it is the relation said to hold between, say, *Socrates* and the famous Greek philosopher of that name. It is envisaged as a permanent and static relation: it does not alter over time, and that is why one can still identify that particular philosopher in that particular way, even though he has been dead for thousands of years. Tomorrow his name will be *Socrates*, just as it was yesterday.

This traditional explanation is still reiterated by philosophers. Thus one finds the term *reference* defined (somewhat circularly) as 'the relation between a referring expression and that to which it refers.' The same philosopher adds: 'Referring expressions are names, like 'Julius Caesar', or definite descriptions, like 'the conqueror of Gaul' (Mautner 1997: 475). This leaves it quite unclear whether an expression still counts as a 'referring expression' if there turns out to be nothing to which it refers, or more than one candidate for the role of referent. Thus what is wrong with the traditional explanation is not difficult to spot. First, there is the possibility of referential ambiguity: nothing prevents different people from having 'the same name' or being given 'the same description'. Second, in any case there is no unique relation between a name or a definite description and a referent. In other words, it is illusory to suppose that a single, determinate set of connections links the name *Julius Caesar* or the description *the conqueror of Gaul* to a certain person. What links there are between the referring expression and the referent may be different for different people. What *A* knows (or thinks he knows) about Julius Caesar and the history of Gaul may not correspond at all to what *B* knows (or thinks he knows). For certain purposes this difference may not matter; but it nevertheless shows that the theoretical explanation in terms of relations is flawed. (Unregenerate believers in reocentric semantics will contend that it makes no difference what *A* or *B* believe, since what matters is the 'real' relation obtaining between the referring expression and the referent. But this removes the question from the domain of communication altogether, and is thus of no interest to integrationists. For further discussion, see Harris 2006a: 25.)

We do not propose here to go into the endless philosophical controversies, mainly associated with Frege, Russell, Wittgenstein and Strawson, that dogged the theory of reference in the twentieth century (for which see Linksy 1967);

but we think it worth pointing out that linguists have compounded confusion by trying to avoid the issue altogether, while still treating names and referring expressions as linguistic categories. Thus, for example, Crystal describes the term *noun* as being 'traditionally defined as "the name of a person, place or thing"', adding that 'the vagueness associated with the notions "name" and "thing" (e.g. is *beauty* a thing?) has led linguistic descriptions to analyse this class in terms of the formal and functional criteria of syntax and morphology' (Crystal 1997: 264). But this has not stopped linguists from adopting the term *proper noun* (a continuation of the traditional *proper name*) and attempting to redefine it as, for example, a noun 'that cannot be used with determiners in the way common nouns can' (Crystal 1997: 312). Thus the fact that (allegedly) one can say *the city* but not *the London* is what marks out *London* as a proper noun. Whether this kind of attempt to steer clear of semantics at all costs is either successful or desirable where proper names are concerned is dubious. (Nothing, apparently, prevents one from saying either *the city I knew as a child* or *the London I knew as a child*; so is *London* in that case a common noun? Are there, perhaps, two nouns *London* that happen to share the same form?)

When it comes to reference, the linguists' confusions and evasions multiply. Crystal gives a blatantly relational and reocentric definition of the term *referent* as 'the entity (object, state of affairs, etc.) in the external world to which a linguistic expression relates' (Crystal 1997: 326). But then he adds: 'for example, the referent of the word *table* is the object "table"'. The trouble with this is that 'in the external world' there is no such object: there are just very many tables of all kinds of shapes, sizes and materials, some of which are pieces of domestic furniture, others being flat surfaces in various types of artifact and machine, still others being sets of numerical figures, subterranean water levels, and so on. Whether or not all these 'tables' have something in common does not alter the fact that, as defined by Crystal, the word *table* has no referent. So reference can presumably be a relation between a linguistic expression and nothing.

Nor is anybody's bacon saved if it is supposed that what Crystal meant to say, or was trying to say in slapdash fashion, is that *table* is a word that can be used as part of a referring expression (such as *this table*) to indicate, in an appropriate context, a particular object. For then it is not the noun *table* that 'refers', but the person using the expression *this table* in that particular context. And that is a matter of *parole*, not of *langue*. Matters get worse when Crystal refers for clarification to the entry *denotation*. For there one learns that the 'denotative meaning' of a term is its 'referential meaning'. 'For example, the denotation of *dog* is its dictionary definition of "canine quadruped"' (Crystal 1997: 109). So now, it appears, there is no question of a relation at all, except that of identity: the dictionary definition itself *is* the denotation. But if we say 'John Stuart Mill must have turned in his grave the day this *Dictionary of Linguistics and Phonetics* was published' we are referring to a particular dictionary, not to a dictionary definition, or to the denotation of the term *dictionary* either.

* * *

An integrationist theory of reference takes quite a different starting point. It has no room for the idea of static relations between words and the world. From an integrationist perspective, reference is always a matter of contextualization, pertaining to a particular communication situation. There is no way of divorcing reference from the circumstantial parameter of human interactions.

This is very obvious in the case of nonverbal signs, such as pointing, but it is no less fundamental in the case of words. A proper name does not 'refer' to anything independently of the circumstances in which it is uttered or written; and the notion that it does, or could do, is generated by metalinguistic abstraction. If *A* succeeds on a number of occasions in using the name *Socrates* in such a way as to give *B* to understand that he is talking about one particular Greek philosopher who was Plato's master and condemned to death for impiety, that is not because of some permanent relation between Socrates and the name *Socrates*, but because on each and every occasion *A* has deployed an appropriate technique of contextualization in those circumstances. It is easy, however, for *A* to overlook his own role in the act of reference, and suppose (mistakenly) that reference is somehow assured by a prior bond tying the referent to the name. This belief is a survival from primitive word magic. *A* is all the more likely to succumb to the mistake if he realizes that there is no such bond tying a deictic expression like *this philosopher* to Socrates, or to any other particular philosopher. *A* supposes, therefore, that the essential difference between names like *Socrates* and referring expressions like *this philosopher* is, precisely, that the name itself guarantees the reference, without any effort on his (or anyone else's) part.

In short, people deceive themselves by their own talk about names. They tend to treat personal names as labels that are permanently attached to their bearers, rather like identification marks tattooed on the skin from birth. But names are not like that. As numerous bigamy cases bear witness, it is possible for an individual to lead quite different lives under different names in different places. There is no inalienable connection between name and bearer; but people tacitly imply that there is when they say of the bigamist, 'Ah! That was not his real name.'

For integrationists, reference emerges from an integration of activities. Just uttering the name *Socrates* does not constitute an act of reference to a particular ancient Greek philosopher unless, in the circumstances, it is part of an attempt that *A* makes to direct *B*'s attention (or his own attention, or both *B*'s attention and his own) to the philosopher in question. That attempt will be in vain if, in the circumstances, there is no way of distinguishing that philosopher from anyone else in antiquity who might have borne the name *Socrates*.

Realizing that fact was what led Russell to formulate his theory that proper names are just abbreviated descriptions. No more disastrous *non sequitur* has ever been committed in philosophy of language. From the fact that further identificatory procedures are always necessary in order to contextualize the use of proper names, it does not follow, as Russell evidently thought it did, that the name is just a substitute for the description. (He might just as well have argued that one can supplement the use of the proper name *Socrates* by pointing to a statue of Socrates and concluded that names are substitutes for statues.)

How do people ever know that their acts of reference have been successful? In a variety of ways, depending on the circumstances. When you sign a cheque, your act of self-reference is successful if what you have written is your own name; and if you want to make assurance doubly sure you could always get a friend to verify it. If *A* and *B* manage to use the name *Socrates* in such a way that they find they agree about the main points in the life of this individual, and can distinguish him to their own satisfaction from anyone else who might have borne that name, they can be reasonably confident that they are talking about the same person. A sceptic might object that none of this offers any guarantee against the possibility of referential error. You may absent-mindedly have signed someone else's name on your cheque, and the friend who verifies it may be hopelessly shortsighted. Both *A* and *B* may be jointly mistaken about Socrates. The sceptic is right on all counts. There is no foolproof certainty. But human communication does not operate on the basis of certainties of this order. If it had to, of one thing there is no doubt: there would be very little communication between human beings.

What is required to establish Socrates as referent for the name *Socrates* is not some cast-iron assurance or verification of the 'real' existence of such a philosopher with that name, at the right period, who 'really' did and said the various things attributed to him, but a communication situation in which participants agree, tacitly or overtly, to proceed on the basis of certain assumptions, i.e. assumptions about the referential function of that name. Given those assumptions, the use of the name can then be integrated into further discussion.

Someone will probably protest: 'But when people talk about me, they are referring to a person who really does exist. My existence is not some kind of communicational convention, as integrationists seem to suppose. Unless I did exist, there is no chance that people would be interested in talking about me or to me. Isn't my existence therefore the essential grounding of my referential status?'

We sympathize with this objector. However, we think the objection involves a confusion of two quite separate issues. Let us grant that the objector exists and can be referred to by name and in many other ways that verbal and nonverbal signs make possible. Let us also grant that his existence (and all the many activities and other facets of it) supplies the basic reason why he is the referent involved in many acts of reference, initiated both by himself and by others. Nevertheless, the reason *why* that particular network of referential activity flourishes is not what explains *how* it is possible. Existence in flesh and blood or some other physical form is not a necessary condition for acquiring referential status, nor does referential status automatically come with it. Referents can also be the products of human fear, imagination, ignorance and lies.

This difference between our theory of reference and that adopted by many philosophers can also be brought out by considering the notion of 'referential failure' in logic (Hodges 1977: 31, 162–3). The canonical example is *The king of France is bald.* This is held by some to be false, and by others to be neither true nor false, because at present (sc. 'in the real world') France is not a monarchy.

Thus there is no referent for the referring expression *the king of France.* Contrast this with the integrationist view that referential failure arises because, in a given context, interlocutors fail to agree on certain assumptions concerning what they are talking about. If *A* assumes, for whatever reason, that there currently is a king of France, whereas *B* assumes, again for whatever reason, that there is no such person, then this a case of referential failure. But should both interlocutors agree that there is such a person, and agree on at least enough other assumptions about him to sustain a discussion, then in that communication situation *the king of France* has a referent.

What is there to choose between these two approaches to reference? Is there a theoretical balance in favour of one or the other? It seems to us that the integrationist has the explanatory advantage of being able to account for the fact that people do commonly discuss counterfactual situations. It makes sense to say, for instance, 'If there were a king of France, it would fall to him to appoint the French prime minister', and likewise makes sense for someone else to disagree with this and suggest that the king of France would have no such prerogative. Under the standard doctrine of referential failure, such an argument would be an argument about nothing at all, given the absence of a referent for the expression *king of France.* It seems to us, on the contrary, to be perfectly clear *what* the interlocutors would be talking about, and thus there would be no question of referential failure. A hypothetical king of France has no less of a claim to referential status than an actual one.

* * *

From this point on in the discussion we shall bring into play the concept of 'referential focus', which does not feature at all in orthodox linguistics. We wish to maintain that even when *A* and *B* have satisfied themselves and each other about their referential use of a name, there may still be a difference of referential focus in the way they use it. For example, the name *Hitler* may be used by historians or by the same historian in ways that differ in respect of referential focus, even when there is no doubt or disagreement at all about who Hitler was. Such a difference emerges in cases like 'Hitler became chancellor in 1933' and 'Hitler invaded Austria in 1938'. The difference is often discussed in terms such as the following: 'When it is said that Hitler became chancellor in 1933, the reference is to Hitler the person, but when it is said that Hitler invaded Austria one does not mean that Hitler in person did it. This is really a shorthand way of saying that Hitler's troops invaded Austria.' Usually, such explanations stop short of claiming that the name *Hitler* is referentially ambiguous, and that *Hitler* in one case refers to Hitler and in the other to Hitler's troops. Instead, a doctrine of 'ellipsis' is invoked. Or else a doctrine of 'metonymy'.

None of these subterfuges is satisfactory from an integrationist perspective. One might just as well say that not only 'Hitler invaded Austria' but also 'Hitler became chancellor' is elliptical, standing in the latter case for something like 'The person who adopted the name *Hitler* became chancellor'. But this leads straight back to Russell's contention that proper names are substitutes for descriptions (which is, in effect, an elliptical theory of proper names).

Nor are these cases of metonymy. They are not instances of *pars pro toto*, but of another way of considering the referent. The integrationist explanation is that statements like 'Hitler became chancellor' are integrated into historical discourse in a different way from statements like 'Hitler invaded Austria'. The referent is the same in both cases, but the focus is different. In one case the focus is on the referent as an individual and in the other on the referent as the initiator or planner responsible for certain actions or policies. 'Hitler became chancellor' goes with statements like 'Hitler married Eva Braun', whereas 'Hitler invaded Austria' goes with statements like 'Hitler killed millions of Jews'. The levels of discourse are different: nevertheless, they are integrated into a single historical account in virtue of the fact that the referent is understood to be the same in both. Were it not so – i.e. were there a referential disjunction between the *Hitler* of one level and the *Hitler* of the other – the historian would be open to the serious criticism of failing to explain how the invasion of Austria related to the actions of the person who was chancellor of Germany.

Referential focus differs from what Frege called 'mode of presentation' of the referent (Frege 1892). As far as we are concerned, the difference between the expressions *Morning Star* and *Evening Star* is not a difference in mode of presentation of the same referent. In different contexts, two uses of the expression *Morning Star* may differ in referential focus, whereas for Frege they would not differ in mode of presentation. The same applies to *Evening Star*. (For example, when Milton speaks of the Evening Star as 'love's harbinger' the referential focus is manifestly different from that in the case of an astronomer discussing the appearance of the planet Venus in its western elongation. But in Frege's terms there would be no difference in 'mode of presentation' between Milton's use of the expression *Evening Star* and the astronomer's.)

We contend that differences of referential focus may apply not only to proper names, but to referring expressions in general, and indeed to signs of all kinds. Focus is one aspect of meaning. Since a sign gets its meaning from the context in which it functions as a sign, and the activities (both mental and physical) that it thereby integrates, referential focus depends on contextualization. Just as there are many facts about Hitler that would be relevant for Hitler's biographer (e.g. that he was the son of a customs official), but of little or no interest to the historian of modern Germany, so there are many facts about dictators that might be important for a psychologist or a political theorist, but can be safely ignored by the lexicographer writing an entry for the word *dictator*.

The mistake made by modern general lexicographers (from Murray onwards) was to suppose that some determinate subset of facts about referents supplied the essential basis for an adequate definition of a class name. In this they were aided and abetted by Mill's misguided theory of denotation and connotation. They failed to recognize the lesson that might have been learnt from their colleagues who compiled specialist dictionaries for limited domains of inquiry. The reason why it is possible to give physicists and chemists adequate definitions of the names of metals by specifying such properties as atomic number, relative atomic mass, relative density, melting point, etc. is that in the discourse of academic physics and chemistry the referential focus of these words is very narrow. The referents (i.e. the metals) are distinguished in terms of *those* properties, and not in terms of their value on the open market, their relative scarcity, their uses in the manufacture of pots and pans, their availability in natural deposits, or anything else. Consequently, the information supplied about a relatively small subset of properties of metals is sufficient to enable scientist *A* to understand *which of the named metals* scientist *B* is talking about.

The mistake made by some semantic theorists, and possibly by many scientists, was – and is – to suppose that this very narrow referential focus is possible only because science has (at last) discovered what metals 'really are' and identified them accordingly. But that is an irrelevance as far as referential focus is concerned. It would make no difference if, in the twenty-second century, advances in science showed the whole basis of the currently accepted periodic table to be mistaken.

The problem for the general lexicographer, who purports to be giving definitions for the total inventory of words in languages like English and French, is that the technique so successfully deployed in restricted domains such as physics and chemistry cannot be extended to general vocabulary. And the reason is not the absence of anything corresponding to the periodic table for other areas of human inquiry. The reason is that words have no *general* referential focus, nor even anything that approximates to one: the very idea is self-contradictory. Focus implies the deliberate exclusion, from a particular communicational context or type of context, of all facts deemed irrelevant thereto. Generalized focus makes no more semantic sense than private property that belongs to no one.

To approach this point from a different angle, let us consider again the case of proper names. If Russell's theory of proper names were right, it should be possible in principle to compile a dictionary of all proper names. This would presumably be something like a biographical dictionary or *Who's Who*, extended to all named individuals, living or dead, existing or fictitious, plus all named places, artifacts and events – a kind of encyclopedia in which every entry had a proper name as its lemma. The entries in each case would consist of definite descriptions.

Let us assume for purposes of the example that the compiler of this dictionary had no difficulty about deciding exactly what a proper name was. (In our view, a very difficult question, but we will take it that the compiler has been supplied with a list of proper names by God, or Plato's 'name-giver', or some equally well qualified figure.) The task is then to provide the list of descriptions adequate for the identification of each referent, distinguishing as many as there are different referents with the same name. This latter condition is manifestly crucial, since otherwise all that remains is an undifferentiated series of descriptions, but the user has no means of telling which descriptions belong to which referent. One would also, presumably, like the dictionary to indicate cases where the same referent goes under more than one proper name. Otherwise the user might be misled into supposing that the number of referents is larger than it is. Finally, since the number of referents with proper names increases day by day and hour by hour, let us suppose that the compiler's Herculean labour is curtailed by stipulating that the dictionary need be complete only down to the year 2000.

Let us further assume that on the list of proper names the compiler finds *Hitler*. It is clear that one of the compiler's tasks must be to distinguish by description the German dictator who played a major role in twentieth-century European history from every other person or creature who bore the same name. We have already argued above that the referential focus of the name *Hitler* may differ from one context to another, even within the same general mode of discourse (e.g. historical). We think it obvious that, depending on the referential focus, rather different possible descriptions of Hitler may be relevant. Thus, for instance, it might be the case that the well-known German dictator is the only person or creature satisfying the definite description 'the son of a customs official, born in Austria in 1899'. If so, that single description would suffice to identify without referential ambiguity one bearer of the name *Hitler*. But such an identification would be unhelpful, to say the least, to any user who consulted the dictionary in order to find out who was this person called *Hitler* whose name seemed so frequently to crop up in European histories of the period from 1918 to 1945. Being the son of a customs official and being born in Austria in 1899 are facts which hardly seem to explain all the historical fuss. So what *more* description does the compiler of Russell's dictionary of proper names have to put in, if the dictionary is not to become an object of ridicule?

The trouble is that the facts about Hitler are infinite in number. They cannot all go in. Even the facts about Hitler that uniquely distinguish him from anyone else with the same name are infinite in number. They cannot all go in either. No one wants to know *everything* about Hitler. No one even wants to know everything about Hitler that distinguishes him from anyone else with the same name. So under the lemma *Hitler* the compiler of Russell's dictionary will have to leave something out – will be obliged to leave out more than is included. How will this selection be justified?

It might seem a reasonable strategy to pick out those facts that the user of the dictionary might find most useful in understanding references to the referent. This, roughly, is the strategy followed by compilers of all biographical reference works. In other words, a certain referential focus is assumed, or certain probabilities with a certain range. ('People will look up *Bloggs* because Bloggs is well known as the person who . . ., or for having done . . ., or for not having done . . ., or for being the first to . . .') Well and good. But there is strictly *no* fact about Bloggs that might *not* – in the right context – become relevant or even central to people's interest in Bloggs. New facts about Bloggs might just have been discovered that put most of the old facts in a quite different light. (The relevant facts may even be negative facts. Yesterday it was revealed that Bloggs was not, as had been thought, the illegitimate son of the emperor of Ruritania; or not the pseudonymous author of that scurillous attack on the papacy; or not someone who fought for the Taliban in Afghanistan.) Referential focus is a historical phenomenon as well as a context-sensitive phenomenon. But above all it is a communicational phenomenon

Mutatis mutandis, all the above applies – we contend – not just to the bearers of proper names, but to all the things and events it might ever occur to people to communicate about. That is why those who compile general dictionaries are forced to assume, whether they like it or not, that certain facts about the world are of more interest than others – at least, for the type of dictionary-user they have in mind. Their definitions are tailored to those assumptions of referential focus, whether they realize that consciously or not.

Some lexicographers try to get by on the very minimum, and this means in practice the most general of assumptions. In Chapter 7 we have cited various definitions of the word *shrimp*. The lexicographer who opted for defining *shrimp* as just 'a small crustacean' is, in effect, hoping that the referential focus that prompted consultation of the dictionary is not so narrow as to render this account of what a shrimp is quite useless for the user's purposes. But it obviously *will* be for any user who already knows that shrimps are small crustaceans and wants to know whether the word *shrimp* is used to refer to any specific class of small crustaceans. At the other end of the scale, the lexicographer who defines *shrimp* by giving a detailed description of the creature's body and the biological classification of its genus assumes a referential focus on the topic which is far narrower. Neither assumption is 'right' or 'wrong' as compared with the other: they are just different assumptions about 'shrimp-talk'; just as including or omitting information about the occupation of Hitler's father in a biographical dictionary makes different assumptions about 'Hitler-talk'.

This explains both how it is that in one and the same society (1) many different definitions can pass for definitions of the same word, and (2) how it is that people can still disagree about the definitions of words in common usage. It elucidates (3) what is happening when someone proposes a stipulative definition or invents a new word, or both at once. Referential focus is involved in all these cases. But it also explains more, and more controversially. It explains why the theorist's distinction between 'real' and 'lexical' definition, although impeccable in principle at a certain level of abstraction, is something of an irrelevance when it comes to the details of lexicographical and legal practice. What counts in the end is always how the use of a word is, or could be, or should be integrated into the complex of activities involved. There is, we venture to suggest, no practical issue of this kind which is ever resolved, or even could be resolved, by insisting that lexical definition is one thing and real definition another. What resolves such issues is a *decision*, not a definition of either kind.

This is not to say, or imply, that talk about words is always parasitic on talk about reality. Nor is it to side with those postmodernists who claim that all talk of reality is parasitic on talk about words; or, as it is sometime put cryptically, that reality itself is a 'linguistic construct'. For an integrationist, these two positions are head and tail of the same misconception. Words, along with many other communicational devices, are an intrinsic part of human integration into the ways of social life, and the communicational use of words is always a form of integrated action. It is in virtue of that integration that it becomes possible to separate out, for certain communicational purposes, talk about words from talk about things. That separation, and the ease with which it is made, is one of the hallmarks of a literate society, where the written sign provides a convenient mode of triangulation for identifying the spoken sign, and vice versa. But, for all that, definition belongs neither to one side of the verbal/non-verbal divide nor to the other, any more than language itself does.

* * *

We should like to offer some further comments on indeterminacy in law. The topic has been discussed in relation to two interlocking issues. The first is the question of whether legal outcomes are determined by legal rules. Legal realism and Critical Legal Studies (CLS) are both understood as arguing that legal outcomes are substantially underdetermined or indeterminate in relation to legal rules, a position that is often labelled 'anti-formalist'. This can also be understood as equivalent to the claim that 'all cases are hard cases' (Solum 1996) or the assertion that 'legal questions lack single right answers' (Kress 2003: 253). The second is the wider question of how theories of meaning and interpretation that argue for various forms of indeterminacy impact on thinking about law. These theoretical approaches can be broadly categorized as 'anti-foundationalist': they include positions often labelled 'poststructuralist', 'postmodern', or 'deconstructive', as well as certain readings of Wittgenstein. Anti-foundationalism is closely associated with a sceptical focus on language and interpretation. It gives rise to two distinct understandings of indeterminacy. Indeterminacy as narrowly understood implies that legal outcomes are not determined by legal rules as expressed in legal texts. Indeterminacy as broadly understood is associated with the idea that law is 'incoherent and contradictory' (Kress 2003: 253). Neither of these is to be equated with the integrationist's 'radical indeterminacy'.

In the deconstructionist camp, notions of incoherence and contradiction are dominant. The question thus arises whether deconstruction as an intellectual movement or as an approach to reading texts has anything of importance to say to jurisprudence. Deconstruction, we are told, involves looking for 'multiple meanings of key words in a text, etymological relationships between words, and even puns to show how the text speaks with different (often conflicting) voices' (Balkin 1996: 368). Texts are not to be viewed as meaningless but rather as 'overflowing with multiple and often conflicting meanings'. Deconstruction often selects as its target entrenched binary oppositions, so that 'conceptual oppositions in legal thought' which have 'ideological effects' can be unmasked: in the operation of law 'their instability or fuzziness is disguised or suppressed so that they lend unwarranted plausibility to legal arguments and doctrines' (Balkin 1996: 369). Deconstruction had obvious appeal for scholars who saw themselves as promoting politically progressive social agendas, particularly those involved in the Critical Legal Studies movement and feminism. The claim that 'meanings were inherently unstable' lent credence to the argument that 'legal decision making was indeterminate', and thus that legal decision making was in reality political; the view that social structures were marked by 'instability and indeterminacy' gave support to the notion that they were contingent and not the product of a claimed 'necessity'; deconstruction also offered a technique for 'trashing' particular legal doctrines or arguments, since all texts could be shown to be undermined by their own logic. But Balkin argues that CLS's appropriation of deconstruction was problematic, as there seemed to be the implication that 'an autonomous subject was manipulating indeterminate language', whereas deconstruction denied that the meaning of a text was under the control of an autonomous subject (or author) (Balkin 1996: 370). Further, deconstruction – at least as Balkin presents it – is a general theory of texts, and can be turned against any alternative legal or rhetorical order. It is just as capable of destabilizing concepts like 'women's interests' as 'patriarchy' (Balkin 1996: 370–1). Indeed, the most curious aspect of the political history of indeterminacy is the assumption that denials of indeterminacy are automatically conservative and attacks on foundationalism inevitably politically progressive.

One attempt at a knockout argument against the strong indeterminacy thesis – that 'in every possible case, any possible outcome is legally correct' – is the argument from easy cases. Kress uses the 'pervasiveness of easy cases' as one strand of the argument that 'indeterminacy is at most moderate' and this level of indeterminacy 'does not undermine the law's legitimacy' (Kress 2003: 253). If it can be shown that 'there is at least one possible case in which at least one legal outcome is legally incorrect', then the strong indeterminacy thesis will have been disproved (Solum 1996: 490–1). Thus a family trip to the beach in which no business dealings were discussed cannot violate an anti-trust law, and, while one can imagine situations where someone might be convicted on these facts (e.g. corruption, perjury), that outcome would be legally incorrect. Solum considers whether 'rule-scepticism', which he finds in Kripke's interpretation of Wittgenstein, can nonetheless be adduced in favour of strong indeterminacy, but rejects this on the grounds that this would imply that 'there are no rules for the application of language to any situation'. This is equivalent to the proposition that 'any sentence can mean anything', and thus that 'no sentence means anything or that human communication is impossible' (Solum 1996: 494). This view is also termed 'semantic scepticism' (Coleman and Leiter 1993: 568) and it amounts to the claim:

> that there are no facts that constitute or determine a sentence's meaning, so that language is indeterminate at the most basic level: there are no objective facts that make it the case that language means one thing rather than another. Thus, there is no point to claiming that a legal rule can be satisfied by some actions but not others since the meaning of the rule is always 'up for grabs.'

Solum considers the alternative view that legal outcomes are underdetermined by law, a position that cannot be refuted by the argument from easy cases. Decisions to proceed to litigation rather than settle are frequently based at least in part on a judgement that the case has a degree of legal indeterminacy. Are not legal decisions in many litigated cases therefore arbitrary? Solum follows Kress (1990) in distinguishing between 'metaphysical indeterminacy' (the indeterminate status of law itself) and 'epistemic indeterminacy' (which relates to the question of whether law can be fully known). Epistemic indeterminacy does not however mean that judges' decisions are arbitrary, since one should not equate arbitrariness with the existence of more than one defensible legal outcome (Solum 1996: 498).

A further distinction in the jurisprudential literature is that between indeterminacy of reasons and indeterminacy of causes (Solum 1996: 496). Indeterminacy of reasons concerns the grounds on which decisions are made, in that legal reasons may be seen as impoverished or 'too rich' and in conflict with one another, so that they do not support any particular outcome (Coleman and Leiter 1993: 575). Causal indeterminacy 'implies that something other than law determines the result in particular cases'. Coleman and Leiter argue that indeterminacy itself does not undermine law's legitimacy unless it can be understood as a failure of 'warrant'. A decision is warranted 'to the extent that rational judgment can be defended in the face of disagreement caused by the fact that different norms support conflicting conclusions' (Coleman and Leiter 1993: 579).

It would be no doubt possible to create a long list of distinct forms of legal indeterminacy, but it is hard to see a principled difference between indeterminacy of reasons and indeterminacy of causes, in particular given that for any given decision there must be a further meta-indeterminacy, i.e. the undecidability of precise locus of the indeterminacy. For example, it might be argued that linguistic structures and meanings are determinate, but the reasoning processes that are applied create indeterminacy of legal outcomes. But it would be impossible to demonstrate this distinction in operation, since in looking at the language of the legal text one is already caught up in the reasoning that the specific facts and context of the case require.

* * *

Is a legal text ultimately different from any other text as regards determinacy? Legal indeterminacy has been linked to literary indeterminacy by Stanley Fish. Fish argues that to deny that norms are embedded in language does not equate with the view that interpretation is random or arbitrary. E. D. Hirsch had offered 'The air is crisp' as an example of a sentence which is 'accessible to all speakers of the language', with a 'sharable and determinate', as well as potentially private or individual associations ('Crisp air reminds me of my childhood in Vermont'). Fish comments: 'The obviousness of the utterance's meaning is not a function of the values its words have in a linguistic system that is independent of context; rather, it is because the words are heard as already embedded in a context that they have a meaning that Hirsch can then cite as obvious' (Fish 1980: 309–10). While denying that texts have determinate meanings, Fish locates the possibility of communication in situations, and in the assumptions and practices brought to situations: 'meanings come already calculated, not because of norms embedded in the language but because language is always perceived, from the very first, within a structure of norms' (Fish 1980: 318). These norms or beliefs are 'communal and conventional' (Fish 1980: 321); in other words, they are the property of what Fish calls 'interpretative communities'. This concept was required to explain 'both agreement and disagreement', such a community being

> not so much a group of individuals who shared a point of view, but a point of view or way of organizing experience that shared individuals in the sense that its assumed distinctions, categories of understanding, and stipulations of relevance and irrelevance were the content of the consciousness of community members. (Fish 1989: 141)

This shared set of norms and assumptions is required to account for agreement as to how interpreters 'constitute . . . the same text'. This is not attributable to the 'self-identity' of the text, but to 'the communal nature of the interpretative act'. Differences with regard to texts are not then settled with reference to the text itself; for what would be at stake in a textual dispute concerns 'the interpretative "angle" from which the text was to be seen, and, in being seen, made' (Fish 1989: 141–2).

In an essay entitled 'Law wishes to have a formal existence', Fish defines formalism as follows:

> the thesis that it is possible to put marks so self-sufficiently perspicuous that they repel interpretation; it is the thesis that one can write sentences of such precision and simplicity that their meanings leap off the page . . .; that one can devise procedures that are self-executing . . . independent of the difference between the agents who might set them in motion. (Fish 1999: 168)

According to Fish, the objections to this view of law derive from two major sources, a 'humanistic' concern that if the law is defined in formal terms it is thus divorced from morality, and, secondly, the view that 'a purely formal system is not a possibility' (Fish 1999: 168). Fish focuses on law as a process whereby assertions that interpretation is formally constrained involve in fact an effort to stabilize what is being supposedly relied on, i.e. 'the plain meaning of absolutely clear language' (Fish 1999: 170).

In the construction of written contracts, the general rule is that the terms of the contract are considered to exhaust the meaning of the contract, and there are restrictions on so-called 'parol evidence', i.e. evidence about what the parties said in relation to the contract before and during its execution. This raises the more general question of the borderline between 'intrinsic evidence', e.g. the language of the relevant contract, and 'extrinsic evidence', e.g. information about the intentions of the parties, practices specific to particular trades, the behaviour of the parties, e.g. the existence of a 'course of dealing' independent of, or alongside, the contract. Evidence that relates to misrepresentation, mistake, duress or undue influence is not excluded by this rule. Clearly if someone induces another to sign a contract by threatening 'if you don't sign this contract I will kill you', this ought to render the contract void. Fish points out that this 'extrinsic evidence' also includes 'the entire history of the parol evidence rule' itself, which is brought to bear in coming to the conclusion that a text has a particular 'literal' meaning (Fish 1999: 171). Thus a determination of what is inside the text 'will always be a function of whatever "outside" has been already assumed' (Fish 1999: 173). The issue is not therefore one of literal versus contextual readings but 'the relative persuasiveness of alternative contexts as they are set out in ideologically charged narratives' (Fish 1999: 180).

Fish's argument, while it covers much of the same ground as other anti-foundationalist theories, does not in the end evince much sympathy for anti-formalist critiques of law. Anti-foundationalism for Fish does not amount to a denial of the existence of foundations, but is 'a thesis about how foundations emerge' as 'local or temporal phenomena' (Fish 1989: 30). The view that legal argumentation masks its own inherent indeterminacy (Fish 1999: 193), if offered as part of a political critique, presupposes that law falls short of a standard of 'rational determinacy', i.e. it measures law by an unattainable standard. For Fish, law is obliged to fashion out of 'alien materials' its own autonomy and authority; its very possibility of continuing as a practice rests on acts of 'forgetting'. The practice of law is distinct from the academic study of law, which can purse interdisciplinary analysis of the foundations and operations of law. This philosophical inquiry cannot however disrupt law's closure, since that closure is necessary for law's operation, 'though the shape of its closure will be endless revisable' (Fish 1999: 202). In a world 'without foundational essences', law must take this 'self-occluding and perhaps self-deceiving form' because it is the task of law 'to stand between us and the contingency out of which its own structures are fashioned' (Fish 1999: 203).

In finding a form of determinacy 'outside' the text, i.e. in the shared norms of the interpretative community, Fish attempts to defuse the argument that the indeterminacy of language requires us to recognize semantic chaos and what he terms 'a universe of absolute free play' (Fish 1980: 268). But his more general argument about the nature of texts and interpretative communities seems to rely on the very distinction between 'inside' and 'outside' that he rejects in law. The 'inside' of the text is indeterminate; the 'outside' constructs the text through community-based norms of reading and interpretation. It is in any case quite problematic to attribute differences in the interpretation of texts to membership of different interpretative communities. The concept has arguably very little explanatory value in the context of law, since there is no independent way of identifying a particular interpretative community of lawyers beyond pointing to a contentious textual issue. It is thus no more informative than explaining the outcome of an election by appeal to the existence of different 'interpretative communities' of voters.

Fish's position on indeterminacy, while it is preferable to the political posturing of much deconstructive criticism of law, raises a profound question with regard to the social understanding of law and language. Is the operation of law only possible on the basis of misrepresenting to all concerned the nature of language and of legal rules? (This is – dare we say it? – an elitist solution to the problem of indeterminacy: 'Don't tell the people.') A parallel suggestion would be that lexicography is only possible on the basis of a fiction that words are fixed form-meaning pairings, capable of particular kinds of precise representation (e.g. in phonetic transcription) and of being defined in systematic ways.

It seems to us at least worth considering the possible consequences of the institutional recognition of linguistic indeterminacy, both for lexicography and for law.

In lexicography, one predictable consequence would be that the general dictionary would lose whatever authority was vested in generalizations that go beyond the evidence presented. The lexicographer's pronouncements would cease to be oracular and be subject to the same critical scrutiny as those of other social analysts. This might lead eventually to the abolition of context-free definitions altogether and their replacement by semantic descriptions based on what we called in Chapter 7 a 'communicational' concept of word-meaning.

In law, the question of indeterminacy is inextricably bound up with competing stipulative definitions of law itself. On the formalist view, law is 'essentially definitional', i.e. it 'comes into being through the specialized meanings of words' (Dimock 2001: 203). If one takes this view, and regards meanings and interpretations as in principle public and stable, then law will be seen as substantially determinate. The 'right answer' in any given case will be that determined by the language of the authoritative text.

The alternative – as we see it – is to treat law in a non-formalist way, i.e. as the pragmatics of the entire process whereby cases are decided. It is then difficult to find houseroom for the determinacy question, since cases are decided one by one against the background of written texts such as laws and contracts, but also as products of human procedural, socio-cultural, ideological and political contingencies, rhetorical competition, the limitations of human powers of concentration and memory, incompatible policy priorities, and so on. Taking a non-formalist approach, it would hardly be feasible to show that law as such was either determinate or indeterminate, since it would be recognized *ab initio* that the actual grounds for each legal decision are not necessarily revealed by the semantics of the relevant texts, but are nonetheless part of law. There is in short no single place where the 'right answer' can be found.

* * *

It should come as no surprise that it proves to be impossible to mount a theoretically convincing case for semantic determinacy either in the domain of lexicography or in that of law. The history of modern philosophy shows the topic to be a disaster area in which a number of distinguished thinkers came to grief.

Frege found himself trapped in his debate with Benno Kerry in the 1890s into conceding something akin to the admission that words have no fixed meanings. In the pages of the *Vierteljahrsschrift für wissenschaftliche Philosophie* (1892) Frege was forced to agree not only that he and Kerry were using the word 'concept' in different senses, but that no one 'can require that my mode of expression shall agree with Kerry's'. This sounds like a distant echo of Locke's claim that every individual is free to attach whatever meaning he wishes to any word he chooses. However, doubtless foreseeing that to appear to embrace a thoroughgoing semantic solipsism would make the whole debate between himself and Kerry seem futile, Frege adds a hedging footnote in which he declines to inquire into the thesis that 'the same word is never taken in quite the same way even by men who share a language'. Instead, he simply affirms his own conviction that 'different expressions quite often have something in common', which is the 'sense' or the 'thought' expressed. The reason why he believes this then becomes clear: if it were otherwise,

> logic would simply be crippled; for the task of logic can hardly be performed without trying to recognize the thought in its manifold guises. Moreover, *all definitions would then have to be rejected as false.* (Frege 1892: 46fn. Our italics.)

Aristotle might well have turned in his grave at such a blasphemous thought. But there is obviously a tension between this and Frege's admission earlier in the same paper that

> we cannot come to an understanding with one another apart from language, and so in the end we must always rely on other people's understanding words, inflexions, and sentence-construction in essentially the same way as ourselves. (Frege 1892: 45)

Apart from being a gross *non sequitur,* this leaves the particular debate between Frege and Kerry (and all such debates) in a kind of limbo. There appears to be, on the one hand, an admission of linguistic indeterminacy (i.e. recognition that even within the same linguistic community there may be no complete agreement about the meanings of words); but, on the other hand, a conviction that any such disagreement cannot be serious enough to undermine the workings of logic. Where this guarantee come from Frege's readers are never told. In short, Frege wants to have the best of all possible worlds, i.e. wants *both* linguistic indeterminacy (when debating with opponents) *and* ideal fixed codes (the latter operating at some level of abstraction where lack of linguistic determinacy does not affect the universal validity of logic or some universal inventory of definitions).

It is ironic that Frege, renowned for his anti-psychologism and neo-Platonist semantics, should end up stranded on this particular reef; for the only way his two requirements can be reconciled is presumably by postulating as a psychological universal that the human mind is so constructed that linguistic indeterminacies always cancel one another out, leaving reasoning intact. Mankind, Frege asserts confidently, 'has a common stock of thoughts'. But how one can know which these are, and how they relate to thoughts that do not belong to this common stock, are questions that manifestly bedevil any attempt at a coherent debate about language. Thus, if Frege is taken seriously, it remains profoundly unclear whether any of us can possibly know what we are talking about.

Popper finds himself in a similar impasse. Pressing the notion of indeterminacy further than Frege, he declares that 'the idea of a precise language, or of precision in language, seems to be altogether misconceived' (Popper 1976: 24). He thinks that 'it is impossible to speak in such a way that you cannot be misunderstood'. At one stroke, this condemns attempts at definition as futile. But he wishes nevertheless to salvage from this communicational catastrophe some hope for progress towards the acquisition and linguistic statement of genuine scientific knowledge. Hence his much-discussed doctrine of fallibilism. This is linguistic theorizing masquerading as philosophy of science. As Popper's critics have pointed out, the notion that one can never verify the truth of a claim, but detect its falsification nonetheless, is self-stultifying. Indeed, in his more desperate moments Popper admits that 'we never know what we are talking about' (Popper 1976: 27). For one who never knew what he was talking about, Popper talked a great deal, and convinced many naive scientists to the contrary.

Wittgenstein struggles with indeterminacy in the late notes posthumously published in *On Certainty*. His problem is that he wants to cling on to the concept of a 'rule', while admitting that 'rules leave loop-holes open' (Wittgenstein 1969: §139). Rules, he maintains, are 'needed for establishing a practice'. But because of the loopholes, in the end 'the practice has to speak for itself'. Had he been a lawyer, he might perhaps have realized how illusory it is to suppose that the practice ever 'speaks for itself'. If it did, there would be wholesale unemployment in the legal profession.

* * *

In conclusion, to summarize our own position, we would like to make it clear that any view which associates indeterminacy with semantic chaos, textual incoherence or pervasive self-contradiction has little in common with, and can derive little support from, an integrationist semiology. Integrationism is committed to a 'lay-oriented' analysis of communication in the following sense: that, where language is concerned, there is no basis of knowledge or expertise other than that available to any lay member of the community. This basis is the experience acquired by participation in the processes of interaction with others – parents, siblings, neighbours, friends, enemies, strangers. All the metalinguistic terms and concepts used in asking and answering questions about language are ultimately derived from – and have to be explicated by reference to – someone's first-order linguistic experience. If that explanatory chain cannot be satisfactorily established, then the linguistic theorist – not the lay person – has been led astray. It is not the professional grammarian or lexicographer who has a superior ('scientific') view of how words function in social praxis and the lay person who is ignorant or perverse on that subject, but the other way round. Or, to put the point somewhat differently: although not everyone is a lawyer, *everybody is a linguist* – not only graduates with a doctorate in 'linguistics'. And necessarily so. For all human beings engage in analytic reflection about their own linguistic experience and use words to describe it. This is a *sine qua non* of engagement in language as a mature member of society.

The pessimistic evocation of Babel lurking in deconstructive, anti-foundationalist and other sceptical theories of language and of law does not correspond to anyone's first-order linguistic experience. To see attempts at definition as doomed in advance to failure, and to regard texts and other products of linguistic activity as perpetually and necessarily self-undermining, is to take the hypothetical view of an omniscient outsider – a view from nowhere. It implies an idealized semantic order against which the existing state of affairs is perceived as chaotic. Integrationism, on the other hand, sees linguistic indeterminacy as a corollary of the fact that, in the communicational process, signs do not 'have meanings' but are 'made to mean'. This is not to reject or call in question the very possibility of human communication. On the contrary, it points to the only basis on which human communication can – and does – proceed.

References

Abelson, R. (1967), 'Definition', *The Encyclopedia of Philosophy*, ed. P. Edwards, New York: Macmillan, 2, 314–24.

Amos, S. (1874), *The Science of Law*. New York: Appleton.

Aristotle, *Complete Works. The Revised Oxford Translation*, ed. J. Barnes. Princeton: Princeton University Press, 1984.

Arnauld, A. and Nicole, P. (1683), *La logique ou l'art de penser*, 5me éd. rev., ed. L. Marin. Paris: Flammarion, 1970.

Austin, J. (1879), *Lectures on Jurisprudence*, 4th edn. London: Murray.

Austin, J. L. (1956), 'A plea for excuses', *Proceedings of the Aristotelian Society*, 57, 1–30.

— (1962), *How to do Things with Words*. Oxford: Clarendon.

Bacon, F. (1605), *The Advancement of Learning*, ed. G. W. Kitchin. London: Dent, 1915.

— (1625), *Essays*. London: Dent, 1994.

Balkin, J. M. (1996), 'Deconstruction', in D. Patterson (ed.), *A Companion to Philosophy of Law and Legal Theory*. Oxford: Blackwell, pp. 367–74.

Barney, J. R. (2003), 'In search of "ordinary meaning"', *Journal of the Patent and Trademark Office Society*, 85, 101–30.

Bennion, F. (2002), *Statutory Interpretation: a Code*, 4th edn. London: Butterworths.

Bentham, J. (1776), *A Fragment on Government and An Introduction to the Principles of Morals and Legislation*. London: Payne. Ed. W. Harrison, Oxford: Blackwell, 1960.

— (1782), *On Laws in General*. Ed. H.L.A. Hart, London: Athlone, 1970.

— (1843), 'Essay on logic', *Works of Jeremy Bentham vol. VIII*, ed. J. Bowring. Edinburgh: Simpkin, Marshall, 1838–43, pp. 213–93.

Berenson, B. (1950), *Aesthetics and History*. London: Constable.

Bix, B. (1993), *Law, Language and Legal Determinacy*. Oxford: Clarendon.

Blanché, R. (1970), *L'axiomatique*. Paris: Presses Universitaires de France.

Bloomfield, L. (1935), *Language*. London: Allen & Unwin.

Bolton, K., Hutton, C. and Ip P.-F. (1996), 'The speech-act offence: claiming and professing membership of a triad society in Hong Kong', *Language & Communication*, 16, 263–90.

Bouquet, S. and Engler, R. (eds) (2002), *Écrits de linguistique générale par Ferdinand de Saussure*. Paris: Gallimard.

Boyle, R. (1661), *The Sceptical Chymist*, Oxford. Repr. London: Dent, 1911.

Burchfield, R. (1985), *The English Language*. Oxford: Oxford University Press.

Cardozo, B. (1921), *The Nature of the Judicial Process*. New Haven: Yale University Press.

Carnap, R. (1937), *The Logical Syntax of Language*, trans. A. Smeaton. London: Kegan Paul, Trench, & Trubner.

Carroll, L. (1871), *Through the Looking-Glass*. London: Macmillan, 1872 [i.e. 1871].

— (1896), *Symbolic Logic*. London: Macmillan.

Carter, L. and Burke, T. (2002), *Reason in Law*, 6th edn. New York: Longman.

Cassirer, E. (1910), *Substance and Function*, trans. W. C. Swabey and M. C. Swabey. Chicago: Open Court, 1923. Repr. New York: Dover, 1953.

Chafee, Z. (1941), 'The disorderly conduct of words', *Columbia Law Review*, 41, 381–404.

Chomsky, A. N. (1965), *Aspects of the Theory of Syntax*. Cambridge, Mass.: MIT Press.

Coleman, J. and Leiter, B. (1993), 'Determinacy, objectivity and authority', *University of Pennsylvania Law Review*, 142, 549–637.

Cornford, F. M. (1941), *The Republic of Plato*. Oxford: Clarendon.

Cunningham, C., Levi, J., Green, G. and Kaplan, J. (1994), 'Plain meaning and hard cases', *Yale Law Journal*, 103, 1561–625.

Crystal, D. (1997), *A Dictionary of Linguistics and Phonetics*, 4th edn. Oxford: Blackwell.

Darwin, C. (1859), *The Origin of Species*. Repr. of 6th edn, London: Dent, 1971.

Dewey, J. (1938), *Logic. The Theory of Inquiry*. New York: Holt.

Dickinson, J. (1929), 'The law behind the law', *Columbia Law Review*, 29, 113–46; 285–319.

Dimock, W. C. (2001), 'Rules of law, laws of science', *Yale Journal of Law & the Humanities*, 13, 203–25.

Dworkin, R. (1996), 'Taking rights seriously', in F. Schauer and W. Sinnott-Armstrong (eds), *The Philosophy of Law: Classic and Contemporary Readings with Commentary*. New York: Harcourt Brace, pp. 74–89.

Eco, U. (1995), *The Search for the Perfect Language*, trans. J. Fentress. Oxford: Blackwell.

Einstein, A. (1961), *Relativity: The Special and the General Theory*, 15th edn., trans. R. W. Lawson. New York: Crown.

Endicott, T. (2002), 'Law and language', *The Stanford Encyclopedia of Philosophy*. (Winter 2002 Edition), Edward N. Zalta (ed.), URL = www. plato.stanford.edu/archives/win2002/entries/law-language/, accessed 17 July 2006.

Ewing, A. C. (1947), *The Definition of Good*. New York: Macmillan.

Fann, K. T. (ed.) (1969), *Symposium on J. L. Austin*. London: Routledge & Kegan Paul.

Fish, S. (1980), *Is there a Text in this Class? The Authority of Interpretative Communities*. Cambridge, Mass.: Harvard University Press.

— (1989), *Doing What Comes Naturally. Change, Rhetoric, and the Practice of Theory in Literary and Legal Studies*. Durham: Duke University Press.

— (1999), 'The law wishes to have a formal existence'. Repr. in H. A. Veeser (ed.), *The Stanley Fish Reader*. Oxford: Blackwell, pp. 165–206.

Fletcher, G. P. (1996), *Basic Concepts of Legal Thought*. New York: Oxford University Press.

Fodor, J. A. (1998), *Concepts. Where Cognitive Science Went Wrong*. Oxford: Clarendon.

Frank, J. (1970), *Law and the Modern Mind*. Gloucester, Mass.: Smith.

Frankfurter, F. (1947), 'Some reflections on the reading of statutes', *Columbia Law Review*, 47, 527–46.

Frazer, J. G. (1921), *Apollodorus, The Library* (2 vols), Loeb Classical Library.London: Heinemann.

Frege, G. (1892), 'On concept and object', trans. P. T. Geach, in P. T. Geach and M. Black (eds), *Translations from the Philosophical Writings of Gottlob Frege*, 2nd edn. Oxford: Blackwell, 1960, pp. 42–55.

— (1893–1903), *Grundgesetze der Arithmetik*, 2 vols, Jena. Quotations are from P. Geach and M. Black (eds), *Translations from the Philosophical Writings of Gottlob Frege*, 2nd edn. Oxford: Blackwell, 1960, pp. 137–244.

— (1918), 'Thoughts', trans. P. T. Geach and R. H. Stoothoff, in *G. Frege, Logical Investigations*, ed. P. T. Geach. Oxford: Blackwell, 1977.

Fuller L. (1958), 'Positivism and fidelity to law – a reply to Professor Hart', *Harvard Law Review*, 71, 630–72.

Garner, B. (2003), 'Legal lexicography: a view from the front lines', *English Today*, 9, 33–42.

Glock, H-J. (1996), *A Wittgenstein Dictionary*. Oxford: Blackwell.

Goble, G. W. (1933), 'Law as science', *The Scientific Monthly*, 37 (3), 229–40.

Golanski, A. (2002), 'Linguistics in law', *Albany Law Review*, 66, 61–121.

Gray, K. and Gray, S. (2005), *Elements of Land Law*, 4th edn. Oxford: Oxford University Press.

Greenbaum, S. (1988), *Good English and the Grammarian*. London: Longman.

Grice, H. P. (1975), 'Logic and conversation', in P. Cole and J. L. Morgan (eds), *Syntax and Semantics, Vol. 3, Speech Acts*. New York: Academic, pp. 41–58.

Harris, J. W. (1980), *Legal Philosophies*. London: Butterworths.

Harris, R. (1981), *The Language Myth*. London: Duckworth.

— (1987), *Reading Saussure*. London: Duckworth.

— (1996), *The Language Connection*. Bristol: Thoemmes.

— (1998), *Introduction to Integrational Linguistics*. Oxford: Pergamon.

— (2003), *The Necessity of Artspeak*. London: Continuum.

— (2004), *The Linguistics of History*. Edinburgh: Edinburgh University Press.

— (2005), *The Semantics of Science*. London: Continuum.

— (2006a), *Integrationist Notes and Papers 2003–2005*. Crediton, Tree Tongue.

— (2006b), 'Integrational linguistics and semiology', *The Encyclopedia of Language and Linguistics*, 2nd edn. Oxford: Elsevier, 5, 714–18.

Harris, R. and Wolf, G. (eds) (1998), *Integrational Linguistics: a First Reader*. Oxford: Pergamon.

Hart, H. L. A. (1954), 'Definition and theory in jurisprudence', *Law Quarterly Review*, 70, 37–60.

— (1982), *Essays on Bentham: Studies in Jurisprudence and Political Theory*. Oxford: Clarendon.

— (1994), *The Concept of Law*, 2nd edn, with a postscript edited by P. Bulloch and J. Raz. Oxford: Clarendon.

Hartmann, R. R. K. and James, G. (1998), *Dictionary of Lexicography*. London: Taylor & Francis.

Hempel, C. G. (1952), *Fundamentals of Concept Formation in Empirical Science.* Chicago: University of Chicago Press.

Henly, B. (1987), '"Penumbra": the roots of a legal metaphor', *Hastings Constitutional Law Quarterly*, 15, 81–100.

Hobbes, T. (1651), *Leviathan*, ed. C. B. Macpherson. Harmondsworth: Penguin, 1968.

Hodges, W. (1977), *Logic.* Harmondsworth: Penguin.

Hohfeld, W. N. (2001), *Fundamental Legal Conceptions as Applied in Judicial Reasoning*, ed. D. Campbell and P. Thomas. Aldershot, Hants.: Dartmouth.

Hudson, A. (2003), *Equity and Trusts*, 3rd edn. London: Cavendish.

Hurley, P. J. (1988), *A Concise Introduction to Logic*, 3rd edn. Belmont: Wadsworth.

Hutchinson, D. S. (1997), *Plato. Definitions*, in *Plato. Complete Works*, ed. J. M. Cooper. Indianapolis: Hackett, pp. 1677–86.

Johnson, S. (1747), *The Plan of a Dictionary of the English Language.* London: Knapton & Knapton *et al.*

— (1755), 'Preface' to *A Dictionary of the English Language.* London: Knapton & Knapton *et al.*

Jori, M. (1994), 'Legal systems', *The Encyclopedia of Language and Linguistics*, ed. R. E. Asher. Oxford: Pergamon, 4, 2122–9.

Kant, I. (1781), *Critique of Pure Reason*, trans. J. M. D. Meiklejohn. London: Dent, 1934.

Kaplan, J., Green, G., Cunningham, C. and Levi, J. (1995), 'Bringing linguistics into judicial decision-making: semantic analysis submitted to the US Supreme Court', *Forensic Linguistics*, 1, 81–98.

Kelsen, H. (1997), *Introduction to the Problems of Legal Theory. A Translation of the First Edition of the Reine Rechtslehre or Pure Theory of Law*, trans. B. Litschewski Paulson and S. Paulson. Oxford: Oxford University Press.

Kelvin, W. T. (1883), 'Electrical units of measurement', in W. T. Kelvin, *Popular Lectures and Addresses* I, 2nd edn. London: Macmillan, 1891.

Kenny, C. S. (1902), *Outlines of Criminal Law.* Cambridge: Cambridge University Press.

Kneale, W. and Kneale, M. (1988), *The Development of Logic*, rev. edn. Oxford: Clarendon.

Kress, K. (2003), 'Legal indeterminacy', in D. Patterson (ed.), *Philosophy of Law and Legal Theory.* Oxford: Blackwell, pp. 253–91.

Langford, C. H. (1952), 'Moore's notion of analysis', in P. A. Schilpp (ed.), *The Philosophy of G. E. Moore*, 2nd edn. New York: Tudor, pp. 319–42.

Linsky, L. (1967), *Referring.* London: Routledge & Kegan Paul.

Llewellyn, K. (1950), 'Remarks on the theory of appellate decision and the rules and canons of how statutes are to be interpreted', *Vanderbilt Law Review*, 3, 396–406.

Locke, J. (1706), *An Essay Concerning Human Understanding*, 6th edn, ed. A. C. Fraser, 1894. Repr. New York: Dover, 1969.

Longuet-Higgins, H. C. (1972), 'The frontiers of psychology', in A. J. P. Kenny, H. C. Longuet-Higgins, J. R. Lucas, and C. H. Waddington, *The Development of Mind.* Edinburgh: Edinburgh University Press, 1973, pp. 1–15.

Love, N. (1985), 'The fixed-code theory', *Language & Communication*, 5, 1–17.

MacCormick, N. (1994), *Legal Reasoning and Legal Theory*. Oxford: Clarendon.

Malone, K. (1940), 'On defining *mahogany*', *Language*, 16 (4), 308–18.

Mautner, T. (ed.) (1997), *The Penguin Dictionary of Philosophy*, rev. edn. London: Penguin.

McLaverty, J. (1986), 'Locke's influence on Johnson's Dictionary', *Journal of the History of Ideas*, 47 (3), 377–94.

Mellinkoff, D. (1963), *The Language of the Law*. Boston: Little, Brown.

Mersky, R. (2004), 'The evolution and impact of legal dictionaries', *Legal Reference Services Quarterly*, 23 (1), 19–39.

Mill, J. S. (1859), *On Liberty*, ed. G. Himmelfarb. London: Penguin, 1974.

— (1884), *System of Logic*, 8th edn. London: Longman, Green. Repr. London: Longman, 1970.

Moore, G. E. (1912), *Ethics*. London: Oxford University Press.

— (1952), 'A reply to my critics', in P. A. Schilpp (ed.), *The Philosophy of G. E. Moore*, 2nd edn. New York: Tudor, pp. 533–677.

Mullins, M. E. (2000), 'Coming to terms with strict and liberal construction', *Albany Law Review*, 64: 90–8.

Murray, J. A. H. (1884), *A New English Dictionary on Historical Principles*, Part I, Preface and General Explanations. Oxford: Clarendon.

— (1911), 'English language', *Encyclopaedia Britannica*, 11th edn. Cambridge: Cambridge University Press, 9, 587–600.

Murray, K. M. E. (1977), *Caught in the Web of Words. James A. H. Murray and the Oxford English Dictionary*. New Haven: Yale University Press.

Ogden, C. K. and Richards, I. A. (1923), *The Meaning of Meaning*. London: Routledge & Kegan Paul.

Pearson, K. (1892), *The Grammar of Science*, London, Scott. Repr. ed. A. Pyle, Bristol: Thoemmes, 1991.

Peierls, R. E. (1955), *The Laws of Nature*. London: Scientific Book Guild.

Plato, *Complete Works*, ed. J. M. Cooper. Indianapolis: Hackett, 1997.

Priestley, J. B. (1927), *The English Novel*. London: Benn.

Prior, A. N. (1962), *Formal Logic*, 2nd edn. Oxford: Clarendon.

Popper, K. (1976), *Unended Quest. An Intellectual Autobiography*. London: Fontana.

Posner, R. (1990), *The Problems of Jurisprudence*. Cambridge, Mass.: Harvard University Press.

Putnam, H. (1975), 'Is semantics possible?'. Repr. in H. Putnam, *Mind, Language and Reality*. Cambridge: Cambridge University Press, pp. 139–52.

Quine, W. V. O. (1960), *Word and Object*. Cambridge, Mass.: MIT Press.

Reid, T. (1764), *An Inquiry into the Human Mind on the Principles of Common Sense*. Edinburgh: Millar, Kincaid & Bell.

Robinson, R. (1954), *Definition*. Oxford: Clarendon.

Robson, W. (1935), *Civilization and the Growth of Law: A Study of the Relations between Men's Ideas about the Universe and the Institutions of Law and Government*. London: Macmillan.

Ruskin, J. (1871), *Munera Pulveris*, rev. edn. Repr. London: Allen, 1907.

Russell, B. A. W. (1919), *Introduction to Mathematical Philosophy.* London, Allen & Unwin.

— (1940), *An Inquiry into Meaning and Truth.* London: Allen & Unwin. Repr. Harmondsworth: Penguin, 1962.

Ryle, G. (1931), 'Systematically misleading expressions'. Repr. in A. G. N. Flew (ed.), *Essays on Logic and Language (First Series).* Oxford: Blackwell, 1951, pp. 11–36.

Saussure, F. de (1922), *Cours de linguistique générale,* 2nd edn. Paris: Payot.

Scalia, A. (1997), *A Matter of Interpretation: Federal Courts and the Law.* Princeton: Princeton University Press.

Schroth, P. W. (1998), 'Language and law', *American Journal of Comparative Law,* 46, 17–39.

Searle, J. (1969), *Speech Acts. An Essay in the Philosophy of Language.* Cambridge: Cambridge University Press.

Silva, P. (2000), 'Time and meaning: sense and definition in the *OED*', in L. Mugglestone (ed.), *Lexicography and the OED. Pioneers in the Untrodden Forest.* Oxford: Oxford University Press, pp. 77–95.

Solan, L. (1993), *The Language of Judges.* Chicago: University of Chicago Press.

— (2004), 'The Clinton scandal: some legal lessons from linguistics', in J. Cotterill (ed.), *Language in the Legal Process.* London, Palgrave, pp. 180–95.

Solum, L. B. (1996), 'Indeterminacy', in D. Patterson (ed.), *A Companion to Philosophy of Law and Legal Theory.* Oxford: Blackwell, pp. 488–502.

Smith, A. (1776), *The Wealth of Nations,* repr. London, Dent, 1910.

Somervell, D. C. (1928), *A History of Western Europe 1815–1926.* London: Benn.

Stebbing, L. S. (1930), *A Modern Introduction to Logic.* London: Methuen.

Stone, J. (1964), *Legal System and Lawyers' Reasoning.* London: Stevens.

Strawson, P. F. (1952), *Introduction to Logical Theory.* London: Methuen.

Sullivan, Ruth (n.d.), 'The plain meaning rule and other ways to cheat at statutory interpretation', www.aix1.uottawa.ca/~resulliv/legdr/pmr.html, accessed 17 July 2006.

Tarski, A. (1956), *Logic, Semantics, Metamathematics,* trans. J. H. Woodger. Oxford: Clarendon.

Taylor, T. J. (1992), *Mutual Misunderstanding.* Durham: Duke University Press.

Thayer, J. B. (1898), *A Preliminary Treatise on Evidence at the Common Law.* Boston: Little, Brown. Repr. South Hackensack, NJ: Rothman, 1969.

Thumma, S. and Kirchmeier, J. (1999), 'The lexicon has become a fortress: the United States Supreme Court's use of dictionaries', *Buffalo Law Review,* 47, 227–301.

Tiersma, P. M. (2000), *Legal Language.* Chicago: University of Chicago Press.

Toolan, M. (1996), *Total Speech. An Integrational Linguistic Approach to Language.* Durham: Duke University Press.

— (2002), 'The language myth and the law', in R. Harris (ed.), *The Language Myth in Western Culture.* London: Curzon, pp. 159–82.

Waismann, F. (1965), *The Principles of Linguistic Philosophy,* ed. R. Harré. London: Macmillan.

Walker, D. M. (1980), *The Oxford Companion to Law.* Oxford: Clarendon.

Walton, D. N. (2002), *Legal Argumentation and Evidence.* University Park, Pennsylvania: Pennsylvania State University.

Werbach, K. (1994), 'Looking it up: dictionaries and statutory interpretation', *Harvard Law Review,* 107, 1437–53.

Whately, R. (1840), *Elements of Logic,* 7th edn. London: Fellowes.

Whewell, W. (1847), *The Philosophy of the Inductive Sciences,* 2nd edn. London: Parker.

Whitehead, A. N. and Russell, B. A. W. (1910), *Principia Mathematica.* Cambridge: Cambridge University Press.

Williams, G. (1945–6), 'Language and the law', *Law Quarterly Review,* 61, 71–86, 179–95, 293–303, 384–406; 62:387–406.

Wilson, R. and Galpin, B. (1962), *Maxwell on the Interpretation of Statutes,* 11th edn. London: Sweet & Maxwell.

Winston, J. E. (1999), *Describing Species. Practical Taxonomic Procedure for Biologists.* New York: Columbia University Press.

Winter, S. (2001), *A Clearing in the Forest: Law, Life, and Mind.* Chicago: University of Chicago Press.

Wittgenstein, L. (1969), *On Certainty,* trans. D. Paul and G. E. M. Anscombe. Oxford: Blackwell.

— (2001), *Philosophical Investigations,* trans. G. E. M. Anscombe, 3rd edn. Oxford: Blackwell.

Wyld, H. C. (1934), *The Best English,* S. P. E. Tract No. XXXIX. Oxford: Clarendon.

Zander, M. (1999), *The Law-making Process,* 5th edn. London: Butterworths.

Cases cited

Adler v George [1964] 2 QB 7
Berkey v Third Avenue Rly (1926) 244 NY 84
British Amusement Catering Trades Association v Westminster City Council ([1987] 1 WLR. 977; [1988] 2 WLR 485
Bronston v United States 409 US 352 (1973)
Brown v Gould [1972] Ch 53
Cabell v Markham 148 F2d 737 (2nd Cir 1945)
Chapman v United States 111 S. Ct. 1919 (1991)
Church of the Holy Trinity v United States 143 U.S. 457 (1892)
Corkery v Carpenter [1951] 1 KB 102
Fisher v Bell [1961] 1 QB 394
Garner v Burr [1951] 1 KB 31
Gompers v United States 233 U.S. 604 (1914)
Hudson v Marshall [1976] Criminal Law Review 523
Investors Compensation Scheme Ltd v West Bromwich Building Society (1998) 1 W. L. R. 896
IRC v Broadway Cottages [1955] 1 Ch 20 (CA)
John Angus Smith v United States 508 U.S. 223 (1993)
Liversidge v Anderson [1942] AC 206 (HL)
MacPhail v Doulton [1971] AC 424
Magor and St. Mellons Rural District Council Appellants v Newport Corporation Respondents [1952] A.C. 189 (HL)
Margate Pier Co. v. Hannam (1819) 3 Barn. & Ald. 266
Marvel v Merritt 116 U.S. 11 (1885)
McBoyle v. United States 283 U.S. 25 (1931)
Nix v Hedden 149 U.S. 304 (1893)
Nixon v United States 113 S. Ct 732 (1993)
NOW v Scheidler 114 S Ct 798 (1994)
Partridge v. Strange & Croker 75 Eng. Rep. 123 (K.B. 1553)
Pepper v Hart [1993] AC 593
Re Tuck's Settlement Trust [1978] 2 WLR 411
R v Caldwell (1981) 73 Cr. App. R. 13 HL
R v Judge of the City of London Court [1892] 1 QB 273
Re Allen [1953] Ch 810
Re Baden's Deed Trust (No 2) [1973] Ch 9
Re Barlow's Will Trusts [1979] 1 WLR 278

Re Gestetner Settlement [1953] Ch 672
Re Gibbard's Will Trust [1967] 1 WLR 42
Re Gulbenkian [1968] Ch 126
Re Rowland [1963] Ch 1 (CA)
Royal College of Nursing v Department of Health and Social Security (1981) ALL ER 545
Seaford Court Estates Ltd. v Asher [1949] 2 KB 481 (CA)
Sparfax v Dommett (1972) The Times, 14 July
Sprange v Barnard 1789 2 Bro CC 585
Stevens v Gourley (1859) 7 CB (NS) 99
Stradling v Morgan (1560) 1 Plowden 201
Sussex Peerage Case [1844] 11 Clark and Finnelly 85
Thames Heliports Plc v LB of Tower Hamlets (1997) 74 P & CR
United States v John Angus Smith 957 F.2d 835 (1992)
United States v Phelps 877 F2d 28 (1989)
Whitely v Chappell (1868–9) 4 LRQB 147

Index